# Iran:
# The Untold
# Story

## Also by Mohamed Heikal

THE CAIRO DOCUMENTS

THE ROAD TO RAMADAN

THE SPHINX AND THE COMMISSAR

# Iran: The Untold Story

An Insider's Account of
America's Iranian Adventure
and Its Consequences for
the Future

by

Mohamed Heikal

PANTHEON BOOKS, NEW YORK

**Library of Congress Cataloging in Publication Data**

Haykal, Muḥammad Ḥasanayn.
  Iran: the untold story.

  Reprint. Originally published: London: A. Deutsch, 1981.
  1. Iran—Politics and government—1941–1979.
I. Title.
DS318.H4   1982     955'.053     81-16963
ISBN 0-394-52275-3       AACR2

Manufactured in the United States of America
First American Edition

# CONTENTS

Ah Love! could thou and I with Fate conspire
To grasp this sorry Scheme of Things entire,
    Would not we shatter it to bits – and then
Re-mould it nearer to the Heart's Desire!

> Omar Khayyám, translated by Edward Fitzgerald

How many divisions has the Pope?

> attributed to Stalin

For heaven's sake, who is this Khomeini?

> Empress Farah, April 1978

# PREFACE

It is not hard to appreciate the particularly traumatic effect which the Iranian Revolution has had both on the American government and on American public opinion. For years, after all, the Shah had been regarded as one of the most trustworthy friends and most valuable allies that the United States had been fortunate enough to acquire in the post-war world. Inevitably the destruction of his apparently impregnable position came as a terrible shock, even to those who had every reason to be well informed about what was going on. When I was talking to Henry Kissinger last summer in Switzerland I asked him if the Revolution had taken him too by surprise, and his answer was that it had, 'completely'. Then of course there was the year-long agony of the hostages, which provoked a sense of bitterness and frustration of a different nature from any of the other recent trials Americans have had to face.

But above all, the Iranian Revolution was a peculiarly difficult phenomenon and Khomeini a peculiarly difficult individual for Americans to understand, let alone to feel any sympathy for. A year ago, in the summer of 1980, I was asked to address the conference of the International Press Institute in Florence on the subject 'Communications Across Frontiers', and took recent events in Iran as an example of the problems faced by communicators in the modern world. I made what seemed to me the valid point that, just as we have to learn another man's language if we want to be able to talk to him, so we have to learn something about a people's history if we want to find any basis of understanding with them. The audience I was addressing was composed of highly intelligent men and women who were for the most part themselves in the business of communication, but I found them singularly unresponsive. Many, particularly the Americans among them, seemed to think I was trying to make excuses for the excesses of the Revolution, but this was far from being my intention and in any case was none of my business. My point was simply that it is very easy to pass judgement on events, but much harder to sit down and attempt to understand how they happened. Yet without that understanding any reaction is bound to be unprofitable. I regret to say that so far I have seen little sign that the

American government or American public opinion appreciates the significance of the Iranian Revolution, highly important though it is that they should do so. It is all the more important because the Iranian Revolution, for all its special peculiarities, is unlikely to prove unique, either in its Islamic or in its revolutionary aspects.

At the time of writing (August 1981) there appear to be, broadly speaking, three main attitudes in the West as to how the Revolution in Iran could or should develop. The first—and this attitude is perhaps more popular in Europe than in America—sees the Revolution as having already shot its bolt. The expectation is that there will be a period of civil war, followed by a successor regime, probably made up from elements which were at first associated with the Revolution but which have since fallen foul of Khomeini and the mullahs. In this connection the names of Abolhassan Beni-Sadr and Massoud Rajavi are most often heard, particularly since their spectacular escape from Tehran last July.

I know and respect both men, and had a five-hour discussion with them in Paris soon after their arrival there, but I believe it would be a mistake to regard them, either separately or together, as offering the nucleus for an alternative to the present regime. It is argued that Beni-Sadr can claim a degree of legitimacy since he was the first President of the Iranian Republic, elected to that office by overwhelming public support. But this is to overlook the fact that he became the popular choice simply and solely because it was known that he enjoyed the backing of Khomeini. Beni-Sadr is a man whose merits are easily appreciated by western observers. He is Sorbonne-educated, an economist, and though a wholehearted supporter of the Islamic Revolution, at home in the cultural atmosphere of France. He is a man of words, and perhaps a man of ideas, but definitely not a man of action.

Rajavi was the head of the Mujahiddin Khalk, who have proved the most effective opposition to the mullah regime and who, by masterminding the explosion at the headquarters of the Islamic Republic Party in June which took the lives of seventy-two leading members of the party including Ayatollah Beheshti, number two to Khomeini, showed a capacity for urban terrorism which his followers have been able to maintain in his absence. When we were talking Rajavi showed considerable interest in an article by George Ball he had read in the *Washington Post*, arguing that the combination of Beni-Sadr and Rajavi could be accepted as a viable alternative to Khomeini and the mullahs. He asked me if I thought the article had any special significance. He himself obviously thought it did, since he claimed it was George Ball's report on the Gulf which persuaded President Carter to abandon his support for the Shah. I think this claim much exaggerated, nor do I think too much should be read into this particular article.

I am sure that Rajavi, like many of his supporters inside Iran, is sincere in his support for the general principles of the Islamic Revolution, though not in the form it has taken. As he said to me in Paris: 'At the time of the 1951 oil crisis, Mossadeq once remarked that Iran could manage an economy without oil. In the same way I would say we can manage the Islamic Revolution without the mullahs.'

The second attitude in the West towards the Iranian Revolution is to let the country stew in its own juice. Those who hold this point of view are not interested in finding alternatives to Khomeini, in the shape either of Beni-Sadr or Rajavi or anybody else. They argue that in Iran, as in other countries that have undergone a devastating political earthquake, the revolution can be relied on to eat its own children; only when this has happened, they say, can there be any talk of alternative regimes. Iran must touch bottom before anyone can expect to see it rise again or help it to do so.

I believe this attitude to be dangerously short-sighted. Iran is not an ordinary country. For so many reasons—its long frontier with the Soviet Union, its oil, its commanding geographical position in the Gulf—it is impossible simply to turn one's back on Iran. To do so shows nothing but political bankruptcy, a refusal to face facts.

The third attitude is to work for a return of the monarchy. I do not believe that such a possibility is taken seriously except in limited circles inside the United States, for even if a Pahlevi restoration was intended to be liberal compared with the Shah's autocracy (Louis XVIII rather than Louis XVI), no attempt to enact the events of 1953 all over again has the slightest prospect of success. This should be dismissed as no more than typical of the dreams émigrés everywhere have always cherished to console themselves for their defeat.

I said in my concluding chapter (page 209) that the army remains the only organized force inside Iran, and that it is from inside the armed forces that new leaders may be expected to emerge. I see no reason to revise this opinion. It will, however, be ironic if this happens, since it was always the army that Khomeini saw as his main antagonist. As he said to me the last time we met: "The Shah was nothing; so was Savak. Ours was a revolution against the army."

If, after three years of revolution, the army remains a crucial element in the political life of the country, this is due to a number of factors, including separatist movements among the minorities the army has had to combat, as well as, above all, the war with Iraq. When I was talking to Beni-Sadr in Paris, he told me that to begin with, Khomeini thought there would be no war. Because of the Iranian Revolution's enormous prestige, he thought it inconceivable that anyone would dare to attack it. So he suspected that all the evidence being presented to him about Iraq's preparations for war was invented by people inside army intelligence who wanted the Revolution to feel itself dependent on the armed forces.

But most of the now purged armed forces had adjusted themselves to the new situation, as an incident Beni-Sadr told me about illustrates. There was a moment in the autumn of 1980, a few weeks after the war had started, when the fall of Dezful, which was considered a key to the defence of Iran, seemed imminent. Beni-Sadr, in his capacity as head of the armed forces, flew to Dezful, where the local commander informed him that he only had six tanks and one gun operational. He felt that defeat or capitulation was inevitable unless the air force could intervene effectively. Most air force pilots had been imprisoned for suspected loyalty to the Shah, but some had been released, and these Beni-Sadr summoned to a meeting. 'Do you know who you are now, gentlemen?' he asked them. They asked him what he meant. 'You remember the battles which the Persians in the past fought against the Tartars? The situation was desperate then, and it is desperate now. Then the situation was saved by Rustum; now it must be saved by you. You are the new Rustums.' It is significant that at this crisis Beni-Sadr should have invoked the legendary hero of pre-Islamic Persia as a spur to the pilots' loyalty. His appeal was successful. The battle for Dezful was won.

But even if the armed forces were to play a more prominent part in Iranian affairs, say as a result of the death of Khomeini, this would not necessarily mean that the Revolution was over. It would be much more likely to represent one more phase in a continuing revolutionary process. All revolutions go through a series of distinct phases. To begin with, there is the time of euphoria, when old dreams seem to be realized and new ones to be born, and when the air is filled with slogans. At this stage the revolution can afford to be generous and can embrace many divergent opinions. Thus it was that the Iranian Revolution gratefully accepted the services of people outside the mainstream of the mullahs' thinking — men like Bazargan, Sanjabi, and even Beni-Sadr — who lent it the prestige and expertise it badly needed.

The second phase in a revolution comes when reality shows itself increasingly at odds with dreams and when slogans are not enough. It is then that those on the periphery of the revolution find themselves in trouble, not necessarily because the revolution is looking for scapegoats but because of the innate difficulty of reconciling state and revolution, one of the most testing tasks facing any revolution and one to which Lenin devoted a pamphlet with that title. In Iran this perennial problem was complicated by the fact that the leaders of the revolution were men of religion — a dictatorship not of the proletariat but of what Beni-Sadr calls the 'mullaritariat'. Their ideas about economics, about the social organization of the country, about its intellectual life, all make cooperation between them and other groups exceedingly difficult. And matters are not made any easier by the personality of Khomeini, who, as I have said, is a bullet projected direct from the feudal and religious world of the seventh century to the twentieth-century world of space travel, nuclear weapons, and the manipulation of genes.

A third phase in revolutions is the time of terror, of revolutionary terror and counter-revolutionary terror, of the Vendée and the Committee of Public Safety. It is somewhere between the second and third phases that the Iranian Revolution finds itself as I write.

Analogies cannot be pressed too far. Khomeini, now in his eighties, may not survive further into the revolution than did Lenin, but this does not mean that he will be succeeded by a Stalin. The armed forces may produce a Bonaparte, but this does not mean that Iran will go through the full cycle of consulate, empire, and Bourbon restoration. It can, however, be safely said that whatever course the Revolution now takes, many of the ideas which came with it will be found to have stuck, just as the ideas of the French and Russian revolutions have survived to this day in spite of all the upheavals their countries have gone through.

We should look to history, not for justification of contemporary prejudices, but for guidance on how to act. This would save us from the oversimplified 'solutions' put forward by theoreticians who feel that they have to produce instant answers. And, since Iran is going to remain a bone of contention between the super-powers whatever happens, Americans have a special responsibility to look at the Iranian Revolution as dispassionately as possible. They should surely have appreciated, from the fate of General and Mme Chiang Kai-chek, that even the most glamorous and friendly rulers are not necessarily going to stay for ever, and that a strong lobby in Congress is no substitute for firm support at home. Had this been remembered there might have been less readiness to take the Shah and Soraya or the Shah and Farah at their own valuation. There might also be less enthusiasm now for the Marcoses.

Friendship between nations is not something that can be hired or bought. If Americans are to play the fully effective role in world affairs that is their due, they must realize that the Third World is looking for new relationships based on true reciprocity and justice. It would be wrong to suppose that in their search for what they see as overdue changes, to be effected if necessary by revolution, Third-World countries are opposed to America. On the contrary, they are naturally closer in ideas and sympathies to America than to the Soviet Union. I recall a recent conversation I had with a Russian friend, who told me that he thought the debacle the Soviet Union had suffered in the Middle East over the last decade, which started with the expulsion of Soviet experts from Egypt in 1972 and was followed by wide repercussions throughout Asia and

Africa, had cost the Soviet Union no less than $100 billion in material losses, to say nothing of the greater but intangible losses in prestige and influence.

I know that for a foreigner to say these things does not make him popular with Americans. In this respect Americans remind me—and this is going to make me even less popular—of Khrushchev. Americans have a capacity for self-criticism which at times—over Watergate and CIA revelations, for example—seems almost to verge on masochism. But they resent the same sort of criticism when it comes from outside. As Khrushchev used to say to me: 'I can criticize Stalin, but you can't.' Unfortunately, the media in America seem too often to prefer to judge rather than to understand. It is as an exercise in understanding that this book has been written.

Finally, a word about my sources. Some of those who read the typescript of this book suggested that I should have said more about where my information was derived from. Apart from not wishing to overburden with footnotes a book designed for the general reader, it will, I hope, be appreciated that in many cases I was told of events by those who had participated in them, but only on condition that I did not quote them. However, it is now possible for me to give examples of what I mean. Thus, the proposal that Algeria should become a founder member of the 'Safari Club' (p. 113) was revealed to me in an interview with President Boumedienne of Algeria; the suspicion that Somalia might have been the victim of a bargain struck by the two super-powers (p. 116) came out of a talk with the Political Counsellor to President Siad Barre of Somalia. And so on.

I mention in the Introduction some of the sources which were opened to me when I visited Iran after the Revolution. It was in the office of Ayatollah Hashimi Rafsanjani, then Minister of the Interior, that I was shown the file dealing with the activities of the spy 'Hafiz' (p. 17), and in the office of Mehdi Bazargan, then Prime Minister, that I read the account of the incident when the Empress refused to be searched before entering the Shah's apartments (p. 152). Many of the details concerning the activities of the Shah and of Savak I obtained from documents which had been found in the Shah's offices after the Revolution and which were shown to me by Ibrahim Yazdi, then Deputy Prime Minister and Minister for Revolutionary Affairs. So, while I can vouch for the authenticity of my informants, it has not always been possible for me to name them.

Cairo, August 1981                                    Mohamed Heikal

# Iran:
# The Untold
# Story

# INTRODUCTION

THE REVOLUTION IN IRAN took most people in the West by surprise. Governments and public had been happy to regard the country as (to quote President Carter) 'an island of stability' in a violent and volatile region. Yet the upheaval which drove the Shah from his throne and installed in his place an Islamic government dominated by his arch-enemy, Ayatollah Khomeini, was not an isolated phenomenon. It was, as I hope to show in the following pages, simply the latest chapter in a long historical process which had its origins in the national and religious inheritance of the Iranian people, which burst out abortively during the crisis over the nationalization of the oil industry by Dr Mossadeq in 1950–3, and which then went underground until its final eruption in 1978–9.

In this last manifestation the Revolution became something of much more than local significance, including as it did many of the elements which look likely to dominate the decade which we have just entered – a resurgent Islam, the energy problem, the new distribution of wealth in the world, and super-power rivalries. All these combine to make the Gulf the centre of gravity in the world. What happened in Iran affected all of us, so that it might now be not fanciful to apply to Iran the words which Napoleon once applied to Egypt – 'the most important country'.

My association with Iran has been a long one. As a young journalist I became roving Middle East correspondent of the Cairo newspaper *Akhbar el-Yom*, and one of my first major assignments was to cover the Iranian oil crisis in 1950–1. I spent many months in the country, travelling all over it and meeting all the leading politicians of the old regime, such as Seyyid Ziauddin Tabatabai, Qavam es-Sultaneh, and of course Dr Mossadeq and the leading Shi'a divine of that time, his ardent supporter, Ayatollah Kashani. It was at this time that I had the first of many conversations with the Shah, and also made the acquaintance of his twin sister, Princess Ashraf, whose former husband, Ahmed Shafiq, was a friend of mine.

The outcome of this experience was my first book, *Iran on a Volcano*, which appeared in Arabic in 1951 and became something of a best-

seller. For a writer a first book is like a first love – something particularly endearing and never to be forgotten. So it is that for nearly thirty
years since the publication of *Iran on a Volcano* I have followed events
in that country with a particular interest.

In July 1958 there was a revolution in Iraq, one consequence of
which was that all the documents found in the headquarters of the
Baghdad Pact were seized and sent in a special aeroplane to Cairo.
(This was in the early days of the revolution, when Brigadier Abdel
Karim Qasim was still a professed admirer of President Nasser and
before they quarrelled.) I had from its inception attacked the Baghdad
Pact, of which Iran was a leading member, in my newspaper, *Al
Ahram*. Now I had the opportunity to check how far my assumption
of what was going on in its councils was correct. I found this an
interesting experience. I have also since been able to compare the notes
I made while I was a reporter in Iran with what was later revealed by
the publication of official dispatches by the State Department in
Washington. These too made me reflect on the origins of the drama
which came to a head in the opening months of 1979.

There was a time, in the aftermath of the 1967 war with Israel, when
I found myself playing a role in the formation of policy towards Iran.
After the 1967 war many of us in Egypt felt the urgent need for a new
alignment of forces in the Middle East which should not only put an
end to inter-Arab rivalries but should rally the support of all Moslem
states in the area. We felt that our quarrel with Iran, which dated back
to the days of the Baghdad Pact and had led to a rupture of diplomatic
relations, was out of date. It so happened that just at this time the Shah
sent me a friendly message through the owner and publisher of the
leading Tehran newspaper, *Etelaat*, Abbas Massoudi. Mr Massoudi,
who was Vice-President of the Senate, came to Cairo in 1968, and
again in 1969. After long discussions we concerted between us the
necessary steps for a restoration of diplomatic relations, even to the
drafting of a communiqué. I like to think that I helped to persuade
President Nasser of the wisdom of this initiative, which was, in fact,
finally brought to a successful conclusion shortly before his death in
September 1970.

I had received many invitations from the Shah to visit Tehran, and
in 1975 this delayed visit became possible. I had long talks with the
Shah himself, with Prime Minister Amir Abbas Hoveyda, with
Jamshid Amouzegar, who two years later was to succeed him in the
premiership, with General Nematollah Nassiri, head of Savak of ill
repute, and many others. I also managed to see and talk to opponents

of the regime, including many students belonging to factions of both left and right.

Three years later the link with the Iranian drama was for me reopened in a new place and with a new actor. In December 1978 I was in Paris and was invited by members of the entourage of Ayatollah Khomeini to visit him at his modest house of exile in Neauphle-le-Château. This I did, spending several hours in his company and talking privately and at length with him on a wide variety of subjects.

I was to see Khomeini a second time after his triumphal return to Tehran, and once again spent the best part of a day in discussions with him in Qom. I had talks with his son Ahmed, his principal aide, and with his grandson Hussein, another valued member of his entourage. During this visit I had a chance to meet all the members of the Revolutionary Council, including Abolhassan Beni-Sadr, later to become first President of the Iranian Republic for more than a year, as well as most of the religious leaders, politicians and soldiers connected with the new regime. I also talked at length with the students occupying the American Embassy. The Prime Minister, Mehdi Bazargan, who received me in the splendid office where I had last seen Hoveyda (though he refused to make use of the huge circular table of his predecessor, preferring the small ordinary table and chairs which he had installed in one corner of the room), was good enough to produce the private diary which he had kept during the last days of the old regime and to read out to me copious extracts from it. I was also particularly indebted to Ibrahim Yazdi, Deputy Prime Minister for Revolutionary Affairs at that time, in whose office were many important documents relating to the Shah's regime. These shed much light on recent events.

For a short time after the Revolution I found myself again directly involved in Iranian affairs. I explain in Chapter 15 how it was that I became one of those who were drawn into negotiations for the release of the American hostages. The narrative of this book begins with my visit to the occupied American Embassy in Tehran; it is appropriate that it should end with the release of the hostages.

The Iranian scene during the past forty years has been one of enormous complexity. I do not pretend that in this book I have been able to do more than pick out a few of the elements – the movements, the people, the events – which have gone to make up this scene. But I hope that I have been able to convey some of the fascination which this country has always exercised over me, and to give a coherent explanation of what to many people still seems an inexplicable political eruption.

I would like to thank Dr Mohammed Zeki Bedawi, the Islamic scholar and Director of the Islamic Centre in London, and Fred Halliday, for reading my manuscript and for their helpful suggestions. I would also like to thank my colleague Fahmi Huwaidi, who accompanied me on an exacting visit to Tehran. Finally, it is for the third time my pleasure to thank my friend Edward Hodgkin for his help in preparation of the material for a book of mine.

# I

## AT THE

## AMERICAN EMBASSY

THERE HAVE BEEN a number of places where in recent years the struggle between the two super-powers, the United States and the Soviet Union, has been present in symbolic form on the ground for all to see: the Berlin Wall, Cuba, Angola are only a few examples. But nowhere has this confrontation been more dramatically expressed than in the heart of the Iranian capital, Tehran, where the embassies of the super-powers stand as two islands of world rivalry surrounded by the teeming millions of Iranian people.

It is appropriate that Iran should be the setting for this symbolism, for no country is better placed by geography and history to be the scene of such a conflict. The Soviet military intervention in Afghanistan abruptly reminded the world that now only five hundred kilometres of Iranian territory separated Russia from the warm waters of the Indian Ocean. From the dawn of history it is this land bridge between the Middle East and Central Asia which has been the melting-pot of races and civilizations. Here the influences of India and Arabia collide; here outside forces from origins as distant as Mongolia and Greece have penetrated and conquered.

More important for an understanding of recent events is the fact that Iran represents the first eastward region where in the seventh century AD the combination of Islam and Arabism failed to penetrate. West-wards there are groups like the Copts in Egypt and Maronites in Lebanon which accepted Arabism but not Islam; but these are minorities. In Iran there is a whole nation which did the opposite – accepted Islam but not Arabism.

For centuries religion dominated the lives of the peoples in the region – Sunni Moslems in the Ottoman Empire, Shi'a Moslems in Persia. Then, under the impact of western ideas and western arms a new concept emerged – nationalism. In Persia, as elsewhere in the Middle East, North Africa and Asia, thoughtful patriots came to the conclusion that only if their fellow countrymen became aware of themselves as belonging to a proud and ancient nation would they be able to resist the impact of the nation-states of the West. This would unite as equal citizens religious and racial minorities which hitherto had been kept subordinate. This did not mean that the new nationalism was incompatible with religion; on the contrary, whenever the national cause received a setback, it was to the citadel of their religious beliefs that people struggling to maintain their own independence usually retreated.

In the nineteenth century Persia was the diplomatic battleground on which the empires of Britain and Tsarist Russia competed for supremacy. For the last thirty years the same battleground has seen new antagonists, the United States replacing Britain and the Soviets the Tsars. Now that the Gulf is the area which produces 60 per cent of the world's most essential commodity, oil, and owns 70 per cent of the world's proved oil reserves, not to mention the fact that this is the area which generates half the cash which flows each year into the world markets, the stakes are obviously immeasurably higher than they were in the nineteenth century.

Suitably enough the Tehran embassies which symbolize this confrontation are no ordinary diplomatic outposts. For most people the word embassy conjures up the picture of a single building, or even an apartment, with a flag on it. Not so these embassies, round both of which I was lucky enough to be given a conducted tour. The Russian Ambassador in Tehran in 1979 was Vladimir Vinogradov, an old friend from the days when he served as ambassador in Cairo during four critical years following the death of Nasser, which included the October war of 1973. He showed me round the Russian Embassy compound; the students occupying the American Embassy compound were my hosts there.

The Soviet Embassy is a complex of buildings enclosed behind a high wall. Here are several palaces, several smaller houses and bungalows as well as apartment blocks, a hospital and a power station. There is a lake with rowing-boats and swans on it, and a small wood where can be seen a herd of gazelles. In one corner of the compound is the Atabeg Palace – Atabeg being a Turkish word which, ironically enough, means a regent, since it was here in the old days that a Turkish Mamluk used to be responsible for the upbringing of the Persian Crown Prince until he came of age.

Nowadays the palace has been turned into a museum, which is the scene of a big reception for the ambassador's guests on two days in the year – 1 May and the anniversary of the October Revolution. Guests are shown the room which was the scene of the Big Three conference in December 1943, and the ambassador will always remind visitors that Roosevelt chose to stay in the Russian Embassy for the conference and that it was on this occasion that his friendship with Stalin developed: 'I may say that I got on fine with Marshal Stalin,' he reported back to the American people at the end of the conference. The room which was given over to Roosevelt is left as it was when he used it. Churchill used to come across from the British Embassy for the conference meetings (in those days it was still the British and Russian embassies which visibly confronted each other). It was in this room that the seeds of later misunderstandings, of Yalta and the division of Europe into spheres of interest, were sown.

Naturally the Embassy compound is extremely well protected. Supplementing the high wall there is an electric fence. Everybody inside the compound is a Russian national, from the ambassador down to the cooks. In normal times the staff of the Embassy amounted to between 120 and 140, with about thirty-six guards.

The American Embassy is not so full of historic associations as the Russian – it lacks a lake with swans and a wood with gazelles – but it is no less impressive for being strictly contemporary. It covers an area of sixty acres in the centre of the city, triangular in shape, and includes about thirty buildings of one sort or another – a large central office, the ambassador's residence, the headquarters of the military mission, the information centre, the commercial department, the houses of the service attachés, and so on. Not least important, in either embassy, are the communications centres. The bristling forest of aerial antennae which sprout from all the embassies' roofs gives the impression that here on alien soil Russians and Americans are talking directly to each other, quarrelling in the air.

Here then were these two super-powers ranged against each other, with sharply conflicting interests and aims in the area. In other parts of the world the super-powers may find a common interest in maintaining the existing balance, but not so in Iran and the Gulf. In this area the Americans used to have virtually everything they wanted; they had the oil and the authority; they were the people in possession, and so they wished at all costs to preserve the status quo. The Russians, on the other hand, had been excluded from the area, economically and strategically. Yet it was an area on their borders and where their influence had once been considerable. It was therefore in their interests to see the status quo upset – not violently upset, perhaps, because the Russians are not keen to see violent revolutions on their doorstep – but altered gradually in their favour. So in Iran it was the Russians who looked for change; the Americans who resisted it. In a Third-World country like Iran, where change is long overdue, anyone who tries to preserve the status quo inevitably finds himself taking on the job of policeman, but those who seek change may find themselves faced with something very different from what they expected or hoped for.

So it was that the American Embassy in Tehran became the nerve centre for the control of the whole area. When Iran began to play the role of policeman in the Gulf region, it was the American Embassy which became the police station. The function of the Embassy staff was more than simply to maintain diplomatic relations with the Shah's government; it was rather to act as protector of his regime. This meant that, though power was divided between the Shah in his Niavaran Palace and the Americans, it was the Embassy compound which became in effect the most important single spot in the whole of Iran.

Not surprisingly the CIA element in the Embassy staff was very pronounced. Nobody now questions that what saved the Shah's throne for him in 1953 was intervention by the CIA, and all the American ambassadors who came to Iran after that had CIA connections, until in 1973 the logical conclusion was reached and the then head of the CIA, Richard Helms, was appointed ambassador.

To begin with, the Shah used to see the head of the Tehran CIA station once a week; Saturday morning at 9 o'clock was the time set aside for their two-hour meeting. But as the Shah grew more confident, relations between him and the Embassy began to change. He felt the Americans needed him more than he needed them, while the Americans found their chosen instrument for the control of the area manifesting a spirit of self-glorification so alarming in its implications that one member of the Nixon administration, William Simon, Secretary of the Treasury, could describe the Shah before the Foreign Affairs Committee of the Senate as 'nuts and megalomaniac'. The interests of the Shah and the Americans were no longer identical. One slightly bizarre but no doubt inevitable consequence of this change was that each began to spy on the other, the Shah trying to recruit agents in the Embassy, and the Embassy to recruit agents in the Palace. In this both were to some degree successful.

General Nassiri, head of Savak, the secret police, was caught and shot soon after the Revolution had succeeded. He tried to save his skin by making a full confession, but this failed to move his judges. However, one of the secrets which he revealed to his captors was the name of the Savak agent inside the American Embassy. The agent, who was in fact neither American nor Iranian, had been given the code-name Hafiz – perhaps in choosing the name of Persia's most famous poet Savak had some idea of copying the example of the Abwehr, who chose 'Cicero' as the code-name for the British ambassador's Albanian valet who sold them secret documents from the Embassy safe in wartime Ankara. After General Nassiri had revealed his identity, Hafiz was discreetly approached by the revolutionary authorities, who promised him immunity if he would continue his activities on their behalf. This he did, but, as he was by now thoroughly scared, with only limited success. He was, however, able to hand over two consignments of documents, which included telegrams exchanged between Ambassador Sullivan and Bruce Laingen, the Chargé d'Affaires who took over from him, and Secretary of State Cyrus Vance and the Iranian desk in the State Department during the last days of the Shah and the early months of the Revolution. These landed up on the desk of the new Minister of Interior in the revolutionary government, Ayatollah Hashimi Rafsanjani. After further interrogation Hafiz was taken in one of the Shah's bullet-proof Mercedes to Tehran airport, put on a plane to Paris, and there disappeared.

This meant that by September 1979 the new government was in almost full possession of the exchanges which had gone on between Washington and Tehran over what should be done about the Shah, and it was this knowledge which was largely responsible for the occupation of the Embassy by the students in November, since the telegrams showed that the Shah's journey to the States was something that had been planned for a long time, and not just a response to an urgent humanitarian appeal, as had been claimed.

One of the captured documents, for example, was a position paper by Henry Precht, Director of the Office of Iranian Affairs in the State Department, dated 1 August 1979, and marked 'SECRET/SENSITIVE'. The paper's title was 'Planning for the Shah to come to the United States', and considered 'three broad questions: what new circumstances would justify a change in the US government's position?; what conditions should we seek for the Shah or state prior to his arrival here?; what arrangements should we make for Embassy personnel to provide protection?'

Under the first heading the paper calculated that by the end of the year there was a good chance that Iran would have a new President and a new Majlis, and that then 'we should inform the new government that we wish to clear our decks of old issues on the agenda. One of these old issues will be the status of the Shah.' The Iranians should be informed 'of the intense pressures for the Shah to come here – pressures which we are resisting despite our traditional open-door policy.' But the paper suggested that if no new government emerged by the end of the year 'there may be an argument for going ahead and admitting the Shah anyway to get that inevitable step behind us.' 'In either of these scenarios,' it went on, 'we should aim for a positive change in our position on the Shah by January 1980.' In conclusion the paper stated that, though the threat to Embassy personnel was less serious than it had been in the spring, 'nevertheless the danger of hostages being taken in Iran will persist. We should make no move towards admitting the Shah until we have obtained and tested a new and substantially more effective guard force for the Embassy.'

The fact that the Shah's admission to the States was regarded as an 'inevitable step' by the State Department in August made nonsense of Washington's assertion that his entry in November was only permitted because of a sudden deterioration in his health. Even though his health had in fact deteriorated, this did not alter the Iranians' firm conviction that there was a conspiracy afoot. They were fully aware that the Shah had always wanted his place of exile to be neither Egypt nor Morocco but the United States, with perhaps Switzerland as an alternative home for the winter months. They were aware too of the 'intense pressures' which were lobbying in America on the Shah's behalf, led by Henry Kissinger and David Rockefeller. The Chase Manhattan Bank, of which Rockefeller was Chairman, had been the principal channel through which the Shah's government dealt with the West. It was Chase Manhattan which from 1954 onwards received the money for sale of Iranian oil in the West, and which acted as banker for the Pahlevi Foundation. As over the five years 1974–9 Iran's income from oil averaged $30 billion per annum it can be seen that very considerable sums were involved, and it was hardly surprising that pressures on behalf of so good a customer should have been intense.

In September Ibrahim Yazdi, then Foreign Minister of Iran, was at the United Nations in New York after attending the Non-Aligned Conference in Havana. It was arranged for him to have three meetings with Secretary of State Vance, who was anxious to persuade Yazdi of four points: first, the Americans wanted the revolutionary government to understand that as far as they were concerned the Shah was finished. Second, they still felt the United States and Iran were natural allies because of their common fear of the Soviet Union. Third, the Americans understood and respected both the Iranian Revolution and Khomeini. Fourth, they hoped it would be possible to start a new page in American-Iranian relations, and were open to suggestion as to how this could best be accomplished.

Yazdi went back to Tehran bearing Vance's message with him, and reported to Khomeini. But while he was away the documents extracted by Hafiz had come into the possession of the revolutionary government. These showed not only that the possibility of the Shah's being given asylum in the United States was being strongly urged by many influential people and was being seriously considered by the administration (though the Tehran Embassy was opposed to the idea), but also that the Americans were making efforts to contact dissident elements in the country, particularly among army officers and the minorities in Kurdistan and Azerbaijan. So when Yazdi passed on Vance's four points Khomeini asked him ironically, 'Do you mean they didn't tell you anything about the Shah's going to America?' Yazdi was, not unnaturally, considerably surprised when he was told the reason for this question.

Shortly after this, Laingen, the Chargé d'Affaires, went to see Yazdi and asked for the guards on the Embassy to be reinforced. Yazdi asked him why he thought this necessary. Laingen explained that the Embassy had already been subject to attacks. Yazdi replied that he had been to inspect the Embassy itself, and he did not think there was any need for alarm. Both Yazdi and Laingen of course by now knew of the possibility that the Shah might be going to the States, but neither revealed his knowledge.

Efforts by the Americans to build some sort of bridge to the new authorities in Tehran continued. They had hopes of the Prime Minister, Mehdi Bazargan, and it was arranged that he and Yazdi should meet Zbigniew Brzezinski, Carter's National Security Adviser, in Algiers when they were all there for the Algerian Independence Day celebrations. However, on 22 October the Shah left Mexico City for New York. Before setting out for Algiers Yazdi sent a protest to the American Chargé in Tehran, and it was assumed that this was something which would be discussed with Brzezinski. But when they met, Brzezinski disclaimed all knowledge of the protest, explaining that it must have reached Washington after he had left for Algiers. All he would promise was that when he got back he would look into the matter. By then it was too late. Laingen had explained to the acting Prime Minister in Tehran that the Shah's journey to America was for urgent medical treatment and that he was being admitted solely on humanitarian grounds. But this explanation carried little weight as it was now known to the whole Revolutionary Council that this visit had been under discussion for several months; they were also obsessed by memories of 1953, continually on the alert for a CIA-sponsored counter-coup.

So on 2 November, while the Algiers meeting was still in progress, Khomeini issued a proclamation to the students exhorting them to open their eyes to the conspiracies of that malignant enemy, the United States. The Revolutionary Committee inside Tehran University accordingly completed preparations for the attack on the American Embassy which it had in fact been preparing ever since September, when it first got to know about the documents Hafiz had smuggled out. The man responsible to the Revolutionary Council for student activities was Hojat al-Islam Musawi Khoeiny, though he himself was not a member of the Council, maintaining contact with Khomeini through the Ayatollah's son Ahmed. It was under Khoeiny's auspices that the university committee began its contingency plan to invade the Embassy and seize the rest of the documents which, from the sample Hafiz had brought out, they knew would tell them a great deal about the Shah's policies and activities.

Nothing more dramatically illustrates the erosion of American influence in the country than the fact that for two months the Embassy had apparently no knowledge of the assault which was being planned against it. What had for years been the centre into which all information about the whole Middle East was daily fed now was totally ignorant of what was going on at its own doorstep. Except for occasional formal contacts between Laingen and Yazdi the Embassy staff lived and worked in isolation.

When the world learned from its newspapers and television screens of the attack on the Embassy it got the impression that this was the work of an undisciplined mob, which had been spurred into spontaneous action by news of the Shah's arrival in America and by the exhortations of religious fanatics. This was far from being the case. When Hafiz was interrogated by the revolutionary authorities he gave them all the information about the Embassy he could – where the guards were stationed, what he thought were the weak points in the perimeter and so on. He provided them with a plan of the whole Embassy complex, so that when the attack took place there was a trained task force ready which knew exactly what it was to do. Perhaps forty or fifty students had been involved in this initial planning under the control of Khoeiny, and as many as 450, who called themselves the *murabitun* (the name which, in the early days of Islam, was used for the men in the outposts that guarded the frontiers against

Byzantium), had been briefed for the final assault. The mass demonstration outside the Embassy which the world saw was no doubt made up of many thousands, but it was the *murabitun* who scaled the walls and fences at prearranged points and made for the preselected targets inside. Maybe ten of them were armed with revolvers, but they relied for success mainly on speed and careful preparation. Khomeini had encouraged the idea of action against the Americans, and doubtless knew that something was being planned, but details of the assault on the Embassy were left to Khoeiny and the students.

In three hours it was all over. As soon as the crowd started gathering Laingen went off to the Ministry of Foreign Affairs to protest and ask for protection. By the time he got back, occupation of the Embassy had been completed, so he remained outside and had to serve out his detention inside the Foreign Ministry building. The remaining Embassy staff were uncertain how to react. One of the Marines on the gate was armed with a machine-gun but had no orders to fire, so when the mob taunted him with 'If you want to shoot us, go ahead and shoot' he could do nothing. He was wounded and disarmed. Some tear-gas was used in an attempt to hold back the invaders, and there were steel security doors in some of the buildings which were shut. Meanwhile the shredding machines were working flat out, and other documents were being burned. But it was all to no avail. From later discussions I got the impression that Khomeini was agreeably surprised by the morning's events. He had probably not believed it would be possible for the whole Embassy to be occupied – certainly not in so short a time and with no loss of life.

One consequence of the occupation of the Embassy was that the student body, or rather the elite among them, the *murabitun*, became a political force in its own right. It was they who had prepared and executed the assault; it was they who now had control of the hostages; it was they who had captured and continued to hold the world headlines. At the beginning of December I had the chance to make their acquaintance. I had come, like so many other newspapermen, to Tehran to see for myself what was going on, and like the other newspapermen I hoped, but without being optimistic, to be able to meet some of them. To my surprise, the day I arrived in Tehran I was rung up by one of the students, who said that they had read in a newspaper of my arrival, knew of my friendship with Nasser, and would like to have the opportunity to meet me and exchange revolutionary experiences. 'We have questions we want to ask you,' the message said.

At first I thought the telephone call might be a hoax. A serving ambassador who spoke English had been attached to me by the Iranian Foreign Ministry, and when I told him that I wanted to go to the American Embassy he looked at me as if he thought I was mad. However, I told him that we had better go and see; if it was a hoax no harm would be done. So we set off.

Outside the main gate of the Embassy there was a milling throng of people, and, as I was later to discover, they were there by night as well as by day. If the citizens of Tehran had nothing else to do they would go along to the American Embassy for entertainment and political participation. There they would find speeches and exhortations directed at them from loudspeakers inside the Embassy walls, and other loudspeakers blaring out martial music, while on the pavements outside there were people selling cassettes of Khomeini's sermons, groups studying the Koran and listening to Islamic teaching, some girls in black *chadors* offering pictures of Khomeini and books about Islam and revolutionary justice, while other girls in blue jeans sold the writings of Lenin and Trotsky and assorted Marxist pamphlets. This was the Revolution in its most visible and characteristic form, and ironically it was all taking place in what had formerly been Franklin Roosevelt Street, now called Ayatollah Talagani Street – after the popular divine who had died recently.

After my companion had made his way through the crowd to the Embassy doors and announced us, four revolutionary guards and a girl with a machine-gun emerged. They gave me a boisterous welcome, embracing me – all revolutionaries together! In a rather touching demonstration of their administrative efficiency they presented me and my companion with badges bearing our names, which we had to pin on our jackets, as if we were entering an American defence establishment – not that there was much likelihood of ourselves or our identities being lost. The badges had to be given up when we left.

I spent four hours inside the Embassy with the students – three hours in discussions and one hour in a conducted tour round the compound. To begin with they assured me that they had found the Embassy prepared to stand a five-year siege, and they took me to a building which was crammed with vast quantities of food – cornflakes, eggs, tins of tunafish and sardines, cheeses, and so on. 'Look at that!' they exclaimed triumphantly, flinging open the door. 'That's not preparation for a siege,' I said, 'that's a PX.' 'What's a PX?' they asked. I explained that it was a sort of co-operative grocery store and that all big American institutions abroad, civil or military, had one. I think they felt rather deflated at having to give up the idea of the five-year siege.

It was abundantly clear to me that the students were obsessed with the idea that the Americans might be preparing to mount another counter-coup. Memories of 1953 were uppermost in their minds. They all knew about Kermit Roosevelt's book *Countercoup*, and most of them had read extracts from it. Although, largely owing to intervention by the British, who were anxious that the part they and the oil company had played in organizing the coup should not become known, this book had been withdrawn before publication, a few copies of it had got out and been duplicated. In *Countercoup* (whose subtitle is, significantly, 'The Struggle for the Control of Iran') Roosevelt, then a senior official in the CIA, explains in detail how the operation code-named 'Ajax' was planned and executed. It was, he says, 'a co-operative venture which allied the Shah of Iran, Winston Churchill, Anthony Eden and other British representatives with President Eisenhower, John Foster Dulles and the U.S. Central Intelligence Agency. The alliance was to be formed for the purpose of replacing an Iranian Prime Minister, Dr. Mohammed Mossadegh.' He describes in detail the meeting on 25 June 1953 in the Secretary of State's office, attended by top American service and diplomatic officials, at which he briefed them on Ajax (the first draft for which, incidentally, had been prepared by the British). Secretary of State Dulles picked up the printed paper outlining the plan, which had been placed on his desk. 'So this,' he said, 'is how we get rid of that madman Mossadegh!' It was; and there was not one of the students inside or outside the Embassy that day who did not believe that what had been done once might well be attempted again. There was not one who did not know of the remark, quoted by Roosevelt in this book, which the Shah made to him when Operation Ajax had been successfully completed and Mossadeq had been toppled and placed under arrest: 'I owe my throne to God, my people, my army – and to you!' And of those four to whom the Shah expressed his gratitude, there was only one to whom the students felt any was due from him, and that was the last – the CIA.

Nor was the anxiety of the students without foundation. It was not surprising that the Americans should have searched around for some means of undermining the authority of Khomeini, which seemed in

those days to be daily consolidating itself. They were doing their best
to build up Ayatollah Kazim Shariatmadari as a rival focus of influence, and were working among the minorities with whom they had
in the past had many contacts – the Kurds, the Azerbaijanis, the
Baluchis, the Arabs in Khuzistan. These minorities had all had some
part to play in the Revolution and were looking for their reward. They
feared that if they did not extract some concessions from the central
government now they might never get any, and the Americans were
quite ready to work on their impatience. It was impossible to persuade
the students or Khomeini that the Shah's journey to the States did not
represent the opening of a new stage in the American counteroffensive of which their other activities inside Iran were a part.

I found the students were very conscious that the struggle they had
embarked upon was going to be a long and difficult one. They knew
that their demand for the Shah and his money to be returned to Iran
was unlikely to be met, so they were going to have to prepare
themselves for a prolonged operation. Those inside the Embassy had
divided the work up among a number of committees. There was one
committee responsible for catering – for the food supplies of the
hostages and of their guards. The Americans could of course be
supplied with suitable food from their own 'siege' supplies, sup-
plemented by fresh fruit and vegetables from outside. The students
were not keen to help themselves to the American food, however,
fearing that it might contain pork.

Another committee was responsible for information, for the daily
proclamation and communiqués which were issued and for a daily
briefing for the foreign pressmen waiting outside, another for administration of the Embassy compound, while a political committee
maintained contact with the Revolutionary Council. The *murabitun*
took turns to go back to the university to carry on their studies, and a
continuous stream could be seen going and coming between the
university and the Embassy through the back door. Overall leadership
was in the hands of a body calling itself the Consultative Committee of
the Murabitun in the American Embassy.

This was a most extraordinary community – a closed society, in its
way as isolated and inward-looking as the hostages it had seized, a
community fully conscious of the power it was exercising, proud to
have the eyes of the world upon it. For years these young men and
women had been living a precarious underground existence, many of
them suffering at the hands of Savak. Now anything they said or did
was assured the attention of all the international microphones and

television cameras waiting expectantly outside the Embassy gates. It was an intoxicating change, and sometimes I got the impression that they were talking more to themselves than to anybody else, as if they could hardly believe the freedom of speech and action they had won.

Every member of this community seemed prepared to engage in endless discussions about the nature of Islamic society and Islamic government. They had respect for only one person – Khomeini. They were prepared to defy President Carter or anybody else. They cared nothing at all for talk of international law, maintaining that the Revolution had created its own law and so could acknowledge no other authority than itself. I felt I was among people who were desperately sincere but woefully lacking in experience. When I asked them what was the real object of what they were doing in the Embassy, they told me that they wanted to show up the Americans for what they were: 'We are the first people on earth who have cut the imperialists down to size!' I had to tell them I was sorry, but this was just not true. At the time of Suez, we in Egypt had defeated two old imperialist powers. Other Arabs – the Algerians, for example – had done the same. And what about the Vietnamese? Had they not shown to the world the limitations of American power?

My first meeting with the students took place in the large conference hall of the building belonging to the Commercial Attaché. Our discussions were conducted in a mixture of Arabic and English, one young man who had trained with the Palestinian commandos in Lebanon and knew some Arabic acting as interpreter. But after a while he became tired and there were some criticisms of his translation, so another student came from the back of the hall and suggested we should switch to English with him acting as interpreter. This we did. The whole discussion was recorded on tape because they said they wanted their absent colleagues to hear it.

To begin with there were seventy to eighty students present, about ten of them girls. Most of them were between the ages of about nineteen and twenty-five. Some of the men had beards, but not all. They were dressed in an incongruous mixture of clothes they had worn at home and things they had picked up in the Embassy – jeans and combat jackets. The girls gave the impression of being even more militant than the men – a few of them almost frighteningly so. All of them wore Islamic dress, including *chadors*, but without the veil. (The wearing of the *chador* is not nearly as prevalent in revolutionary Iran as many people outside have been led to suppose; and when some days later I asked a colleague of mine, as a test, to check the number of girls in the Foreign Ministry who were wearing *chadors* he found that only two out of fifty were.) After some time we were joined by other students coming direct from the university, so that by the end there must have been more than 100 of them.

Our discussion was animated and vivid. The main point, to which they continually returned, was that Islam represented the only possible answer to the West. There was no hint that any of them had any use for communism. Profound as was their respect for Nasser, and of course for Mossadeq, they felt that these two had stressed nationalism more than Islam, and they argued that this had led them into dangerous compromises. And for the *murabitun* compromise was a word full of the most sinister connotations. I explained to them that I was an unrepentant believer in Arab nationalism. I pointed out that the two main ingredients which made the Arabs a nation were language and culture, so that if I talked about Arab history and Arab nationalism I was automatically to a great extent talking about Islam. But they refused to accept this argument.

At times the discussion became quite heated. It made me very conscious of the difficulties which obliged Sanjabi, Beni-Sadr, and Yazdi to resign as Foreign Minister, and which made it so difficult for their successor, Qotbzadeh, to operate at all. As Yazdi later explained to me, he found it impossible to talk to the students. They could afford to be idealists, he said; the Foreign Minister could not. It was a dilemma which had been inherent in the Revolution from the outset – the conflict between dogma and human nature, between religion and history, between the absolute and the relative.

The last words I heard from the students were 'We have obliterated twenty-five years from the history of Iran.' They insisted that they had occupied the Embassy buildings because it was these that had been made the headquarters of the counter-revolution; it was in them that the arrest of Mossadeq and the assassination of Hussein Fatemi, the two leaders of the first stage of the Revolution, had been planned. So now, after a quarter of a century, the forces of the Revolution had wiped out the shame of its first defeat.

# 2

# THE BEAR AND THE LION

THE *murabitun* spoke about obliterating twenty-five years of Iranian history, but the humiliations resulting from foreign interference which are so vivid in their memory, and in the memory of almost every Iranian, go back a long way before the counter-coup of 1953. Persia, like the rest of what in those days was known as the Near East, had been profoundly affected by the winds of change which blew in from the West with increasing violence as the nineteenth century progressed. True, Persia had never been part of the Ottoman Empire, but as this greatest of all Islamic states, which had once been a barrier against western penetration and, since its rulers were Caliphs, the guardian of Islamic legitimacy, declined into the Sick Man of Europe, Persians too awoke to the challenge of new forces and new ideas.

Many of those Moslems who watched the apparently inexorable advance of western influences turned for assurance and help to religion. The Ottoman Empire was supposed to have a religious basis, yet it was collapsing. Why? The answer, they felt, must be that its rulers had betrayed their religious inheritance. Western-style nationalism was meaningless; the only course, they believed, was a return to the true spirit of Islam. So it was that movements of puritan fundamentalism broke out in outlying regions of the Empire – Wahhabis in Arabia in the second half of the eighteenth century; Sanussis in Libya and the Mahdiyya in the Sudan in the second half of the nineteenth. But there was an element of tribalism in all such movements which restricted their impact, and eventually they survived only by allying themselves with some powerful family, which meant that two of them developed into hereditary monarchies.

A response to the challenge of the West which was to have more widespread and lasting effect is associated with the name of one of the great thinkers of Islam, a name which is held in much respect by the leaders of the Iranian Revolution today – Jamaleddin el-Afghani. Afghani (1839–97) travelled widely, to India, Russia, France and England, as well as living for long periods in Cairo and Constantinople. Everywhere he saw the Moslem world under pressure from the West, and particularly from Britain. It was not so much a direct military assault that he thought Moslem countries had to fear (though that had of course brought about the occupation of Egypt) as their subtle undermining by western thought, by the corrupting influences of materialism, rationalism and missionaries. These it was which had brought the Moslem world to its current state of weakness. But if Moslems examined their religion and understood it properly they would be strong enough to resist the West, physically as well as spiritually. Islam, he reminded them, was much more than a matter of prayers and ceremonies; it should order every aspect of society, man's relations with his fellow men, with the authorities of the state, and the state's relations with other states. If only people realized it, Islam was the one perfect, comprehensive religion. But it needed a Renaissance, a Reformation.

One of the countries where Afghani saw the corrupting influence of the West most in evidence was Persia. (He had in fact been born in Persia, though, as his name implies, he preferred to be regarded as a Sunni from Afghanistan.) There he found two great European powers, Britain and Russia, quarrelling, as he said, 'over the dead body of Persia.' Nor was there much exaggeration in such a judgement. This was the time of Nasruddin Shah, a ruler whose extravagance and financial incompetence can only be compared with those of the Khedive Ismail. But whereas the most famous of the concession hunters who thronged Egypt in Ismail's day, de Lesseps, did at least build the Suez Canal, the most notorious of the Europeans who hoped to plunder Persia, Baron Julius de Reuter, achieved nothing. As Curzon wrote of the concession granted to Reuter by Nasruddin Shah in 1872, 'When published to the world, it was found to contain the most complete and extraordinary surrender of the entire industrial resources of a kingdom into foreign hands that had probably ever been dreamed of, much less accomplished, in history.' The concession covered existing and potential undertakings of every description – railways and tramways, mines, canals, roads, public works, mills, factories, telegraphs, banks, and the farming of the customs for twenty-five years. And all this for an annual payment of £10,000! The news of the concession provoked so much indignation that the Shah's throne was endangered. Popular resentment, to which were added official Russian protests, forced the Shah to back down. The concession was cancelled.

Eighteen years later came a second act in the concession drama. On 8 March 1890 the Shah's government granted to an Englishman, G. F. Talbot, a concession covering the production, sale, and export of all tobacco in Persia for a period of fifty years. In return Talbot was to pay the Shah £15,000 a year, plus one quarter of any net profits accruing to the company formed to exploit the concession. This time an unusually effective way of dealing with another bitterly resented foreign intrusion was found; the leading *mujtahid*, Haji Mirza Shirazi, issued a *fetwa* (an authoritative opinion) declaring the use of tobacco in any form by the faithful to be a sin. This *fetwa* was obeyed with a unanimity which astonished foreign observers. Rioting spread, and the concession was withdrawn. Before this happened the British Minister in Tehran had significantly reported to the Foreign Office: 'We are in the presence of revolution.'

The government and the foreign concessionaires had been defeated by an alliance of mullahs and reformists, both backed by the growing sense of national consciousness. It was the same mixture of forces which was to be responsible for a real revolution sixteen years later. In the interval, discontent continued to grow. Afghani was expelled from Persia in 1891, and then on 1 May 1896 one of his followers assassinated Nasruddin Shah after a reign of forty-nine years. He was succeeded by Muzaffaruddin Shah, a weak rather than vicious character.

In all those parts of the Middle East which were subjected to interference by European powers, or in some cases to the actual presence of European troops, the 1890s and 1900s were years of political ferment. The inability of their own autocracies to withstand the European democracies gave impetus to demands for political reform. This period saw the creation in Egypt of Mustafa Kamil's National Party, in Turkey of the Committee for Union and Progress, and in Persia the series of demonstrations and protests which forced the Shah in 1906 to grant a constitution and to summon the first Majlis (parliament). It is this constitution which the popular movement of 1978–9 insisted the Shah should implement, and it is the men who originally fought for it – men like the *mujtahids* Mohammed Tabatabai and Abdulla Bahbahani – who became heroes of the later revolution.

Not that the reformers enjoyed their triumph for long. The situation in Persia was complicated by the fact that here two of the great powers, Britain and Russia, faced each other in almost equal strength and with almost equal determination. This meant that it was not difficult for the Shahs to play off Britain and Russia against each other to their own advantage. Little more than a year later, Muzaffaruddin Shah, with Russian backing, fought back; the constitution was abrogated, the Majlis bombarded and dispersed.

What particularly distressed the Persians about the whole affair was the behaviour of Britain. It was to be expected that the Tsars, who were resisting the idea of a constitution in their own country, would oppose the introduction of one just over their borders. But the British had encouraged the constitutional movement, which looked to British parliamentary practice as a model. It was the fact that over 10,000 reformists demanding a constitution took sanctuary in the British Embassy compound, and stayed there for several weeks, which largely forced the Shah's hand. But only a year later, in August 1907, after long and secret negotiations, the governments of Britain and Russia announced that they had signed a convention which divided Persia into three parts, a large Russian sphere of influence in the north, a smaller British sphere of influence in the south, and a neutral zone including Tehran in the centre.

The need for such a convention was dictated by the situation in Europe, and particularly by the growing strength of Germany, with its *Drang nach Osten*, which alarmed London and St Petersburg equally. But there was also a new ingredient in the mixture of which much was to be heard – oil. The importance of this fuel was becoming increasingly appreciated in the industrialized West, and Persia was one of the countries where it was believed it might be found. All the geological evidence pointed to the north of the country, the Russian zone, as being the most promising area for search, but it was at Mesjid i-Suleiman in the British zone in the south that oil was first struck in 1908. For many years the wells of south-west Persia were to be much the most productive in the Middle East.

In the First World War Persia, though nominally neutral, became a theatre of war, in which British and Russian armies occupied parts of the country in order to check the advance of Germany and Turkey. As far back as 1879 the Russians, at the Shah's request, had raised a gendarmerie force in the north, called the Cossack Brigade, with Russian officers and Persian NCOs and enlisted men. It was this Brigade which in 1907 had bombarded the Majlis and re-established the Shah in his capital. But when the Russian Revolution broke out in 1917 the Russian officers withdrew, leaving the Brigade in the hands of its Persian NCOs.

One of the most capable of these was a sergeant called Reza Mirza, and it was through the intervention of the commander of the British forces in Persia, General Edmund Ironside – the British being concerned to fill the vacuum caused by Russian withdrawal – that Reza Mirza was appointed deputy commander of the Cossack Brigade.

In the immediate aftermath of the war Persia was in a state of chaos, but, like the rest of the Middle East, profoundly influenced by the growth of national feeling which the war had stimulated. The Arabs were everywhere demanding the independence which they believed the Allies had promised them; Egypt was in ferment; in Turkey Mustafa Kemal was reforming the nucleus of a shattered empire into a smaller but homogeneous nation state. It was not surprising that in the circumstances Reza Mirza Khan (as he became when an officer), a man of iron will and determination, should have gained control first of his own Brigade, then of Tehran, and finally of the whole country.

The last of the Qajar Shahs was deposed, and Reza Khan was encouraged to follow the example of his neighbour, Mustafa Kemal, who had just got rid of the last Turkish Sultan, and declare Persia a republic. But this was the heyday of monarchies of the Middle East. Not only was there King Fuad of Egypt, with his eye on the vacant caliphate, but new thrones were being created for the sons of Hussein, self-appointed King of the Hejaz – for Feisal in Baghdad and for Abdulla in Amman. In Arabia Abdel Aziz ibn Saud was now a king too, and consolidating his power. So when the ayatollahs expressed their opinion that a republic was alien to the traditions of Persia Reza Shah did not need much persuading. He was proclaimed shah in 1925, and performed his own coronation on 26 April the next year.

Reza Shah was of peasant origin and quite illiterate, though he taught himself to read and write after he became an officer. To consolidate his throne he had to create some form of legitimacy which might replace that of birth. He did this in a number of ways. He looked back beyond the Qajars whom he had supplanted to an earlier stage of Persian history, taking for the title of the dynasty he hoped to found the name of the language of pre-Islamic Persia – Pahlevi – and changing the country's name from Persia to an earlier form, Iran. Unfortunately his greed rivalled that of the worst of his Qajar predecessors, whose property he appropriated. It was estimated that when Reza Shah abdicated in 1941 he owned two thousand villages and had a quarter of a million of his subjects working directly for him on the land.

In the late 1930s Reza Shah had another idea. His eldest son was now of an age to marry. What could better demonstrate the acceptance of his house than to ally it with the oldest royal family in the Middle East, the House of Mohammed Ali in Egypt? It would mean changing the constitution, which laid down that the wife of the shah must be Iranian by birth, but Reza Shah was not the man to let a little thing like that stop him.

So a tentative approach was made to Cairo, and in the Chief of the Royal Cabinet, Ali Maher Pasha, it found a sympathetic listener. Ali Maher had been the king's man in the days of Fuad and was determined to be equally useful to Fuad's son, Farouk, who had succeeded to the throne in 1937. A memorandum by Ali Maher, which was found in Abdin Palace after the 1952 revolution, shows him thinking in terms which Queen Victoria or Bismarck would have understood, but which seem a little out of place in the Middle East in the 1930s. King Farouk had four sisters; might not these, Ali Maher suggested, become the instruments to extend Egyptian influence throughout the area? With luck thrones might be found for them all, and Tehran would do as a start.

Farouk was agreeable, and so early in 1939 the Crown Prince, Mohammed Reza, arrived in Cairo. The eldest of the four, the beautiful Fawzia, was chosen to be the future empress. To the sophisticated Egyptian court the young man they now scrutinized with so much curiosity appeared embarrassingly shy and uncertain of himself. Had they known more about his upbringing they would perhaps have been less surprised and shown more understanding.

The Prince had been six years old when his father marched on Tehran on the first stage of his climb to power. The boy had therefore been born and passed his formative years in the austere surroundings of barrack life. Then the scene changed dramatically. He suddenly found that he had to get used to living in palaces; he was confronted by strange faces and new duties. It was now too that his education began, and, though he was an intelligent child and keen to learn, his schooling became a nightmare to him.

In the course of one of the talks I had with him, the Shah gave me two examples of what it was like to be Crown Prince under Reza Shah. He told me how Reza Shah used to make a point of periodically coming along to see how his eldest son's education was progressing. These 'days of inspection', as they were called, were prepared for with desperate thoroughness by teachers and pupil alike. They would go over together time and time again the questions the Prince was likely to be asked and the answers he was to give, until surely he must be able to acquit himself in a manner that would do credit to all. But when the monarch, with flashing eyes and bristling moustache, strode into the room in full military uniform, the teachers were reduced to quivering incoherence and the Prince's mind became a total blank. The monarch shouted, hurling barrack-room abuse at everyone within reach – the son was clearly a nincompoop and his so-called teachers idiots. It took them a long time to recover, and then the threat of the next 'day of inspection' would loom ahead.

The second example from his childhood which the Shah told me of was when his father decided that all the book-learning he was supposed to be having was a waste of time, and that the only training a future ruler of Iran needed was how to be a soldier. So instructions were given that his bed should be removed, and that in future he was to sleep on the ground. It was only after the intervention of his mother, known as Taj el-Muluk, that his bed was eventually returned to him. She came from a landowning family, had married Reza Khan soon after he became an officer, and retained some influence over him. She bitterly resented it when later he married two more wives, though she accompanied him on his exile to Africa and was with him when he died.

The Crown Prince had a twin sister, Princess Ashraf, who was to play an important part in politics during her brother's reign. She is a woman with a very strong personality, and she told me that in her presence Reza Shah, who greatly admired the toughness of her character, so like, he felt, to his own, had once protested that nature must have made a mix-up in the womb of his wife, because Ashraf ought to have been the boy and Mohammed Reza the girl. The old Shah was never good at concealing his feelings, and his bluntly expressed disapproval – contempt almost – for his son can have done nothing to increase the young man's self-reliance.

Princess Fawzia received a great shock when she first met her betrothed. She had been shown photographs of him in which he looked fairly personable, but in the flesh he appeared sickly and miserable. Farouk understood her feelings, and adopted a patronizing attitude towards the Shahpur (his official title as Crown Prince). The Crown Prince reciprocated by detecting in Farouk what he described as 'criminal tendencies'. All the same, Farouk instructed Ali Maher to talk his sister round – to point out to her how important it was for Egyptian influence to be extended through the Middle East and for a future ruler of Iran to be half Egyptian by blood. Fawzia, who was sensible as well as charming, agreed to go through with the marriage for reasons of state, but, as she said later, she felt she was being made to play a part in a historical novel, and a part which she did not at all understand. The reactions of the Queen Mother, Queen Nazli, were forthright. All right, she said in effect, let the marriage go ahead. But for goodness' sake get someone to teach the young man the rudiments of etiquette; he has no table manners.

So the marriage took place on 15 March 1939, and turned out, rather surprisingly, to be not unhappy. But it was never an easy one for Fawzia. She found the Tehran court very provincial after Cairo, and Reza Shah's first wife, Taj el-Muluk, accused her, not without reason, of finding the old Persian aristocracy – the numerous Qajar princes and princesses and people like Qavam es-Sultaneh – easier to get on with than Reza Shah's military cronies and their wives. But she refused to be browbeaten by her father-in-law. After what her husband had told her she had dreaded her first meeting with the old tyrant, but she stood up to him.

Almost immediately the war came, and changed everything. Middle Eastern royalty viewed the conflict between Germany and the Allies very differently. The Hashemites in Iraq and Jordan and King Ibn Saud betted on an Allied victory, but Farouk and Reza Shah expected – and hoped for – a German victory. The Shah, a dictator in his own country, had a natural sympathy for other dictatorships, while Farouk, whose political judgements were always superficial, inherited connections with Fascist Italy through his father King Fuad. Both rulers were, like so many others, shocked by the fall of France and assumed that this would lead to a speedy Axis victory. The Shah was in continual contact with the Germans, and Farouk, whose scope in British-occupied Egypt was limited, maintained his contacts with them through a special envoy in Tehran, Youssef Zulficar, his own father-in-law, with whom he communicated directly without going through the Ministry of Foreign Affairs.

After the fall of France the Shah's cooperation with the Germans became more blatant, and the number of German 'businessmen' in Tehran more ostentatious. It cannot have surprised him that, when the Germans invaded Russia in June 1941, British and Russian troops invaded his country and compelled him to abdicate in favour of his son.

Mohammed Reza once described to me the last meeting he had with his father. He said it was the first time in his life he had seen him behave like a father, and not, as always before, like a king or a commander-in-chief. There were tears in the old man's eyes when they met, and the young man felt too moved to speak. The father's first remark was a question: 'Can you keep the throne?' The son said nothing. 'I didn't fail to keep the throne,' the father went on, 'but forces stronger than me defeated me. I kept the throne for you. Will you be able to keep it?' The son could only nod. Reza Shah continued: 'Pay attention, my son. Don't resist. We and the whole world are facing a storm that is bigger than any of us. Bow your head till the storm passes.' And then he added: 'Get a son!' He repeated this: 'Get a son!' And then he went out of the room and into exile in South Africa, where he died.

There was a curious sequel to all this, which affected relations between Iran and Egypt. Reza Shah took with him into exile a beautiful old jewelled sword which he had chosen from the fabulous imperial treasury of Iran to wear at his coronation. When he died his widow put the sword in the coffin beside him, and asked for permission for the body to be sent back to Iran for burial. But the British and Russian authorities, who were still in occupation, refused. So the coffin was sent to Egypt, where it was given a temporary resting place in the Rifa'i mosque.*

After the war was over it became possible for burial in Iran to take place, and the coffin was flown back to Tehran. But when the coffin was opened it was found that the sword was missing. Taj el-Muluk knew that it should be there, because she had put it there herself, and thought that the only possible explanation of what had happened to it (which was in fact the true one) was that Farouk had heard about the sword, had the coffin opened, seen the sword, and liked it so much that he had appropriated it.

Poor Fawzia was made to suffer for this. Her mother-in-law made her life miserable with her taunts – 'So this is the way royalty behaves in your country, is it? The House of Pahlevi may not be so old as the House of Mohammed Ali, but at least we aren't common thieves,' and

---

* It was here that after his death in Cairo in 1980 the second Pahlevi shah, Mohammed Reza, was to be buried. When the exiled Shah reached his final place of asylum in the spring of 1980, his host, President Sadat, planned to build him a suitably luxurious villa on the Mediterranean shore close to his own summer retreat near Alexandria. Work had already begun on this when the Shah had to go into hospital again for further treatment for cancer. There were fears that he might not survive the operation. Work was suspended on the Mediterranean villa and begun on a tomb for him in the Rifa'i mosque. Thereafter, according to whether the bulletins from the hospital were optimistic or pessimistic, work was continued on the villa or the tomb.

so on. There was naturally a lot of gossip about this, and there was a revival of criticism, in which the formidable Princess Ashraf joined, that the Queen was not an Iranian as constitutionally she should have been. To make matters worse, Fawzia had only been able to produce a daughter, not a son. When she went back to Cairo for a holiday in 1948 Farouk decided that the House of Mohammed Ali had endured sufficient insults from those parvenus in Tehran; Fawzia was ordered not to go back and a divorce was arranged in November, in spite of the fact that she had by now grown quite fond of Tehran and of her husband.

# 3
# ENTER THE EAGLE

THE DECADE between 1941 and 1951 saw the seeds sown of the crisis which was to convulse the world in 1979. For over a century Iran had been buffeted between the rival interests of two expanding giants, the British and Russian empires. But it had been a poor country, with nothing except its geographical location to tempt outside interference. Now the scene was changing. A new state, America, was joining in the old power rivalries, and the world's most desirable commodity, oil, had become a stake in the struggle.

When British and Russian troops made their coordinated entry into Iran in August 1941 the country became a highway for the conveyance of arms and supplies to the Russian front and one of the main sources of oil for the Allied war effort. But after Pearl Harbour the Americans came into the war, and it was then that the picture began to undergo a complete transformation.

For the people of Iran the British and the Russians were the old giants and enemies with whom they were familiar, but America was a newcomer to the scene. Surely it might be possible to call in the new world to redress the balance of the old. Persians knew little about the Americans, but what they did know they liked. They remembered the American economist Morgan Schuster, who had made a gallant effort to reorganize Persia's finances in 1911 until he was jockeyed out of his job by Russian intrigue. And at a time when Britain and Russia had their backs to the wall at Alamein and Stalingrad, America seemed to be a country of almost unlimited resources and, more important, of almost unlimited goodwill. The Americans were the goodies in white hats the world was familiar with from Hollywood, who would ride up on their splendid horses and deliver the unhappy captives (including Iran) from the baddies. If the Americans had a fault it was perhaps that these gallant cowboys appeared to know too little about the outside world, including countries like Iran – that they were too politically naive. On so many occasions in these hectic months after Pearl Harbour, as more and more Americans in and out of uniform poured into the Middle East, the princes and politicians who met them would come away shaking their heads in astonishment – these people seemed to them to know nothing, to have everything to learn.

In fact, though individual Americans may have been ignorant and innocent, the American government and American businessmen knew exactly what they wanted in the Middle East, and were determined to get it. The two things they wanted were air facilities, to begin with for the purpose of the war effort but with an eye to strategic and commercial considerations when the war was over, and oil concessions. On these two desiderata much was to be built.

From the point of view of both air communications and oil Iran was obviously a key country, and in the four years which were to elapse before the war ended America was to consolidate its position there in a quite remarkable manner. If two of the main features of the post-war world were to be the confrontation of America and Russia in the Cold War and the replacement by America of British influence in the Middle East, it can be said that in Iran by the end of 1945 both these features were already clearly established. It is instructive to watch the process by which this was achieved.★

In their efforts to consolidate a new position in wartime Iran the Americans started with a number of advantages. The welcome which the Iranian people were prepared to accord them has already been mentioned. This was an asset which, because of past history, neither Britain nor Russia could ever hope to enjoy, and the Americans, though determined to work as loyal allies in the defeat of the Axis, were naturally anxious to preserve the purity of their reputation. As late as December 1945, after the war was ended, the American Secretary of State, Dean Acheson, was to declare: 'The United States is in a better position than either Great Britain or the Soviet Union to take the lead in the discussions concerning Iran because we are freer from suspicion of having selfish interests in the country than either of the other two Powers.'

It was to a large extent this reputation for being disinterested helpers which had secured for the Americans another asset of incalculable value – the confidence of the Shah. When British and Russian troops moved into Iran they were able to build on already established political foundations. The British, through the Anglo-Iranian Oil Company, had influence with politicians and among the tribes of South-West Iran (the AIOC used to pay a part of the royalties due to the government direct to the leaders of the Bakhtiar tribe, which dominated the country in which the oilfields were situated). The Russians too had

---

★ See the relevant chapters in *Foreign Relations of the United States*, several volumes of which have been published by the Historical Office of the Department of State.

their men, and though the communist Tudeh (Masses) Party had been driven underground by Reza Shah it only needed a little judicious encouragement to become a political force to be reckoned with. The Americans realized that it would be a waste of time trying to outbid the British and Russians in the business of buying political influence. They saw that the Shah needed them as much as they needed the Shah.

When the Americans appeared on the scene Mohammed Reza was a thoroughly demoralized young man. He was shocked by what had happened to his father, appalled by the responsibilities that had been thrust upon him, bewildered by all the new faces and problems surrounding him, and conscious that he had no exceptional qualities with which to meet the challenge. He was, not surprisingly, mistrustful of the many British and Russian officials with whom he had now to be in contact. He knew that the older generation of politicians had little time for him, and he reciprocated their dislike. Seyyid Zia Tabatabai, who had helped Reza Khan to organize his coup in February 1921 and was then for a few months Prime Minister, still regarded himself as a republican; Ahmed Qavam es-Sultaneh came from one of the old aristocratic families which, as the Shah well knew, despised him and his father as upstarts; Dr Mohammed Mossadeq too was a wealthy landowner whose mother had been a Qajar. The only one among the leading politicians for whom the Shah felt any sympathy was Hussein Ala, a man of humbler origins and more of a diplomat than a politician. He became Minister of Court and to some extent the mentor of the young monarch.

In their attempt to woo the Shah the Americans started badly. As if to symbolize the importance of Iran's future international role, Tehran had been the venue for the first Big Three conference at which the course of the war was plotted and the foundations for the post-war settlement laid. At this conference, in November–December 1943, Roosevelt had been invited by Stalin to stay at the Russian Embassy. There the Shah had paid courtesy calls on both world leaders, but whereas Stalin had returned the call, walking without guards or attendants to the Palace and spending three hours in conversation with his host,★ Roosevelt had made no such gesture. Instead, when he got

---

★ It was during this visit that the question of the supply of Russian arms (tanks and planes) to Iran was first broached. Stalin offered them, and the Shah accepted the offer, though when he learned how many experts and technicians would have to be sent in with them he felt obliged to decline, much to the Russians' annoyance.

back to Washington he sent the Shah a telegram saying that, because his visit to Iran had necessarily been so short, he could not pretend to know the country well, but that what had struck him most about it was 'the lack of trees on the mountain slopes'. Might he recommend an experimental programme of planting trees 'or even shrubs'? The Shah declared himself impressed by the President's wise advice, and promised a programme of afforestation; but privately he was mortified by what he saw as a snub.

However, other Americans more than made up for Roosevelt's insensitivity. In February 1944 the Shah and some of his senior ministers were flown from Tehran to the American Air Force base at Abadan in a Liberator plane, and on the return journey in a DC3 'the Shah was given an opportunity to handle the controls.' Nor were other members of the royal family neglected. In the same month the Hollywood singing star Nelson Eddy gave a special concert in Tehran which was attended by the Princesses Ashraf and Shams.

The Shah found the Americans good listeners as well as good talkers. He felt able to unburden himself to the American Ambassador, Leland B. Morris, as he could to nobody else. In December 1944 he told Morris of his wish that Iran should be democratic but of his fears that lack of education made this difficult. 'To arrive at this the Shah desired very strongly to establish free education without the exclusion of private education for those able to afford it.' Free education could only be paid for by the exploitation of Iran's agricultural and mineral resources, and for this he looked for 'the whole-hearted support of the United States'.

Morris was impressed. Seven months later in a dispatch to the State Department he summed up his opinion of the Shah: 'He is today of a mental maturity that belies his 25 years. He is deeply distressed over the poverty and disease among his people, their low standard of living and bad working conditions and appreciative of the fact that if Iranian patriotism is to be revitalized in order to stem the tide and appeal of communism, drastic and urgent steps must be taken to relieve the misery in his country.' Islam, said the Shah, could not be a sure barrier against communism 'when hunger, disease and misery are left un-checked.' And he added once again his earnest hope that the United States would 'lend him every possible assistance toward solving the grave problems with which he is faced.'

Another advantage enjoyed by the Americans was the presence of numerous advisers in almost every branch of the Iranian government. As soon as they become involved in the war they had acted in Iran as everywhere else with their customary vigor and thoroughness. Within six months of their first appearance on the scene there were 28,000 American servicemen in Iran, most of them concerned with the delivery of war material to the Russian front, but others with a vast network of ancillary services – signals, road-making, medical and so on, not forgetting, of course, intelligence. An American, Dr A. C. Millspaugh, had been appointed Administrator General of Iranian Finance, with executive authority over virtually the whole economic life of the country; General Clarence S. Ridley was head of a military mission to the Iranian army; Colonel H. Norman Schwarzkopf was adviser, and later director, for the gendarmerie (rural police); General Donald H. Connolly was commander of a separate Persian Gulf Command, with its headquarters in Abadan; General Patrick Hurley was President Roosevelt's Personal Representative in Iran. All these high-powered officials headed considerable staffs of their fellow countrymen. They were acceptable to the Iranian government and people because they were friendly men coming from a friendly nation, but, as happened in other parts of the world, Iranians sometimes found American friendship a bit overwhelming.

Quite early on Washington tried to assess what this massive commitment in Iran was going to imply for the future. On 31 July 1944 Edward R. Stettinius, the Acting Secretary of State, sent an important memorandum to the Chargé d'Affaires in Tehran. The State Department, he said, 'recognizes the increasing importance of American relations with Iran and is prepared to assume a more active and positive role in Iranian affairs than was possible or necessary in the prewar period.' He listed three reasons why this should be so. First, Iran having turned to America for aid, this should be given 'as unselfishly as we may . . . The President and Department have considered Iran as something of a testing ground for the Atlantic Charter and for the good faith of the United Nations.' Secondly, a strong Iran, 'free from the internal weaknesses and dissensions which breed foreign intervention,' would contribute towards a more stable world. The third reason lay in the protection and furtherance of national interests: 'This includes the possibility of sharing more fully in Iran's commerce and in the development of its resources; the strategic location of Iran for civil air bases; and the growing importance of Iranian and Arabian oil fields.'

At this stage of the war the ideals for which Americans were fighting naturally came first. It was also natural that Stettinius, like other officials in government, should be anxious to stress America's desire for the fullest cooperation with her wartime allies: 'The impression should be avoided at all costs that we intend to stand at the side of Iran as a political buffer to restrain our Allies the British and Russians with regard to Iran. We should emphasize rather the importance to the world of a strong and independent Iran as a member of the community of nations and should seek the support and sympathy of our Allies in achieving this end.'

But as the war progressed the alliance came under strain, not least in Iran, where the Americans proved themselves more than able to out-manoeuvre both their partners. Three principal problems emerged: how and when foreign troops in Iran were to be withdrawn; how to maintain the country's territorial integrity; and on what terms oil concessions should be granted. By 21 December 1944, only five months later, Stettinius was referring to Iran as 'the most prominent area of the world where inter-Allied friction might arise'.

The withdrawal of foreign troops was governed by the Declaration on Iran signed by Roosevelt, Churchill and Stalin at the close of the Tehran Conference on 1 December 1943. This paid tribute to the sacrifices made by Iran in the war, pledged Allied assistance to Iran during and after the war, and promised that all foreign troops would be withdrawn from Iran 'six months after the suspension of hostilities with Germany and her associates'. The Iranian government took this promise, with some reason, as meaning six months after VE Day (8 May 1945) and on 21 May sent notes to the three governments concerned which requested that the evacuation of troops should now proceed. However, privately the Iranians made it plain that, though they were greatly concerned to see the British and Russians depart, they were in no such hurry over the Americans. Thus on 1 June the Iranian Ambassador in Washington told Loy Henderson of the State Department (later to become ambassador in Tehran) that the Iranian note about troop withdrawals 'was of course not directed at the American troops but it was necessary to include them in order not to offend the Soviet and British Governments.'

This privileged position was extended to the Ridley and Schwarz-kopf missions. Back in 1944 it had been agreed in Washington that the Iranian army should receive priority for the allocation of arms, and that the mission to it would have to continue after the war, since 'the protection and advancement of our interests in Iran will require the strengthening of the Iranian security forces so that order may be maintained in this area, where world security might be threatened, after the withdrawal of Allied Troops.' By October 1945 the enduring value of the missions was no less recognized, but the reasons for their presence had undergone a slight change of emphasis. In a letter to the Secretary of War, the new Secretary of State, James Byrnes, wrote:

'Continuance of the Military Missions to Iran, at the request of the Iranian Government, is considered to be in the national interest of the United States. Strengthening of Iran's internal security forces by the American Missions contributes to the stabilization of Iran, and, thereby, to its reconstruction as a sound member of the international community. By increasing the ability of the Iranian Government to maintain order and security, it is hoped to remove any pretext for British or Soviet intervention in Iran's internal affairs and, accordingly, to remove such future threats to Allied solidarity and international security. The stabilization of Iran, moreover, will serve to lay a sound foundation for the development of American commercial, petroleum, and aviation interests in the Middle East.'

As things turned out, all British and Russian troops had been evacuated from Iran by May 1946, but only after an international crisis which had put the machinery of the new United Nations to the test and brought the fabric of the Iranian state to the brink of collapse. From the outset the Russians had kept a tight control over the northern zone which was occupied by their troops. They had no intention of sharing responsibility there with their allies and little intention of sharing even with representatives of the Iranian state. Dr Millspaugh found his financial and economic measures frustrated in the north; Colonel Schwarzkopf's gendarmerie were interfered with. On one occasion, for example, at the end of 1944, some gendarmes had been sent into a textile mill at Shahi, 100 miles north-east of the capital, where there was a strike, to act as 'guards'. Soviet troops moved in and disarmed them. The Iranians complained to the Americans of the 'desperate situation' in the north: 'the Russians do not permit the Iranian Government to despatch troops to the northern part of the country, and are in fact acting in such a way that all Iranian administration in the north may soon become impossible.'

Iranian suspicions that Russian behaviour was motivated by more than their usual exclusiveness and mistrust of foreigners, and was in fact aimed at securing permanent control over Iran's northern provinces, were justified. The Russians established puppet governments favourable to their interests in Azerbaijan and Kurdistan, following the pattern of hegemony which they were simultaneously setting up in eastern Europe. They were, however, hampered by the fact that Iran was not covered by the doctrine of spheres of influence as laid down, or implied, at the conferences of Yalta and Berlin, and that consequently in Iran the United States and Britain were prepared to stand firm – and, more important, had the resources on the spot to support such a stand. In this way they had the full backing of the Shah and of his wily Prime Minister, Qavam es-Sultaneh. The Azerbaijan crisis was to be one of the principal causes of the deterioration of relations between Russia and the West and was to have fateful consequences for Iran itself.

The Russians of course considered their behaviour in Iran to be perfectly justified. They had more reason than the Americans for wishing to see friendly to them a country with which they shared a thousand miles of frontier, and their ideas of what constituted friendship were perfectly clear. When they did not like the government in Tehran they accused it of fascist tendencies and of representing no more than five per cent of the population. They managed to jockey one prime minister out of office in November 1944, and accused his successor of allowing the 'forces of reaction' to remain in the saddle while persecuting 'liberal elements'. As occupying power, their control over broadcasts in the north and their exercise of censorship there and in the capital enabled them to attack those Iranians they regarded as their enemies and to build up those they regarded as their friends. All this was watched with growing alarm by the Shah, his government, and the Americans. Soon after the end of the war the American Ambassador in Tehran, Leland Morris, had reached ominous conclusions about Russian intentions. 'Ultimate Russian objectives,' he wrote in a dispatch to the State Department, 'may include access to the Persian Gulf and penetration into other regions of the Near East, but present aims are probably limited to maintenance of buffer zone in Iran as protection against attack from the south . . . I think it likely their principal aim at present is establishment in power in Tehran of so-called "popular" government like Groza regime in Rumania* which could be led by men under Soviet influence amenable to Russian demands and hostile to other foreign nations.' The Ambassador pointed out that Soviet dominance for the Iranian government would be 'definitely harmful to American interests' for four reasons:

---

* After occupation by Russian troops Rumania had been declared a republic, and in elections held in March 1948 the 'People's Democratic Front' had won virtually all the seats. Petru Groza had been made Prime Minister and introduced a constitution and regime closely modelled on Stalin's Russia.

'1. It would mean exclusion of American airlines from Iran.

'2. It would orient Iranian trade toward Russia to detriment of our commercial interests.

'3. It would end all possibility of an American oil concession in Iran.

'4. Most important of all it would mean extension of Soviet influence to shores of Persian Gulf creating potential threat to our immensely rich oil holdings in Saudi Arabia, Bahrein, and Kuwait.'

The battle over oil had been joined. When America had entered the war her oil interests were already established in a number of Middle East countries, though only recently, and were producing in quantities which by later standards seem insignificant. The Americans had appeared first in 1928 as junior partners to Britain in the old Turkish Petroleum Company (later the Iraq Petroleum Company, IPC), in which a group of American companies owned about a quarter of the capital. In 1930 a Canadian subsidiary of Standard Oil of California (BAPCO) had been given a concession in Bahrein, the products of which were marketed through Caltex, and in 1933 Gulf Oil had secured a half share, with British Petroleum holding the other half, in a new company granted the concession in Kuwait. The country which was to become far and away the biggest scene of American oil enterprise in the Middle East, Saudi Arabia, was a comparatively late starter. It was in May 1933 that a sixty-year concession for El-Hasa province was awarded, against competition by IPC, to the California Arabian Standard Oil Company (CASOC), later to become the Arabian-American Oil Company (ARAMCO), but the first well only came into production in September 1939, the month the war in Europe started, and by 1944, in spite of the American government's awareness of the need for Middle Eastern oil for the war against Japan, production had only risen to 1,050,000 tons.

In the same year production in Iran was 13,270,000 tons, almost four times that of its nearest rival in the area, Iraq. It is not surprising that Iran should have been the country which most attracted oilmen everywhere whose thoughts were turning to the post-war pattern of oil. In March 1944 a representative of the Standard-Vacuum Company had arrived in Tehran and presented his proposal for a concession to the Prime Minister, Ali Soheily. He found a sympathetic hearing. Soheily told him he would give the Americans 'every ethical opportunity' to compete with their rivals, since he remained keen on getting American oil interests into Iran. He said he was 'particularly opposed to having the entire southern coast of Iran tied up under British concessions.' It was clear that, in expressing his wish to see American participation, the Prime Minister was also expressing the point of view of the Shah.

Next month the Standard-Vacuum representative was joined in Tehran by two representatives of the Sinclair Oil Company on a similar mission. The British were also in the field for an extension of their concession, and on 16 May the American Chargé d'Affaires reported: 'All firms making preliminary arrangements for support for their proposals by rival factions in Parliament. Matter is being discussed in newspapers.' In July two petroleum geologists, A. A. Curtice and Herbert Hoover Jr, who had been commissioned by the Iranian government as advisers, arrived on the scene.

But September saw a more significant visitor. Sergei Kavtaradze, a Vice-Commissar for Foreign Affairs, appeared in Tehran accompanied by several oil technicians. The ostensible purpose of his visit was to examine some of the existing oilfields in the Russians' zone of occupation, but in fact the proposal which they put to the Shah was that they should be given exploration rights over 200,000 square miles in the north with the guarantee of a concession after that. A week after this proposal was made, a special session of the Majlis, many of whose members were on the payroll of the Anglo-Iranian Oil Company, decided that there should be no further discussion of any new oil concessions until the war was ended.

The obvious gainers by this Majlis decision were the British, who were well and profitably dug in in the south, and there was some natural suspicion that they had had a hand in it. But whatever the truth, there was nothing much the Americans or Russians could do about it, though the Russians made their anger and disapproval plain. Soviet troops armed with tommy-guns paraded through the principal streets of the capital, and there were several demonstrations by Tudeh Party supporters demanding the resignation of the Prime Minister. Various other acts of intimidation prompted the American Ambassador to comment on 1 November: 'Measures which smack of Hitlerian methods continue to be used in increasing crescendo by the Soviet authorities here.'

Although the Prime Minister (Saed) did resign, to be succeeded by Bayat, the Majlis showed no sign of being intimidated by Russian threats. On the contrary, on 2 December a new law was presented by Dr Mohammed Mossadeq and adopted almost without discussion after only two hours' debate. This law made it illegal for any minister to undertake oil negotiations without consent of the Majlis. The penalty for breach of the law was up to eight years' imprisonment and permanent debarment from public office. 'The success of this tour de force,' reported Morris, 'was undoubtedly made possible only by the personal prestige of Dr. Mossadeg.'

Once again British guile was suspected of being behind a move which appeared to serve Britain's interests so well, though a better knowledge of Mossadeq's character would have suggested a different interpretation. What is certain is that it was the violence of Russia's reaction to the loss of the desired concession, and other evidence that the Soviets were consolidating their position in the north, which helped to make Iran more dependent on its new and far from unwilling protector, the United States. On 24 November 1945 Hussein Ala, whom the Shah had sent as his first ambassador to Washington, told President Truman: 'In this critical situation, I earnestly beg you, Mr President, to continue to stand up for the rights of Iran, whose independence and integrity are being trampled under foot. Your country alone can save us . . .'

The effect of the ending of the war was to bring into sharper outline the factors which had already begun to dominate the Iranian scene. Hostility between America and Russia intensified; Russian designs on Iran became more open; Britain's role diminished, and the Shah tried harder to assert himself.

The crisis over Azerbaijan was to put both the Americans and the Shah to the test. Both had to feel their way in conditions to which they were unaccustomed. Although, as has been seen, the American government had early decided that it had a vital interest in keeping Iran out of the Soviet orbit, this was a new part of the world to the American public and to most American officials. As one ambassador in Tehran was to write, 'Most of the world is completely unaware whether Azerbaijan is a river, a mountain, or merely a new religion.' And even at the top there could be a dangerous lack of understanding. In March 1946, prompted by alarmist reports from Tabriz of Soviet troop movements, a map was prepared in the Department of State with arrows indicating a four-pronged Soviet advance, against the Turkish and Iraqi frontiers, against Tehran, and against the oilfields in the south. This product of a subordinate's zeal was shown to the Secretary of State, James F. Byrnes, who remarked that 'it now seemed clear the USSR was adding military invasion to political subversion in Iran.'

Beating one hand with his fist he exclaimed: 'Now we'll give it them
with both barrels.' Later President Truman was to claim that it was as a
result of an American ultimatum that the Russians had withdrawn
their troops from Iran – a claim which could not be substantiated.

The situation was indeed serious enough without these em-
broideries. According to the tripartite declaration of December 1943
all Allied troops should have been out of Iran by 2 March 1946, but the
Russians showed no sign of going. On the contrary, they seemed
prepared to dig themselves in. The only matter in doubt was whether
the establishment of the puppet Pishevari government in Tabriz was a
preliminary to the annexation of Azerbaijan or was intended as a
means of pressure by which to secure an oil concession. Qavam
es-Sultaneh, who had been appointed Prime Minister in January 1946,
journeyed to Moscow in March in an attempt to secure a Russian
withdrawal. There he met Stalin, who, after some rather unconvinc-
ing excuses, raised the question of an oil concession. The Russians
were obviously mortified by the fact that the British had held on to
their concession in the south while they had got nothing in the north.
Molotov suggested a joint Russo-Iranian company to develop northern oil in which the Russians would hold a controlling 51-per-cent
interest. Qavam pleaded that the Majlis decision made this impossible.

As the Azerbaijan crisis developed, the three principal participants
found themselves frequently at loggerheads. The Shah feared that a
coup might be attempted in Tehran, and at one time contemplated the
possibility of withdrawing from the capital to some safer location. He
wanted to be sure of American backing and he mistrusted his Prime
Minister. The Americans were instrumental in bringing Iran's case to
the Security Council, and were concerned to keep the Shah and his
ministers up to the mark. Qavam was playing a lone hand and managed to deceive the Russians, the Americans, and his own sovereign.

To many Iranians the scene looked all too familiar. Once again their
country was becoming the plaything of the big powers; once again
weakness at the top was spreading decay through the whole nation.
The threat of foreign intervention, and the apparent inability of the
Shah to defend the nation's interests and integrity, greatly strengthened support for the National Front under the leadership of Dr
Mossadeq.

But for the moment the initiative lay with Qavam, and he was
convinced that oil was the crux of the crisis. Acting in this belief he
manoeuvred with great skill, luring the Russians with the prospect of a
concession covering most of the north of Iran, in which, for twenty-

five years, they would have the controlling interest they demanded. As a further earnest of his good intentions he removed the ban on Tudeh meetings, suppressed anti-Russian newspapers and ordered the arrest of public men known to be anti-Soviet. In exchange he managed by the end of March to obtain from the Russians a firm date for troop withdrawals.

Qavam's readiness to make concessions to the Russians, his talk of the 'inevitability' of an oil concession for them, his willingness to withdraw Iran's complaint from the Security Council and to substitute bilateral negotiations ('when dealing with a lion you must cajole it and feed it, not attempt to match your claws against his') alarmed the Shah and the Americans. By the end of April the American Chargé felt the danger was that Qavam's policy of 'modified appeasement' would eventually leave him with no choice but either to become a complete puppet of the Russians or to be overthrown to make way for someone prepared to act the part.

The Shah, as has been seen, had never liked Qavam, and had only appointed him Prime Minister under pressure. On 8 May Qavam was reported as telling the American Chargé, 'in the utmost confidence', that he found the real obstacle in the way of a solution to the Azerbaijan crisis was not Pishevari, the puppet Prime Minister installed in Tabriz by the Russians, but the Shah, who wanted to use force. Qavam thought the trouble was that the Shah took his nominal position as commander-in-chief of the armed forces seriously, and did not realize that sending the army into Azerbaijan would be to court a fiasco. Three weeks later the Shah was reported as expressing his 'increasing dissatisfaction' with Qavam and his conviction that 'forceful measures would have to be taken to prevent Iran from becoming a puppet to the Soviet Union.' He tried to get assurances of 'more direct' American support, but was told that the only effective support America could give was through the United Nations. On 6 June the Ambassador, Allen, reported privately to Loy Henderson, the Director of the Office of Near Eastern and African Affairs at the State Department:

'In addition to seeing a good deal of the Shah and Qavam, I have had to receive innumerable delegations of Iranians, almost all of whom insist that the United States must play a more positive role in internal Iranian affairs. I have repeated almost *ad nauseam* that the United States is exerting every effort to prevent internal interference in Iranian affairs and that we cannot adopt the very tactics to which we object so strenuously, and insist that the United Nations is Iran's best safeguard. However, Iranians are so ac-

customed to outside interference they resemble a man who has been in
prison a long time and is afraid to walk out in the sunlight. The only way
they can think of to counteract one interference is to invite another.'

Allen was afraid this answer failed to satisfy his interlocutors, who
usually went away with the impression that the United States was not
interested in the fate of their country. They might have been reassured
on this point had they been able to see a memorandum prepared a few
months later giving the assessment by the Joint Chiefs of Staff of the
importance to the United States of Iran:

'The Joint Chiefs of Staff consider that as a source of supply [oil] Iran is an
area of major strategic interest to the United States. From the standpoint of
defensive purposes the area offers opportunities to conduct delaying operations and/or operations to protect United States-controlled oil resources in Saudi Arabia . . . Quite aside from military counteroffensive
action in the area, the oil resources of Iran and the Near and Middle East are
very important and may be vital to decisive counteroffensive from any
area.'

The memorandum suggested that 'token assistance by the United
States to the Iranian military establishment would probably contribute
to the defence of the United States strategic interest in the Near and
Middle East by creating a feeling of good will toward the United
States in the central government of Iran and would tend to stabilize
and strengthen the government.' So it recommended supplying Iran
with 'non-aggression items and military material in reasonable
amounts' – the beginning of a long and escalating history of arms
supplies.

If, as Qavam said, oil was the 'crux of the matter' for the Russians it
had by now become so for the Americans also. But just as it would
have been embarrassing for them to be discovered interfering in Iran's
internal affairs when this was precisely what they were accusing the
Russians of doing, so it would have been awkward to be seen lobbying
for oil concessions when they were encouraging the Iranian government to stand firm against Russian demands for a concession in the
north. The interest in Iranian oil shown by American companies
during the war, blocked by Majlis action forbidding all consideration
of new concessions till the war had ended, was of course known, and
Qavam was prepared to hold out the prospect of a concession in
Baluchistan as a reward. But when the Embassy in Tehran went as far
as to ask Qavam whether he would be willing to receive negotiators

acting for American oil companies, Washington was quick to send a reproof (8 April 1946): 'We are anxious that impression should not be obtained that we be influenced in our recent actions before Security Council by selfish interest in Iranian petroleum . . . We do not wish any discussions with regard to possibility of Americans obtaining oil rights in Iran carried on by representatives this government or American oil companies at least until Soviet Troops have evacuated Iran or until law prohibiting such negotiations is no longer effective.'

While Russia and America had their eyes on the oil which might be forthcoming from Iran in the future, the third country involved, Britain, was preoccupied with present oil supplies. The AIOC's refinery at Abadan was the biggest in the world. Production from the oilfields in the south-west had risen from 13,270,000 tons in 1944 to 19,190,000 tons in 1946, more than half the total production of oil in the Middle East. Although the British and American governments acted closely together at the United Nations over the Iran crisis, and the British and American ambassadors in Tehran continued to consult each other at frequent intervals, there were areas of reservation, which were to become larger as the crisis over the AIOC's concession deepened. Qavam was not above speaking critically of the British to the Americans, confessing that he kept from them his negotiations over oil with the Russians, assuring the Americans that Britain was not going to get any more concessions and that if any were to be handed out these would go to America, and accusing the British of trying to get him dismissed. All this was no doubt part of the complex game which Qavam was playing, but he was shrewd enough to see where American and British interests diverged, and to exploit these differences for his own purposes.

The Russians were outwitted. Qavam called elections, which they and the Tudeh Party were persuaded would result in a Majlis favourable to the Russian oil concession in the north. On the grounds that elections could not be held until the government's authority was effective throughout the country, the Shah's troops entered Tabriz, the capital of Azerbaijan, in mid-December 1946, and the Pishevari regime collapsed. But when the new Majlis eventually met it voted almost unanimously against the Russian concession. All Moscow could do was to reproach the Iranian Government with a 'treacherous violation' of its undertakings.

# 4

# THE EAGLE ATTACKS

A LITTLE LATER, in the summer of 1950, I paid my first visit to Tehran. Already as a newspaperman I had followed the Second World War's legacy of fighting and political unrest, and in Iran I detected all the symptoms of a profound malaise. The young Shah was still insecure on his throne, though the attempt on his life on 4 February 1949 had been responsible for a surge of sympathy towards him which bolstered his self-confidence. However, the Majlis showed no wish to share power with him; the religious leaders were very active and so was the communist Tudeh Party. But the most noticeable feature of the country was the Americans, who were creating positions of strength for themselves in every part of the national life. This was to some extent being done at the expense of their British allies, whose AIOC was still the main prop of the Iranian economy but was also the focus of fierce political passions which were shortly to erupt.

Although Iran had so far escaped the fate of Czechoslovakia, and had avoided being swallowed up by its northern neighbour, many people still feared that this might happen. A policy document prepared in Washington by the Department of State in January 1949 had described Iran as 'the weakest link in the chain of independent states along the Soviet border in the strategically important Middle East'. Two months later the American Ambassador was reporting back confidentially: 'I think that I would give odds of about one to three that the Sovs will jump the gun on Azerbaijan this year.' 'In my opinion,' he said, 'the Soviet return to Iran is not a question of "if" but is solely a question of "when". The Soviet build-up is so similar to what preceded the Red *Anschluss* of the Baltic States as to be truly alarming.'

How to strengthen the weak link, plug the Iranian gap? As usual, the Americans had to consider three approaches – arms, aid, and alliances. Delivery of surplus military equipment had already started in 1949, but more than this required congressional approval. The Shah wanted modern weapons; he wanted his forces to undergo training in the United States, and he wanted in the course of 1949 and 1950 to build up an army of 300,000 men. With this force he calculated he could hold sufficient areas in the south and south-west of the country against a Soviet attack to prevent loss of the oilfields: to hold the whole country, he thought, would require an army of half a million.

These were figures of fantasy, and probably advanced simply as bargaining counters, but the Shah and his ministers felt they had a legitimate grievance. The 'Truman Doctrine' had in May 1947 brought to their neighbour Turkey the guarantee of American protection. Why should it not be extended to Iran? 'They see in the execution of American policy,' wrote Ambassador Wiley in April 1949, 'a discrimination against Iran which might be most dangerous to them – as though US were putting up a road sign for benefit of the Russians, "detour via Iran".' The aid America was giving Turkey had 'become an obsession to Iranian leaders,' he said. The Prime Minister appealed in writing for direct American aid, and Wiley thought it should be granted: 'It would stiffen the Iranians' spine by making it clear we consider Iran in the same category as Turkey as far as eligibility for assistance is concerned.' And though Iran's capacity to absorb military aid was limited, 'we must scrupulously avoid any consideration of "token aid" in dealing with Iran and proceed on the basis of our judgment as to its capacity effectively to absorb military aid.'

Demands for economic assistance were equally importunate. The Shah described (July 1949) American aid to his country as 'measly'. The Iranian Ambassador in Washington thought $500 million might be a suitable figure; then a few weeks later suggested a figure of $147 million. When the Mutual Defence Assistance Programme legislation in August linked Iran, for aid purposes, not to Turkey and Greece, but to Korea and the Philippines, and made it share a measly $27 million with them, the Ambassador argued that this would 'result in chagrin, disappointment, and even resentment in Iran.'

What about alliances? The North Atlantic Treaty had been signed in April 1949; Turkey had become a member in 1952. Pact-making was in the air. The Shah spoke vaguely about 'reinforcing' the Saadabad Pact – a treaty of non-aggression signed by Turkey, Iran, Iraq and Afghanistan in 1937 which had never had any real life and was by now completely dead. There was some talk of a Mediterranean Pact, to include Turkey, Greece, Egypt, and perhaps some other Arab countries, and the Iranian Embassy in Washington thought that Iran should be considered the most important country in such a pact. But Dean Acheson, the Secretary of State, shot the idea down. In April 1949 he advised: 'The Department has given no consideration to the question of a Mediterranean or Middle Eastern Pact, is not in a position to do so until the ramifications of the North Atlantic Pact are clarified, and cannot encourage or discourage consideration of such a pact by countries possibly party to such a regional arrangement.'

No alliance would of course be any use if the internal state of the country was insecure and its government weak. When the Director of Greek, Turkish and Iranian affairs in the State Department, William M. Rountree, visited Iran in March 1950 he found the situation there 'dangerous and explosive'. There were three reasons for this: '(1) increased activity of the Tudeh Party, (2) the current internal economic depression, and (3) the incredible disorganization, confusion and uncertainty among the government leaders.'

On 25 March 1950 the Shah appointed as Prime Minister an elderly politician, Ali Mansur, who was widely accused of corruption – a move which, according to Wiley, was 'received with consternation and stupefaction even by the royal family and inner court entourage.' The Americans were committed in theory to a policy of non-intervention in Iran's internal affairs, but were finding this increasingly difficult to sustain. Being new to the game they lacked the subtlety with which the more experienced British manipulated Iranian politics and politicians. A paper to the State Department prepared in April 1950 by the Assistant Secretary of State, George McGhee, headed 'The Present Crisis in Iran', showed how far the Americans had already in fact taken over responsibility for the country. It recommended that 'the United States should express to the Shah its concern over events in Iran, should describe to him the reforms the Iranians could put into effect themselves, and should indicate United States assistance will be forthcoming only if a government comes to power willing to and capable of using this assistance to strengthen Iran's internal defences against communism. If necessary, the United States should be prepared to name the Iranian official who it believes most effectively could meet these requirements.' Like the Americans the Shah was feeling that the situation had grown so dangerous that more drastic remedies were perhaps called for, though his thinking, then as later, was turning towards a military solution.

On 26 June the Shah dismissed Ali Mansur and appointed in his place General Ali Razmara, Chief of the Iranian General Staff. 'With the present muddled political and economic situation,' Wiley had reported on 22 May, 'there is growing sentiment for a Razmara premiership even among some of his former political enemies.' Among these enemies had to be counted the Shah's younger half-brother, Prince Abdorreza, a Harvard graduate who had come home with ideas about reorganizing his country's economy. One of the more printable of his comments on Razmara was that he was 'a snake in the grass'.

However, much was hoped of this new broom. Razmara was forty-nine years old, a graduate of St Cyr Military Academy, and had played a leading role in the forcible suppression of the Pishevari regime in Azerbaijan. He had made little secret of wanting the top job, though it was understood that 'the Shah intends, if he can, to keep him on the leash.' Razmara faced a situation of extreme difficulty. In 1948 negotiations had been begun between the government and the AIOC for a Supplemental Agreement to raise the terms arranged between the company and Reza Shah in 1933, by which the company paid the Iranian government a flat rate of £4 million a year, rising with the rise in production to £16 million in 1950. The new Supplemental Agreement, which would have substantially increased the benefits accruing to the government, was signed in July 1949 and immediately went to the Majlis for approval. But the Majlis was dissolved before the agreement could be approved, or even debated, and in June 1950 it was passed for examination to a parliamentary sub-committee of eighteen members, whose chairman was Dr Mossadeq.

Razmara wanted to see the agreement implemented, but the mounting fervour of nationalism and religion, which was concentrating its energies on the demand for the nationalization of oil and had found in Dr Mossadeq a charismatic spokesman, was too strong for him. He had tried to mollify the opposition by asking the Shah to describe him, in the decree announcing his appointment as Prime Minister, not as General Razmara but as Haji Ali Razmara. He was not in fact a haji in the usual sense of the term – someone who has made the pilgrimage to Mecca – but in Iran anyone born on the first day of the Islamic year (as Razmara was) can be called Haji as a sort of courtesy title. So it was as Haji Ali, and in a civilian suit, not in uniform, that Razmara presented himself to the Majlis. He was met with a storm of abuse from Mossadeq: 'You're not a haji! Why try to hoodwink us? You're a general – a fox dressed up as a cat! Go back to the person who sent you!' There was a terrific row, but in the end the Majlis approved Razmara's appointment.

Though now Prime Minister, there was little Razmara could do. The battle-lines between the Palace and Dr Mossadeq's National Front had been firmly drawn, and no compromise between them was possible. Mossadeq was the hero of the hour and nationalization the symbol of a nation's pride. For a political leader, Mossadeq was a strange mixture. Now seventy years old, he was an extremely effective orator of the emotional sort, with all the sadness of the Shi'a. I attended many Majlis debates at this time, and became familiar with his technique. He would start talking to the deputies about the sufferings of the Iranian people, and become so moved by his own eloquence that he would burst into tears. Tears would turn into a fit of coughing and then into total collapse. Deputies would rush up to him, offering glasses of water, eau de Cologne or smelling salts. After a while they would succeed in getting Mossadeq back on his feet, and he would go on with his speech, only to be similarly overwhelmed about five minutes later. Everyone exclaimed about his sincerity, and without a doubt Mossadeq was completely sincere, and by 1950 he had become the embodiment of his people's aspirations; but as a practical politician he was a failure, since he had no idea whatever about organization or administration.

Mossadeq represented the political wing of the nationalist movement. The religious wing was led by Ayatollah Abul Kasem Kashani, who had been exiled to Lebanon by Reza Shah but was allowed back after the war. Both the British and the Soviets suspected America of being behind his return, and he was consequently accused of playing America's game. Many extremist religious groupings were fermenting beneath the surface, the most significant of which was the Fedayin-i-Islam (Sacrificers of Islam), founded and led by Navab Safavi. One day Safavi had read a newspaper article by a well-known journalist called Kosrawi, who in his opinion insulted Islam. He enquired from one of the Qom ayatollahs what the punishment should be for anyone who insults Islam. On being told that the punishment was death he decided to form his own society to carry out this punishment.

Safavi's first victim was Kosrawi, who was a lawyer as well as a journalist, and was assassinated in 1949 by four men who entered the courtroom where he was appearing. The assassins were arrested and confessed, but Kashani sent them his blessing. I attended their trial in the old Adliya court, and a most extraordinary occasion it was. The court was full of flags and decorations, and when the judge came in he asked for an explanation. He was told 'Ayatollah Kashani has ordered these decorations to celebrate the acquittal of the four accused.' 'But I haven't begun to hear the case yet,' the judge protested. 'We know,' was the answer, 'but the Ayatollah has every confidence in your justice.' He was not disappointed. There were crowds of people outside the court building, many of them from Qom, all chanting 'Allahu Akbar!', and the judge dismissed the case.

Another element with which Razmara had to contend was the Tudeh Party. This party had its origins in the work of a professor of chemistry called Erani, who had studied in Germany before Hitler came to power and had had many contacts with German communists. When he came back to Iran he felt that the situation there was very much like that of the Weimar Republic and required the same drastic remedies. Erani died in prison in the late 1930s, but in 1941 some of his disciples founded a communist party called the Tudeh (Masses). Because of its close association with Moscow, the Tudeh Party was always suspect, particularly at this period when, ironically enough, it took up a position opposed to the nationalization of oil, because what Moscow wanted was new concessions, not the nationalization of old ones. However, the Tudeh Party had quite a following among students and intellectuals.


I had my first meeting with the Shah in the early spring of 1951, at Princess Ashraf's house. This was an interesting house because it reflected the Princess's passion for the Emperor Napoleon. There were portraits and busts of Napoleon all over the place, and in her office (she had an office in her house, but her husband had to have his outside) all the chairs and sofas were covered in tiger-skins. There must have been the skins of at least a hundred tigers there. I think Princess Ashraf saw her father as a Napoleonic character and herself as the old tiger's cub. But at this meeting I found her brother extremely depressed; he did not hide his misgivings about nationalization. He pointed out that the AIOC had 53,000 employees. How were their salaries going to be paid if nationalization went through? Where could Iran get the money needed to pay compensation? If this was borrowed it would take as long as the repudiated concession would have lasted (to 1993) to pay off the debt. And how was Iran going to be able to transport and market the oil, even if it could go on producing it? Many of these were quite legitimate questions to ask, as events were to show.

As if his public worries were not sufficient, the Shah was also around this time having trouble with his family. The attempt on his life had made him increasingly concerned with his father's parting advice to 'get a son'. So it was that on 12 February 1951 he married his second wife, Soraya Esfandiari. But his twin sister, Princess Ashraf, disapproved of the match. She thought it had been arranged by their

half-sister, Princess Shams, and objected to the diminished status it
meant for her – since her brother's divorce she had been the first lady
of the land, in effect playing the role of queen. So immediately after the
wedding ceremony she made her disapproval plain by going back to
her house without attending the celebrations which followed.

The Shah's other half-sister, Princess Fatima, was the cause of
much worse trouble. Prince Abdorreza had been studying in
California and brought an American friend called Vincent Hillyer
back with him for the vacation. Princess Fatima met Hillyer and they
fell in love. She announced her intention of going to California to
study, and did so, but promptly got married. The fact that her
husband was not only an American but also showed no intention of
becoming a Moslem caused a predictable outrage all over Iran.*

Then on 20 February Razmara was assassinated as he was entering
the Shah mosque to attend the funeral of a mullah. The assassin was
arrested, still shouting 'Allahu Akbar!' When asked his name all he
would say was 'Abdullah', meaning 'servant of God'; when pressed
for his second name he only added 'Muwaheddy' – 'believer in one
God'. In fact his name proved to be Khalil Tahmusby, a member of the
Fedayin-i-Islam.

Some of the repercussions to the assassination which I recall from
that time give an indication of the prevailing atmosphere. One was a
drawing in a newspaper, *Asnaf*, which showed the hand of an angel
emerging from a cloud and holding a smoking revolver which had just
killed Razmara. The cartoon was captioned 'The Final Kiss'. Another
was a statement issued by Kashani to the effect that the bullets which
had caused the death of Razmara had been blessed by God, and that oil
would be nationalized in spite of the activities of the traitor who had
now been drowned in his own blood. There was also a statement put
out by Safavi which was headed 'Huwa al-Aziz: He [God] alone is
strong'. It was addressed 'To the Shah', giving him none of his titles
and calling him simply 'Pisr Pahlevi' (son of Pahlevi). It peremptorily
told the Shah that he must order the immediate release of the man who
had killed Razmara and must apologize to him for any annoyance
caused by his interrogation at the hands of the police. Most significant
of all was the fact that the government failed to find any imam
prepared to say the prayers at Razmara's funeral. Fahimi, the acting

---

* Eventually the old Aga Khan's help was enlisted, his mother having been a Qajar
princess. He saw the young couple in Paris and persuaded Hillyer to become a
Moslem. But the marriage proved an unhappy one and ended in divorce.

Prime Minister, offered one imam £3,000 to do it, but was told by the imam that he valued his life at a higher rate than this.

The army was naturally demoralized by Razmara's murder. The streets of Tehran were filled with noisy demonstrators, many of them Tudeh supporters, shouting 'Mordibad-i-Truman' (death to Truman). By choosing President Truman rather than the oil company or the Shah as their target the demonstrators showed their commitment to Moscow and the extent to which the Iranian crisis had become caught up in the Cold War. There was an atmosphere of tremendous tension. When I wanted to go to the offices of the AIOC, which were then in a big building near the Central Bank, the Bank-i-Melli, my Foreign Office guide refused to come with me.

Princess Ashraf's husband told me later that when the news of Razmara's assassination was brought to him the Shah was stunned. He simply could not believe that his Prime Minister could be wiped out like this. 'I can't believe it; I can't believe it,' he kept saying. 'I don't know what to do,' he went on. 'I am all alone. Nobody understands my problems. Everybody is in a conspiracy against me; some of them deliberately and some unconsciously. But it is I who have to pay the penalty.'

Some of those most obviously taking part in what the Shah saw as a conspiracy against him were the politicians in the Majlis. A vigorous parliamentary life is a comparatively rare feature in Third-World countries, where effective power is almost always in the hands of a colonial or occupying authority, or in the hands of the one man or small group of men, be they soldiers or civilians, who have replaced the occupiers. Though some Iranians, mindful of the constitutional movement in the early years of the century, have claimed to be heirs to a parliamentary tradition, their country has in reality been no exception. After the absolutist Qajars came two periods of foreign occupation and the dictatorship of Reza Shah. It was only because this was a moment of transition, between occupation and consolidation, that the Majlis was able to enjoy a brief importance. All other centres of power in the country being temporarily paralysed, the Majlis became the focus of popular feeling. With conditions in the country approaching chaos, the Majlis in 1950 found its opportunity, as did the States General in 1790 or the Duma in 1917.

The Shah had to get the approval of the Majlis for the appointment of a new prime minister, so he sent Fahimi, the Deputy Prime Minister, to the Majlis with a list of names of possible candidates. When Fahimi arrived, the Speaker, Fakhir Hikmet, began to say something about 'the tragic events of the last few days', but was interrupted by Mossadeq: 'Mr Speaker, stop all this nonsense. You ought to be standing up with the rest of us to shout "Long live the nationalization of our oil!"' Fakhir Hikmet tried to struggle on with his speech, but Mossadeq again interrupted him, insisting that he should shout 'Long live the nationalization of oil!' So the Speaker had to give up, and instead called on Fahimi to speak, saying he understood he had brought an important message for them to hear. Fahimi went to the tribune. He said that he had been sent by His Majesty the Shah to obtain a mandate from the Majlis so that he could form a new cabinet, pointing out the danger to the country if it remained without a prime minister at this critical juncture. But this produced an outcry from the deputies, and once again Mossadeq took the floor. It was very strange, he said, that the Shah should send someone to ask the deputies to give him their confidence. Who gave the Shah the authority to form a cabinet? That was the business of the Majlis, and by acting in this way the Shah was proposing to violate the constitution.

The Speaker then suspended the session for an hour to give passions a chance to cool, during which time messages were exchanged with the Palace. When the session was resumed Fahimi did not put in an appearance, but the Speaker informed the deputies that he had been told by the Shah that he was submitting three names to them, from among which he trusted they would be able to select a prime minister. These were Fahimi, the Deputy Prime Minister, Ali Soheily, the Ambassador in London, and Hussein Ala, the Minister of Court. One of the National Front deputies took the floor. 'Honourable members,' he said, 'if in the past we supported the monarchy, it was not because of the person of Mohammed Reza Pahlevi, but because of certain political and social considerations. The Shah must realize that the government of this country belongs entirely to the representatives of the people. It is we who nominate the Prime Minister. The Shah must understand that his remaining on the throne is conditional on his observing the constitution. He must stop interfering in politics. Razmara was imposed on us by him against our will. The monarch is only an individual, and individuals are always influenced by those around them. Who can guarantee that the Shah is not influenced by his brothers and sisters and who knows who else?'

Mossadeq started speaking again. Addressing Fakhir Hikmet, he said, 'Go and tell the Shah what you have heard here. Tell him he must always remember that we here are the representatives of the people and that we are the ones who matter.' There was some more debate, and then the Majlis decided to reject all three candidates proposed by the Shah – Fahimi because he was a traitor who had tried to defend Razmara and was opposed to the principle of nationalization; Soheily because he was a friend of Princess Ashraf and it was assumed that it was through her influence that his name had appeared on the Shah's list; and Hussein Ala because, though essentially a decent man, he had been educated in England, spent all his career in the diplomatic service, and was not eloquent in Farsi – besides, he was suffering from a stomach ulcer. The Speaker then announced that Hussein Ala had asked for his candidature to be withdrawn. But in fact after five days the Shah persuaded him to step into the breach. He was accepted by the Majlis and allowed to form a cabinet. But this was of course only until what was now seen as the inevitable step – that the premiership should pass to Dr Mossadeq.

It is not my intention to tell in any detail the story of Mossadeq's premiership. He became Prime Minister on 19 April. The Nationaliz-ation Law was passed on 30 April and signed by the Shah on 1 May 1951. One of the first consequences of this action was that the Oil Company stopped all payments to the Iranian Treasury, whereupon many government servants ceased to receive any pay. I had reason to appreciate the hardship this caused when from time to time my Foreign Office guide found himself, to his embarrassment, without any ready money in his pocket. On 26 May the British government brought a case against Iran before the International Court of Justice at the Hague, which gave judgement on 5 July, recommending in effect that, pend-ing further consideration, oil production should be continued as be-fore. The arrival in Tehran of the American trouble-shooter, Averell Harriman, and a British Cabinet Minister, Richard Stokes, failed to produce an acceptable compromise. All refining ceased on 31 July, and in September Britain referred the dispute to the United Nations, Mossadeq appearing before the Security Council in person to present his government's case.

1952 saw another reference by Britain to the International Court, much more coming and going in Tehran, and finally the rupture of diplomatic relations with Britain by the Iranian government. The Americans continued to play a somewhat equivocal role. They were naturally opposed in principle to the idea of nationalization, but they saw many possible advantages for their own oil companies in Britain's discomfiture. A number of American oilmen appeared on the scene, and much to the chagrin of the British government the American government left it to the discretion of the purchaser whether or not to buy what little oil trickled out of Abadan – oil which Britain insisted was stolen property.

By the spring of 1953 the situation showed a marked deterioration. Although the government put a brave face on things, there was a great deal of unemployment and hardship. Mossadeq and his closest ally, Kashani, were hopeless administrators and now began to quarrel with each other. The Majlis was more or less out of control; the Shah impotent. Many men of importance, including deputies, began to slip away across the Gulf to places like Sharjah and Kuwait, and there they were often quick to get in touch with the British authorities.

The Americans had become increasingly worried by Middle Eastern developments. July 1952 had seen the Free Officers' revolution in Egypt, which ousted King Farouk and replaced him by a revolutionary regime with strongly nationalist sympathies. Nasser had emerged as the leader and symbol of the Egyptian revolution, and had quickly shown that he had no use for the Middle East Defence Organization which the Americans and British were trying to put together. To an uncooperative Egypt was added a hostile Iran. It was with some reason that Stalin, shortly before he died on 5 March 1953, had expressed his confidence that Iran would soon fall into Soviet hands like a rotten apple.

However, the first people to do anything about reversing the drift were not the Americans but the AIOC. Over the years the company had built up a highly efficient intelligence service. Many politicians were on its payroll, and, as has been seen, some of the tribal chiefs in the South-West received direct from the company some of the royalties due to the Treasury. Now, of course, all these recipients of company money had to go without, and this went much against the grain. When emissaries of the company began to hint that a way of removing Mossadeq and Kashani and all their works might be found, they were ready to listen.

In his book *Countercoup*, which, though suppressed, was widely read (in Iran at least), Kermit Roosevelt explains that he had been in touch with anti-Mossadeq elements in Tehran on behalf of the CIA as far back as late 1950 – that is, even before Mossadeq became Prime Minister. Roosevelt had continued to watch the scene and to visit Tehran at intervals until, as he passed through London in November 1952, he was approached by representatives of the AIOC who made it clear that they wanted to see Mossadeq overthrown and they wanted this done quickly. Roosevelt was a sympathetic listener, and was prepared to study, though not to adopt, the plans for subversion which the company had drawn up. The fact of the matter was that the Americans and the company wanted to get rid of Mossadeq for different reasons. The company wanted to get its concession back and to be able to start producing oil once again; the Americans were afraid of what Roosevelt called 'the obvious threat of a Russian takeover' in Iran. He claims that when he briefed John Foster Dulles at the crucial State Department meeting on 25 June 1953 he argued that the Soviet threat to Iran was 'genuine, dangerous and imminent'. Dulles agreed that if the Russians could control Iran 'they would control the Persian Gulf. This has been their dream, their chief ambition, ever since the days of Peter the Great.'

One of the considerations which had prevented the British from taking any violent action against Mossadeq was fear of Russian reaction. The Russo-Iranian Treaty of 1921 gave Russia the right to send troops into Iran in certain circumstances – a fact of which the British were very well aware, since the relevant clause of the treaty had been invoked at the time of the joint Russo-British occupation of the country in 1941. Post-war Britain was clearly in no position, militarily or politically, to challenge Russia single-handed in Iran. But the Americans might be, and they were all the more ready to take this risk after Stalin died in March 1953 and his heirs in Moscow became locked in a desperate, if unpublicized, struggle for power.

Roosevelt had convinced himself – and managed to convince Dulles and other key members of the administration – that when it came to a showdown between the Shah and Mossadeq 'the Iranian army and the Iranian people will back the Shah.' So he went ahead with organizing the showdown, and in spite of a slip-up which nearly brought catastrophe, and which obliged the Shah and the Empress to seek temporary sanctuary in Rome, the counter-coup was successful, and General Zahedi was installed as Prime Minister in Mossadeq's place.

On 4 September Roosevelt gave a personal report on Operation Ajax to an audience at the White House which included President Eisenhower and John Foster Dulles. In his book he explains that he ended his report on a warning note. The operation, he said, had been a success because the CIA's analysis of the situation had been correct. They had come to the conclusion 'that if the people and the armed forces were shown that they must choose, that Mossadegh was forcing them to choose, between their monarch and a revolutionary figure backed by the Soviet Union, they could, and would, make only one choice.' If the CIA was ever to try such an operation again they would have to be just as certain in advance that the army and the people of the country concerned wanted the same things as the CIA did. 'If not,' Roosevelt concluded, 'you had better give the job to the Marines!'

# 5

# TEHRAN – OPEN CITY

BY 22 AUGUST 1953 the counter-coup was over. The Shah was back in his palace and the supporters of Mossadeq were being rounded up or going into hiding. Mossadeq himself managed to hide in a friend's house for a couple of days, but when he heard the broadcast orders for his arrest he decided to go to a police station and give himself up.★

Tehran in fact gave the impression of a conquered city, with troops and police loyal to the Shah executing summary justice on anyone they suspected of being a Mossadeq supporter. Many students and leftists were shot out of hand. Hussein Fatemi, Mossadeq's Foreign Minister and former editor of one of Tehran's leading newspapers, *Bakhtar Amruz*, which had become the mouthpiece of nationalist-minded youth, an idealist who was as violently anti-communist as he was anti-West, was shot dead in the street.

The real seat of authority in Tehran in these days was the American Embassy rather than the Niavaran Palace. It was the CIA which had staged the counter-coup and which was now supervising the aftermath. Loy Henderson, the American Ambassador, a close friend of Kermit Roosevelt and one of those who had taken part in the fateful State Department meeting of 25 June and had agreed, albeit with some reluctance, to the mounting of Operation Ajax, was back in his Embassy after a brief tactical withdrawal to Switzerland. Roosevelt himself had moved into the Embassy from the small house in Shemran which had been his headquarters while the coup was in progress. With him went many of his assistants – men like Richard Helms, who were to make a career in the CIA and whose ideas about its potentialities were no doubt distorted by this early and easy triumph.

The new control was quickly extended from the capital to the provinces. Those towns which had shown conspicuous support for Mossadeq and the National Front, or where the mullahs had been notably hostile in their criticisms of the Shah, were subjected to special

---

★ Afterwards, so his son told me, he was put in a cell with water up to his waist, which brought on such acute rheumatism that he became completely paralysed. He remained in prison for five years before being released, dying soon afterwards.

punitive action by army and police. Qom, Shiraz, Tabriz, and Isfahan (the home of Hussein Fatimi) were the scene of widespread searches and arrests. In Tehran Mossadeq's house was bulldozed out of existence to prevent it from becoming the focus for opposition.

As well as reprisals against the Shah's enemies, there had to be rewards for his friends. All those politicians who had been in eclipse under Mossadeq, the well-to-do who had seen their property confiscated or their businesses ruined as a result of Mossadeq's nationalization policies, the officers who had stood by the Shah – all these, many of whom had had to flee the country, now expected compensation for what they had suffered. And they got it, for though the Treasury was empty the American government was quick to grant a $45 million credit and American oil companies were willing to come across with generous loans in the expectation of benefits to come. For the undoing of oil nationalization was naturally high on the agenda of the new government, and though it took over a year to hammer out the new consortium which was to manage Iran's oil affairs, when it did emerge it was highly satisfactory for the American companies, which now had a 40-per-cent share in what before nationalization had been a British monopoly.

Among those loyalists who received their rewards were Colonel Nassiri, who had delivered to Mossadeq the message dismissing him, and who was promoted to general and put in charge of Savak; General Fazlullah Zahedi, who had led the counter-coup in Tehran and became first Prime Minister after its success; his son, Ardeshir, who had acted as liaison with Kermit Roosevelt, was given the Shah's daughter Shahnaz as bride and was eventually made ambassador in London and Washington; Captain Khatemi, who had piloted the plane which took the Shah to Baghdad and Rome, was made commander of the air force and married to the Shah's sister after her divorce from her first husband, an American; while Jaafar Sharif Emami, who, as Vice-President of the Majlis, had been instrumental in persuading a large number of deputies to flee the country and thus pave the way for a 'constitutional' victory, became head of the Pahlevi Foundation and later Prime Minister. Nor did Kermit Roosevelt lose, since he was appointed adviser to a number of oil companies.

But how was the new government to consolidate itself? In spite of the cheering crowds which the CIA had brought into the streets of Tehran it would have been rash to assume that the Shah had genuinely supplanted Mossadeq in the affections of the Iranian people. Something more was needed.

One of the documents found after the Revolution in the archives of the Marmar Palace is a very revealing memorandum recommending guidelines for the policies which the Shah should try to pursue. It is written in English but not signed, and the presumption is that it was the work of a group set up by the Embassy or the CIA for the purpose. There were seven main recommendations:

1. A concerted campaign should be initiated to present the Shah as the Father of his People – *Fermandeh*, to use an old expression – in the best Iranian tradition.

2. Every available means of propaganda should be enlisted to build up the prestige of the throne and of the Shah personally. In this connection it was pointed out that there existed in the country what amounted to a ready-made constituency for the Shah to woo – the women. More than half the population of Iran consisted of women, and though the men might be governed by old concepts, the women were susceptible to new ones. The emancipation of women would give the Shah a base in every home.

3. The Shah and his new government should do all they could to extend and strengthen the middle class. Limited though it was in numbers, it was the middle class which had been the most effective opposition to Mossadeq. By instinct and interest opposed to adventures and secular in outlook, the middle class could become the natural foundation for the regime.

4. As far as possible new political faces should be brought forward. Senior politicians – men like Ahmed Qavam es-Sultaneh and Seyyid Zia Tabatabai – were too old and unreliable.

5. It was most advisable that the Shah should play a significant part in international affairs, both in the Middle East and on the broader world stage. It had been proved that the leaders of many smaller countries benefited internally from the image created by them externally.

6. The Shah should pay serious attention to religious matters, and so do his best to wrest the religious leadership of the country from the ayatollahs of Qom. He should, for example, make a point of going to a different mosque each week for his prayers.

7. Careful consideration should be given to the organization and control of intelligence, and special attention should be paid to the needs of the air force, because if the air force remained loyal it would, by its mobility, be in a position to deal with any threat of mutiny

by army units. Moreover, because it combined smaller numbers of officers and men with more concentrated firepower, it was easier to keep a tight hold over than an army.

This last recommendation was largely responsible for the way in which the Shah's control over every aspect of national life was consolidated, and in the end was no less responsible for his downfall. Thus it was during these early days that Savak, the secret police, was instituted, to begin with more or less as a branch of the CIA, and coming directly under the orders of the Shah. Other parallel intelligence organizations were set up. There was the Second Bureau in the army, which spied both for, and on, the army; the political police, which came under the Ministry of Interior; and Colonel (now General) Schwarzkopf's gendarmerie, which operated in the regions, and particularly among the tribes.

All these intelligence activities were advised and supervised by Americans. And to ensure that the armed forces could count on a uniformly trained cadre of loyal officers, virtually every officer with the rank of colonel and above was sent to the United States for a period of usually between two and three years for training. Over the twenty-five years of the Shah's effective reign no fewer than 15,000 officers did these long attachments in the States, not to mention many thousands of junior officers and NCOs who went for shorter periods.

All intelligence ended up in the Shah's personal office, which was usually headed by a general. The armed forces were kept apart from each other and from Savak and other intelligence-gathering bodies. There was no such thing as a Joint Chiefs-of-Staff; the commanders of the infantry, artillery, armoured forces, navy and so on reported separately to the Shah. He was determined that they should have no opportunity to coordinate, for coordination might lead to criticism and so even to revolt. What happened in fact was, of course, that when revolt was in the air, and the Shah was vacillating, the heads of the armed forces were unable to produce a coordinated response because they had no machinery for doing so.

The Shah must have read this memorandum and studied it carefully, for he clearly tried to follow its recommendations. In fact he came to take them too seriously and to believe his own propaganda. Thus, not content to accept the idea of appearing to be Father of his People he came to think that the people really did regard him as *Fermandeh*. And though it was beyond his resources actually to create a new middle class, he did succeed in creating a new parasitic class –

merchants and middle-men who were awarded contracts and commissions. These included representatives of some of the leading families in Tehran as well as the bourgeois elements the Shah was supposed to be cultivating, and the distribution of privileges gave the green light for the royal family to take its cut. Moreover, it was the Shah's twin sister, Princess Ashraf, who was given the job of wooing the Shah's new constituency, the women.

It may not have been easy for the Shah to create a whole new social class but he could create new politicians. The old order vanished, and in its place were promoted new people, many of them civil servants. For example Amir Abbas Hoveyda, who was to serve the Shah as Prime Minister longer than anyone else, and who in the end was to refuse to escape execution by flight, had started life as an official of the United Nations, became a diplomat, then was head of the Iranian delegation to the UN in New York, and subsequently was brought back to Tehran to serve as minister and Prime Minister. He was a man with no strong family or other roots, whose entire loyalty was to the Shah. Two other of the Shah's Prime Ministers were equally men of his own creation. Hushang Ansari had been a journalist, correspondent of the Iranian news agency in Tokyo. He favourably impressed the Shah when he was on a state visit to Japan in 1968, so he was brought back and made Minister of Information and later of Finance. Jamshid Amouzegar, perhaps the best of these politicians who reached the top, had started as an engineer.

All these men were in effect the Shah's puppets, debarred by their background from making any serious criticism of his policies even when they disapproved of them. On the same principle of encouraging groups of individuals who owed everything to him, the Shah saw to it that all army communications – radar, W/T, etc. – were manned by Bahais (the small and often persecuted religious minority). One consequence of this particular action was that after the Islamic Revolution, which removed the Bahais, army communications were disrupted.

Another way in which the Shah's regime was consolidated was through control of press and radio. When I visited Tehran leading journalists used to come to me almost in tears, protesting how, as part of the *Fermandeh* myth, they were obliged to have a photograph of the Shah on the front page of their newspapers every day. This cult of the royal personality was carried to such an extent that, for example, on the day when Nasser died, and the principal Tehran daily, *Kayhan*, had made up the front page with, not altogether surprisingly, Nasser's

death as the lead story, the censors ordered the presses to be stopped,
the front page to be remade, with something to do with the Shah as the
lead and Nasser's death as the second lead. The strict censorship was
responsible for many other absurdities; red ink could not be used by
newspapers because it was the colour of communism and revolution,
and no plays could be performed or published which in any way
referred to the assassination of monarchs – not even *Hamlet*.

So, hesitatingly at first, but as the years went by with ever-growing
confidence, the Shah adapted himself to the requirements of his own
propaganda. By nature an essentially weak character, he compensated
by behaving with increasing arrogance. He would explain to his
hearers what he called the inherent weaknesses of oriental societies –
how they needed to be ruled by a dictatorial hand. The people were
ignorant, he said, and only capable of beneficial action if guided to
this end by the state – and as far as this was concerned he was the
state. He really believed that he had a mission to civilize the Iranian
people.


By one means and another all resistance to the Shah was effectively
scattered. Many members of the intelligentsia had been killed or
imprisoned soon after the coup; many others sought permission to
leave the country, and they were followed by students who could not
face the prospect of life under the Shah's dictatorship. Within two or
three years after the coup about 50,000 young men had left the
country, legally or illegally, often going first to Kuwait or Iraq and
then trying to find permanent asylum further afield, in Europe or
America. By the beginning of the Revolution there were 150,000
Iranians abroad, 35,000 of them in the United States, about half
students and half voluntary exiles.

Those who stayed behind faced difficult decisions. They tried to
analyse what had gone wrong. Why had Mossadeq failed? As many of
them saw it, his failure had been to rely on the established machinery
of government, or what passed for the democratic processes. He had,
after all, been duly elected Prime Minister by the Majlis, and he had
undoubtedly enjoyed the backing of a majority of the people as well as
of the deputies. But this had not saved him (any more than it was later
to save Allende). So it was that much of the underground opposition
decided that terrorism was the only weapon open to those looking for
a change. Secret societies began to proliferate, two of them developing
into quite significant organizations. The first, the Mujahiddin Khalk,

founded in the late 1950s, was built round elements from the now illegal and disbanded National Front. It was Islamic in outlook, and adopted many of the progressive ideas current in the Third World. The other, the Fedayin Khalk, was more specifically Marxist in orientation, and was to that extent a successor to the discredited Tudeh Party, which by now had almost evaporated. Both organizations adopted terror as a weapon, and though at first they remained largely ineffective, having been penetrated and neutralized by Savak, they managed to survive. Fedayin Khalk grew more efficient after it had established contact with George Habbash's Popular Front for the Liberation of Palestine (PFLP) and sent some of its members for training with the PFLP in Lebanon.

Three key members of the opposition managed to make their way to Egypt. These were Ibrahim Yazdi, Sadeq Qotbzadeh, and Mustafa Shemran, all of whom were later given leading positions in the new revolutionary government. After arriving in Cairo in the mid-1950s they got in touch with the intelligence services, which were responsible for looking after political refugees. They explained that they wanted training in arms, because they had decided that guerrilla warfare was now the only course open to the Shah's opponents. They were accordingly sent to the camp at Inshass outside Cairo (one of King Farouk's former estates) which was now the place where members of various national liberation groups were trained. There they met Palestinians, as well as Eritreans and many groups from Africa. But after a while they quarrelled with their hosts. The responsible department of Egyptian intelligence wanted the Iranian refugees to join in broadcasts beamed from Cairo attacking the Shah, but they refused, insisting that they had come to Egypt solely to learn how to fight and that the Shah was not going to be overthrown by words. They could not be persuaded that the prospects for armed intervention in Iran were at that time nil, and that in the interim radio propaganda was a very powerful weapon in their armoury. There was a quarrel, and they decided to leave Egypt, some (their number had by now swelled to about fifty) going to the States and some to Lebanon for further training.

While in Egypt they had been reasonably safe from the attentions of Savak, though the Shah's police, as well as the CIA and Israeli intelligence (Mossad), were as active there as they could be. It was around this time that cooperation between Savak and Mossad, as well as between both of them and the CIA, became a feature of the Middle East intelligence scene. The year 1955 saw, in addition to the signature of the Baghdad Pact, the Israeli raid on Gaza and the Egyptian arms deal with Czechoslovakia. Tension in the area was mounting. Israel, as well as the West and particularly America, believed it a matter of paramount importance to keep Iran, the vital link between the Arab world and the Indian sub-continent, immune from contagion from the rising tide of Arab nationalism.

The Israeli Prime Minister, David Ben-Gurion, made first approaches to the Shah through the good offices of the CIA, sending Meier Amit, the director of Mossad, as his messenger. The Shah did not need much persuading of the benefits the two countries could derive from cooperation, and not just in matters of intelligence. Here were two non-Arab states, one on the Gulf and one on the Mediterranean, separated by a sea of Arab nationalism, which was an elemental force both of them had good reason to fear. The Shah had already been impressed by Israeli achievements. He thought they had shown themselves extremely efficient and up-to-date in their techniques. He was prepared to learn from them, particularly in matters of security, so he sent selected key officers, including some from the royal guards, for training in Israel.*

American advice to the Shah took a variety of forms. While the CIA was giving help in the intelligence field the voice from the White House was urging caution. J. F. Kennedy had become President in 1960 and when he turned his attention to Iran it was to urge the Shah to put some order into his country's affairs, to check the corruption for which his family and entourage had become notorious, and to appreciate that a country's security cannot be guaranteed by arms alone. The Shah later told me that he regarded Kennedy's message as more or less an American coup directed against him, but he heeded it to the extent of bringing in as Prime Minister a man the Americans were known to approve of, but whom he personally much disliked, Dr Ali Amini, who had been Minister of Finance under Mossadeq.

It was around this period that the combination of forces which was to dominate the Middle Eastern scene in the 1970s began to emerge – the alliance between oil, arms, and intelligence. An enormous amount of money was being generated by the oil-producing states, and both

---

* As Kermit Roosevelt explains in *Countercoup* (p. 9), Iran and Israel already had 'excellent though informal relations' with each other in 1953. 'These relations,' he adds, 'became closer in later years when certain Israeli friends discreetly joined the CIA in helping to organize and give guidance to a new Iranian security service. This Israeli action was entirely "under the table", essentially a clandestine operation – but it was of great assistance to the Iranians.'

governments and companies were prepared to spend lavishly to protect their investments. Effective protection depended on good intelligence as much as on the latest armaments, hence the willingness to pay large sums to anyone who seemed in a position to supply it. Special publications, professing to give inside political and economic information, multiplied. Many of the CIA operatives who had worked with Kermit Roosevelt in Iran opened offices ready and eager to inform local governments and commercial companies, and found plenty of customers. Often what they offered was of genuine value, but often too it was a bazaar gossip reported – or invented – by third-rate journalists.

Meanwhile the forces of opposition to the Shah were abandoning the capital and making their way 100 miles south, to the city of Qom.

# 6

# THE REVOLUTION
# WITHDRAWS TO QOM

WHY TO QOM? There are, as is generally known, three Holy Cities for all Moslems: Mecca, which contains the House of God, the Ka'aba, and is the place of pilgrimage; Medina, whither the Prophet migrated from Mecca, where he died and was buried; and Jerusalem, towards which in the early days of Islam believers directed their prayers and which was the setting for the Prophet's nocturnal journey to Heaven. To these three the Shi'is add four more – Najaf, the burial place of Imam Ali; Kerbala, the scene of the massacre of Ali's son, Hussein, and his followers; Meshed, the burial place of the Imam Reza; and Qom, the burial place of Fatima, the Imam Reza's sister.

Qom lies on what was formerly one of the principal caravan routes across Persia. In AD 816 Fatima was on her way to visit her brother when she was taken ill at Saveh, fifty miles north-west of Qom. She was carried to Qom, where she died. Legend has it that as she lay on her lonely deathbed, praying in her isolation that God might release her from her agony, the spirits of the Prophet, of his daughter Fatima, his son-in-law Ali, and their son, the martyred Hussein, came round her. Their presence has for ever hallowed the ground on which she lay.

When, at the beginning of the sixteenth century AD, the Safavid kings made Shi'ism the official religion of Persia, the two Holy Cities within the boundaries of their empire, Meshed and Qom, inevitably grew in importance. The tomb of Fatima in Qom was magnificently adorned by Shah Abbas; the city became the centre of religious studies, the place to which all religious leaders made their way and where the pious chose to be buried. Today the outskirts of the city, with their garages, workshops and restaurants, look much like those of any other city in Iran. But once the bridge over the river-bed is crossed, and the old city entered, the special aura of religion is unmistakable.

Qom became, in fact, the religious capital of Persia. First Isfahan, and then Tehran, became the political capital, but kings and mullahs found it more convenient to keep their distance from each other. The kings preferred not to have the leading mullahs closely watching, and probably condemning, the life they led, while for their part the mullahs liked to preserve a geographical as well as a practical independence. So it came about that whenever the religious leaders in Persia have suffered a rebuff at the hands of the state authorities it is to Qom that they have withdrawn to lick their wounds.

But to understand the distinctive characteristics of Shi'ism it is necessary to go back to the earliest days of Islam and to the civil war which broke out among the Moslems only a generation after the death of the Prophet.

The Prophet Mohammed was both the bearer of the message of God and the implementer of the message. With his death the message stopped, though the word of God, the Koran, remained in the world, in history. The challenge which faced the successors of Mohammed was how to reconcile the continuing and unchanging presence of God in history (through the Koran) with temporal rule. This challenge presented itself immediately Mohammed died on 8 June 632.

Mohammed left no will, nor did he designate a successor, and he left no son. Yet somebody to guide and guard the growing community of Moslems was clearly needed, the only question being how he was to be chosen, and on whom the choice should fall.

To Fatima, the Prophet's surviving daughter, it was abundantly clear that the man who should be designated was her husband, Ali ibn Abi Talib. He was not only Mohammed's son-in-law, but also his cousin and virtually his adopted son. Apart from Mohammed's first wife, Khadija, Ali had been the earliest of all converts to Islam, embracing the new faith while still a boy, at an age which meant that he, unlike most other converts, had never done reverence to the idols which adorned the temples of pagan Mecca. It was Ali who had ensured Mohammed's safety when he fled from Mecca to Medina (*hijra*), who had been his lieutenant and standard-bearer in the Moslems' early campaigns and received sixteen wounds at the battle of Uhud. Who could possibly show better qualifications to head the new community? Did not Ali have an almost divine right to the inheritance?

Others thought differently. A hastily assembled meeting of some of Mohammed's closest companions (but not including Ali) chose Abu Bakr, father of Ayesha, the Prophet's favourite wife in whose arms he had died, as Khalifa (successor). In fact Abu Bakr was more than just the Prophet's father-in-law. He was the earliest adult male convert to Islam, and one whose faith had never wavered. Abu Bakr's devotion to the Prophet was absolute, and it was he whom the Prophet had chosen to accompany him on his emigration from Mecca to Medina. This companion of the Prophet, simple, pious, and unswervingly loyal, was well calculated to hold the new community together.

Abu Bakr received the homage (*bay'a*) of the community, including Ali, and for two years, until his death in August 634, he consolidated the ranks of the faithful, many of whom had fallen away on hearing of 'the death of one whom, as God's messenger, they had come to regard as immortal. It was Abu Bakr's achievement to point out to the dismayed believers that worship should be accorded to God, who was immortal, not to Mohammed, who was mortal.

On Abu Bakr's death the election once again eluded Ali, the choice going to the man Abu Bakr had designated, Umar ibn al-Khattab, the great warrior-statesman of the first generation of Moslems, whose armies broke the power of the two empires which for centuries had divided the lands of the Middle East between them, Byzantium and Persia. When Umar died at the hands of a Persian slave in November 644 the council he appointed on his deathbed to nominate a successor chose Uthman ibn Affan. With some reluctance Ali gave his homage to both Umar and Uthman, and it was not until Uthman had in his turn been murdered (June 656) that Ali became fourth Khalifa.

Behind the problems of succession lay a complex of forces – tribal, personal, social, economic – whose repercussions can be clearly traced in the Moslem world today. The people of Mecca, to which the message of God was first brought by Mohammed, belonged to a number of different tribal groups and distinct social classes – merchants, artisans, and slaves. It was, at any rate to begin with, these two latter classes who most eagerly received the message of justice and a new social order given to the Prophet; the merchants, with few exceptions, rejected it. Ali, whose father was so poor that he was obliged to turn to his relatives (including Mohammed) for help with his children's upbringing, was from the outset identified with the dispossessed – the poor and the oppressed. The leader of the merchants was a certain Abu Sufyan, from the Banu Umaiya branch of the Qureish (the tribe to whom almost all the inhabitants of Mecca, including Mohammed, belonged).

Mecca in the seventh century AD was the great trading centre of Arabia, and annual caravans took its merchants to Damascus and beyond. The Caliph Uthman, though an early convert to Islam, belonged like Abu Sufyan to the Banu Umaiya, most of whose members had only accepted Islam late in the day when it was obvious that the new faith would be victorious. Uthman was himself a rich merchant, and during the twelve years of his caliphate the treasure which had begun to flow into Mecca and Medina through the conquests of Umar's armies reached staggering proportions. Umar, a man of great simplicity and piety, firm but just in his rule, tried to check the corruption this new wealth inevitably brought with it: 'If I could live my life again,' he is reported to have said on his deathbed, 'I swear to God that I would take all that has been acquired by the rich and distribute it among its rightful owners, the poor.'

Uthman was not so strict. Anxious to please everyone, making no distinction between his private purse and the public treasury, he was lavish in the distribution of money and goods. To the Banu Umaiya went the leading appointments in the provinces, where they built for themselves splendid palaces, filled with the luxuries of Byzantium and Persia, with slaves and concubines.

Opposition to Uthman multiplied. It came not only from those who felt that they were not being rewarded according to their deserts, but also from those who believed Islam was losing its pristine purity, that the word of God was being smothered by the preoccupations of the world. Discontent spread in the provinces, particularly in Kufa and Basra in Iraq and in Egypt. Early in 656 rebellious contingents marched on Medina, still the capital of the Islamic empire, surrounded the house of the Caliph, and, after forty days' siege, burst in and murdered the eighty-two-year-old Uthman as he sat reading the Koran.

The murder of Uthman was the trigger which touched off a civil war that divided the community of Moslems in the seventh century, and still divides it today in the twentieth. Ali had been in Medina while these violent events were taking place. Though his sympathies were with the insurgents he was bound by his oath to Uthman, and tried unsuccessfully to act as a mediator. He even went so far as to send his two sons to help in the defence of Uthman. Now he was pressed by the insurgents to accept the caliphate but refused to take it from their hands alone. When a majority of the notables of Mecca and Medina, including surviving companions of the Prophet, added their support, he agreed, and was proclaimed Caliph in Medina six days after Uthman's murder.

Some refused the *bay'a* on the grounds that the real community of Moslems had not been consulted. The most significant refusal came from Mu'awiya, the governor of Syria. When the rich provincial capital of Damascus was captured from the Byzantines during the first year of Umar's caliphate it was natural that the family of Abu Sufyan should be installed there as governors. As merchants they had been in frequent contact with the city and its citizens; they possessed the necessary experience and the necessary skills. Now the governorship had passed to Abu Sufyan's second son, Mu'awiya, a man of exceptional ability who had kept his province quiet during the turmoil which distracted most of the rest of the empire. Since he, like Uthman, belonged to the Banu Umaiya it was not surprising for him to demand that the Caliph's murderers should be sought out and punished according to the word of God. He went further, and accused Ali of direct responsibility for the tragic events of Medina.

Ali procrastinated, reluctant to proceed against his own followers and against other Moslems. He tried to replace Mu'awiya and other of Uthman's Umaiya appointments with his own nominees, but the representative he sent to Damascus was refused admission. Both sides began to rally their forces and to prepare for the civil strife which now seemed inevitable.

The crucial battle took place at Siffin on the Euphrates, not far from Aleppo. Moslem was ranged against Moslem. But what were they fighting for? Was it for religion or for power? For principles or for riches? For the rewards of God or for the fruits of office? The composition of the two armies was very different. In Ali's ranks were many puritan warriors who retained the fanatical zeal of Islam's early days; but, as in all armies of individualists and volunteers discipline was slack, each man having his own idea of what should be done. Mu'awiya's army was better organized, with an able commander who knew exactly what he wanted and was determined to get it. This was revolutionary Islam ranged against the developing machinery of a powerful Moslem empire. It cannot be said that the conflict was between right and wrong, between truth and falsehood. Neither side had a monopoly of right and truth; it was this that made the collision between them so bitter and its outcome so enduring.

In spite of Mu'awiya's technical advantages it looked, after three days of intermittent fighting, as though Ali's forces were gaining the upper hand. Mu'awiya then had recourse to an ingenious stratagem. He ordered his men to tie leaves of the Koran to their spears and to proclaim 'Let the word of God decide.' The ruse worked. Ali and Mu'awiya agreed to abide by the terms of an arbitration to be worked out by two representatives they would nominate. In this second stage

Ali was again outmanoeuvred. It was agreed by the arbitrators that both Ali and Mu'awiya should be set aside and a new caliph appointed, but after Ali's representative had proclaimed the deposition of his principal, Mu'awiya's representative went back on his commitment and declared Mu'awiya the true caliph and the avenger of the blood of Uthman.

The world of Islam was thus split down the middle, with two Caliphs, each claiming legitimacy. Ali controlled most of the Arabian peninsula, Persia and Iraq; Mu'awiya Syria and Egypt. This division and compromise disgusted the extreme puritan element, the *khawarij* (outsiders), who rejected both rival Caliphs, claiming that what they were witnessing had nothing to do with matters of faith but was a simple struggle for temporal power. 'Judgement,' they insisted, 'belongs to God alone.' Soon they began to back their beliefs with the assassination of their enemies, and some of them resolved that both Caliphs deserved to die. In January 661 Ali, who still maintained the unguarded habits of the Prophet and Abu Bakr, was assassinated as he was entering the mosque in his capital of Kufa in Iraq. Mu'awiya, who now enjoyed the protection of a more sophisticated court, escaped.

Ali left two sons, Hassan and Hussein, who now represented, as their father had before them, the dynastic tradition in Islam, the family of the house of the Prophet (*ahl el-beit*). As we have seen, there had been, immediately after the death of Mohammed, those who felt the justice of Ali's claims to the succession. These backers or party of Ali (Shi'at Ali) became more clearly defined after Ali himself was dead. More than loyalty to a man or to a family was involved. From the outset Ali had been associated with the dispossessed in Mecca and Medina, and this revolutionary strain in Islam, with its emphasis on the social content of the Prophet's message, was to persist. One of the earliest philosophers of Islam, Abu Zurr al-Ghaffari, was in Ali's camp and quoted a saying attributed to Mohammed: 'There are three things which belong to society as a whole and cannot be claimed by any individual – fire, grass and water.' By thus listing the three essentials for the existence of the Arabs, al-Ghaffari was in effect proclaiming the nationalization of the means of production thirteen centuries before Karl Marx.

Many stories of Mohammed's devotion to his two young grandsons were common currency among the Arabs. They were, however, men of very different temperaments and were to meet correspondingly different fates. Hassan, a pious but unassertive character, soon retired into private life in Medina, where he died eight years later. His

younger brother, Hussein, was more combative. He refused to give
the *bay'a* to Mu'awiya, and, after the latter's death in April 680, refused
it to his son Yezid, who had inherited not only his father's Syrian
possessions but also his claim to the caliphate.

In the autumn of 680 Hussein left Medina with his family and
supporters and marched north across the desert towards his father's
old capital, Kufa. The story of how his small force was betrayed,
abandoned and finally surrounded and slaughtered by Yezid's troops
near the town of Kerbala in Iraq is for Shi'a Moslems a tragedy as
abiding and personal as the Passion of Christ is for Christians. When
he saw that there was no hope, Hussein welcomed martyrdom. There
were to be many more martyrs of the Shi'at Ali in history.

I have thought it necessary to give a brief outline of these early days of
Islam because without some understanding of what happened then it is
impossible for anyone to comprehend what is happening now. Islam
differs from Christianity in that it imposes upon believers not only the
ordinances of divine worship (*ibadat*) but also regulations governing
every aspect of their daily life; it provides the framework for the
organization of the community in this life as well as the means of
salvation for the individual in the world to come.

But, as has been seen, the problem is that, while during his lifetime
Mohammed was both the bearer of God's message to man and its
implementer in action, after his death prophecy came to an end.
Mohammed left behind him the law. But all law requires interpreta-
tion, and in Islam where is this to be found? Controversy between
Sunnis and Shi'is focuses on one of the sayings (*hadith*) of the Prophet:
'I have bequeathed to you that which will always be a guide to you, if
you will take hold of it; the Book of God and the practices of my life.'
The Sunnis take this to mean the Koran and the *sunna*, the ideas and
practices of Mohammed during his lifetime. But to this saying of the
Prophet the Shi'is add another phrase attributed to him: 'the Book of
God, and the practices of my life and of my family (*ahl el-beit*).' The
Sunnis maintain that the successors of Mohammed were no more than
fallible human interpreters of the law; the Shi'is that as Mohammed
was the imam, or interpreter, while he was still alive, so after him there
have been other imams to interpret for the faithful, and that, because
the message of God was received with greatest clarity by Ali and his
family (*ahl el-beit*), the imam must be able to prove descent from Ali
and Fatima, the Prophet's daughter. Against the Sunni reliance on

consensus among believers (*ijma*) the Shi'is trust in what amounts to divine right of the family of Ali. A majority of Shi'is believe that the imams continued visible in the world until the twelfth in succession disappeared in AD 873. They await his reappearance as the Mahdi, the infallible guide who will institute the reign of justice in the world and liberate the poor. But until that day some other means for interpretation of the word is required, and that is to be found in those who have special knowledge and understanding of religious matters, the *fuqaha*, who thus become in effect the deputies of the hidden imam.

Many forces combined to deepen the gulf which had opened between Sunni and Shi'i through the civil strife in Islam's first century. After the murders of Ali and Hussein their followers were scattered and became the victims of fierce persecution. The victorious Umayyad Caliphs, who now ruled the Arab empire from their capital in Damascus, made it a test of belief to insult Ali and his family, and failure to pass this test was punishable by death. To avoid this fate Shi'is came to adopt the principle of *tuqi'a* (dissimulation), which means that it is legitimate to dissemble if one is in the hands of an enemy, or believes with reason that one's life is threatened. Inevitably Shi'ism found adherents among those who for any reasons resented the centralized authority of Sunni orthodoxy – the poor and under-privileged classes, the minorities, and those, such as the Persians, who had accepted Islam when the Arab conquerors swept over them, but who retained a strong feeling of national identity.

When in the middle of the eighth century supremacy in the Arab empire passed from Umayyad Caliphs in Damascus to the Abbasid Caliphs with their capital of Baghdad, it might have been thought that better days would dawn for the Shi'at Ali, for whereas Damascus had always been influenced by the civilization of Byzantium Baghdad was influenced by the civilization of neighbouring Persia. True enough, Persians (and by now almost all Persians were Shi'is) occupied leading positions in government and administration under the Abbasids; they were prominent as writers, poets, philosophers and artists. Yet they suffered from a feeling of subordination. They could enjoy privileges but they could not rule; they could create but not direct. And although during the next thousand years there were to be places and periods in which the Shi'is were in power – Fatimid Egypt and the Yemen, for example – more often they have, except in Persia, been a suppressed and often a persecuted community.

By now, I hope, some of the characteristics of Shi'ism, and particularly of Persian Shi'ism, will have become clear. To begin with there is the identification with the revolutionary tradition of Islam – with the element of social justice in the Prophet's teaching and with the pursuit of social justice even when this involves opposition to the civil authority. Then there is the adoption of the cause of Ali and his family as imams, interpreters and mediators. So far did this process go that they have on occasion become identified with the heroes of pre-Islamic Persia, Ali taking on some of the character of Rustum. Thirdly, there is what has sometimes been called the Kerbala complex, the preoccupation with martyrdom as a particularly blessed and meritorious destiny, thanks to the example of Hussein. Indeed, some Shi'is look on Hussein in much the same light as Christians look on Christ, as a willing sacrifice who will come forward at the Day of Judgement to intercede with God on behalf of the whole nation of Moslems. Fourthly, there is the continuing process of interpretation carried out by those qualified to do this in the absence of the one true imam. Finally, there is the legacy of persecution which has led not only to fierce resentment of all foreign domination and interference but also to the acceptance of dissimulation as a necessary form of protection against this evil. When foreigners accuse the Persians of being a deceitful nation the explanation is that they have, probably unconsciously, come up against the doctrine of *tuqi'a* in practice. It should, however, be pointed out that Khomeini has laid down that Iranians have by now reached a stage of maturity and independence which should make this doctrine, too often abused by them in the past, no longer necessary.

It must be confessed that there is something particularly sad about Persian Shi'ism. The intensity of grief with which the Muharram ceremonies commemorating the martyrdom of Hussein are marked is something no spectator can ever forget. The black turbans of the mullahs and the black *chadors* of Persian woman combine to emphasize this sense of sadness. As a nation the Persians have too often looked back from under foreign or native despotism to a golden age when their country, one of the oldest geographical entities in the world, was the object of universal fear and respect. As believers they have been waiting for a thousand years for the reappearance of the imam, the liberator and saviour. Persia has provided the world with one of its greatest and most enduring civilizations, with a literary and artistic legacy which has few rivals, but this element of sadness and disappointment overshadows it. It is the sense of sorrow and tragedy pervading both the religion and the history of Persia which creates such an explosive mixture.

At the beginning of the sixteenth century the first Safavid Shah, Ismail, made Shi'ism the official religion of Persia. In this way church and state were linked against the Sunni Ottoman Empire which constituted the main threat to the country. Persia's religious life thereafter became organized in a way which differs from that of other Moslem countries. The schools of training for Shi'a religious centred on two mosques, one outside and one inside the country: the mosque of Ali at Najaf, and the mosque of Fatima the Ma'asuma (the sinless) in Qom.

Six distinct grades are open for those who embark on their training at these mosque schools. The initial grade is that of *talib ilm*, a learner. On graduation he becomes a *mujtahid*, which literally means someone who has exerted himself so as to be able to frame an opinion. The third stage is that of *mubelleg al-risala*, or carrier of the message; the fourth, that of *hojat al-Islam*, or authority on Islam; the fifth, that of *ayatollah*, or sign of God. The sixth and final grade is that of *ayatollah al-uzma*, or great sign of God. He then automatically becomes a *margieieh* (a person to be referred to on everything).

Traditionally there are never more than five ayatollahs al-uzma at any one time,* and according to the 1906 Persian constitution they cannot be arrested. So it was that when Khomeini was a plain ayatollah it was possible for the Shah to order his arrest, but when he had become an ayatollah al-uzma his arrest was impossible and he had instead to be exiled.

The nucleus of the Shi'a religious schools is the *hawza* (circle) of disciples who collect round a teacher and accept his interpretations. When a novice has reached the grade of hojat al-Islam he can form his own *hawza*, and the more disciples he gathers the nearer he comes to achieving the next grade, that of ayatollah. But a candidate can only reach the final grade, of ayatollah al-uzma, if he is accepted by the others already in the grade and if he can present them with a theological treatise of sufficient merit. In the case of Khomeini his treatise was entitled *Tahrir al-Wasilah* (*The Liberation of the Means*) – a title of no little significance.

One important difference between Shi'a divines and those in the Sunni world is their independent financial status. In Sunni countries

---

* The number five has a special significance for Moslems. There are the five pillars of Islam (the profession of faith, prayer, alms, fasting and pilgrimage); the five persons of the *ahl el-beit* (Mohammed, Fatima, Ali, Hassan and Hussein); the five daily prayers, and so on.

the state receives the religious offerings and pays the mullahs and ulamas, but Shia *mujtahids* and other divines receive directly from their flock revenues which are devoted to services of the mosque and other pious purposes. According to the Koranic ruling they are entitled to receive one-fifth of the income of all those in their *hawza*. When, in the 1920s, Reza Shah was trying to curb the power of the mullahs he hoped to be able to bring Iran into line with the Sunni system, thereby making the mullahs state functionaries. But he met with such fierce resistance, not only from the divines but from their flocks, who continued to give them financial support, that he had to abandon the attempt. A Persian citizen may be prepared to cheat the tax-collector, but not his ayatollah.

Khomeini put the money he received in his exile from his adherents to good use. In addition to spending generously on schools and welfare work he used it to enlist the most up-to-date machinery of propaganda – duplicating machines and cassettes – by which his sermons and instructions were distributed throughout the length and breadth of Iran.

Khomeini speaks of time-serving divines with a certain contempt; *fuqaha es-Sultan*, 'the Sultan's theologians', is the expression he uses. The tradition of Qom, which he has done so much to foster, is the opposite of time-serving. Revenues to its divines give it financial independence. Its distance from Tehran helps to remove it from the attentions of the central government. Above all, in Qom there is a continuing religious life of great intensity, which makes it a place of refuge in adversity, and a city ready to challenge the rival authority of Tehran when adversity is past.

# 7
# QOM ENCIRCLED

THE ATMOSPHERE inside a city in which religion plays a dominant part, whether it be Rome or Mecca, Benares or Kyoto, is always unlike that in a secular city. In Qom were now to be found not only its usual complement of *mujtahids* with their *hawzas*, teachers and learners, but also a whole new population of refugees, endlessly discussing the events of the past and possibilities for the future. They were particularly concerned, naturally enough, with the role that had been played in the Mossadeq days by the leading Qom divine, Ayatollah Kashani. Had he been right, they asked themselves, to become so involved in politics? Of course, in Islam religion and politics cannot be separated, since Islam is concerned all the time with every aspect of society; but Kashani had taken a leading office in the state, President of the Majlis, and at times had functioned almost as second man in the government. Had this been wise? Had it been sensible to put the whole weight of the religious influence which he symbolized behind a single political issue, the nationalization of oil?

Though the cause with which Kashani had identified himself had been lost, and he himself was now dead, his colleagues in Qom did not feel themselves defeated. They realized that it was the intention of the Shah, as it had been of his father, to produce a separation between religion and the state, but this was something they could never accept. If the Shah had his way, Islam would be confined to *ibadat*, to the performance of ritual prayers and worship, whereas they knew it covered every aspect of life, and that in a truly Islamic society it was the *fuqaha*, the theologians, whose business it was to interpret for the state.

In these difficult days a relatively young *hojat al-Islam* (sixty is not old as religious leaders in Qom go), teaching mainly *fiqh* (jurisprudence) and logic, began to attract attention and to find the numbers in his *hawza* growing. His name was Ruhallah Khomeini. To the questions which were everywhere being asked in Qom he provided answers. Yes, he said, Kashani had made mistakes. His target should have been Islam, not oil, because all the fruits of the earth, including oil, came within the purview of Islam. And with religious instruction Khomeini, then as later, combined political action. He took steps to assist the dependants of those who had been killed in the counter-coup, or who had disappeared or been obliged to go into exile. He dispatched letters to the heads of state of all Moslem and Arab countries asking for contributions to the cause. Only one of the recipients was to reply – Gamal Abdel Nasser. He sent a messenger, a Lebanese working with the Syrian security chief, Colonel Abdel Hamid Sarraj (Egypt and Syria were at this time partners in the United Arab Republic), from Beirut airport carrying $150,000 to be placed at the disposal of the relief committee. But when the messenger reached Tehran airport he was arrested; either Savak or one of the intelligence agencies working with it (CIA and Mossad) had alerted the airport authorities.

The Shah was of course well informed about everything Khomeini was saying in his *hawza*, and he did not like what he heard of this rising star in the religious firmament. He thought it was time to cut him down to size. So in a broadcast he addressed himself to the religious leaders of Iran, not mentioning Khomeini by name, but asking them what they thought of a prominent Shi'i who was prepared to accept money from non-Shi'is.

In his *hawza* the next day Khomeini gave his answer. The time for *tuqi'a* (dissimulation) is over, he said. Now is the time for us to stand up and proclaim the things we believe in. Then he quoted what the Shah had said in his broadcast and commented: 'I don't need money; the contributions from my *hawza* cover all my needs. The money sent by President Nasser was not sent to me but to the relief committee, and was for the needs of widows and orphans – made widows and orphans by the rule of the Shah and of his father before him. I take this opportunity to declare the end of *tuqi'a*.'

With this declaration Khomeini became the first religious leader to denounce *tuqi'a* and to make a frontal attack on the Shah. He soon found other lines of attack. In 1962 the Shah proclaimed what he called the 'Shah–People Revolution', or 'White Revolution', which consisted of a six-point programme including land reform, the emancipation of women, and changes in the electoral law. Hitherto only males had been eligible to vote or stand as candidates, and voters and candidates had had to take an oath on the Koran. The new regulations opened the door to women and non-Moslems. Khomeini opposed them. It is from this period that his reputation as an anti-feminist derives – a reputation that is not undeserved, since it must be admitted that on this and many other matters Khomeini is thoroughly obscurantist.

Khomeini was roused to send the Shah a telegram, but the Shah refused to reply directly. Instead a telegram was sent in the name of the government, which addressed Khomeini as *hojat al-Islam* – a delicate snub since he had by now progressed to *ayatollah*. But all the telegram said was that the Shah hoped Khomeini would see his way to follow the correct course.

Khomeini now enlisted the support of some of the younger mullahs in the preparation of a petition to be sent to the Shah. The other ayatollahs were not yet behind Khomeini. Although the Shah had been unsuccessful in an attempt to get one of the *mujtahids* in Najaf nominated as chief Ayatollah al-Uzma in place of Ayatollah Bargroudi, who had died, and so divert the Shi'a leadership outside Iran, the Qom hierarchy was still cautious. By appealing to the younger element Khomeini was combining the thinking of Qom traditionalists with that of the opposition forces in Tehran.

The petition made three points. First, it called on the Shah to break what it called his 'chains of serfdom' with America. 'Do not,' it urged, 'sacrifice the beliefs of the people and the independence of the nation for the purposes of safeguarding American and Zionist interests.'*

Secondly, the Shah should show his respect for Moslems and for Islamic liberties. He should stop imposing his rule by bullets and deceiving his people by trickeries passing under the name of elections and 'White Revolutions'.

Thirdly, the Shah should employ the growing wealth of the country to combat poverty and ignorance, and so leave the people free to build their own future.

To this petition the Shah again made no direct reply, but he sent a man from Savak, accompanied by a mullah, to Qom to tell Khomeini to do three things: stop attacking the Shah; stop attacking Israel; stop attacking America. If he observed these three conditions, Khomeini was free to say what he liked on other matters. This should be treated as an ultimatum.

The next day, in the Fatima mosque, Khomeini revealed the whole

---

* A study of Khomeini's writings shows that from the earliest days he mistrusted the Jews. He has a profound conviction that from the beginning the Jews have hated Islam and have tried to frustrate it. When the state of Israel was founded Khomeini immediately denounced it. This, and his espousal of the cause of the Palestinians and his concern for the status of Jerusalem, ranged him on the side of the Arab states. This was later to be of considerable importance, because the Shah, by harking back to Cyrus the Great and Iran's Achaemenian past, was trying to wean his people away from their Arab neighbours and, by implication, away from the broad pan-Islamic movement.

transaction. 'What does this mean?' he asked. 'What does the Shah want from me by sending me a messenger from Savak? Why am I not allowed to attack Israel? Has the Shah an Israeli mother or an Israeli father? And why am I not allowed to attack him himself? Is he Ali? No; he is a human being, and if he does wrong we tell him he has done wrong, just as we tell him he has done right when he has done right. And what is this about the United States? Are we supposed to glorify those who enslave us, and have crushed the self-respect of our nation?' Then, in a passage which seemed to have echoes of Lenin in it, he went on: 'Either all the mullahs should join with me or they are no better than revisionists. Unless they speak out, it shows that they have chosen to side with Satan.' In this manner Khomeini tried to force into the open those religious leaders who, from fear or doubt or reliance on the principle of *tuqi'a*, were letting discretion remain the better part of valour.

To choose the Fatima mosque in Qom for this tirade against his sovereign seemed to many at the time an act of almost reckless folly. Yet, like Lenin and many other successful revolutionaries, Khomeini had an almost instinctive sense of occasion and of the telling phrase which would stick in the minds of his hearers and serve to remind them of his words. He ended his sermon by addressing himself once again directly to the Shah: 'I have prepared my heart to receive your bayonets, but never to accept your warning.'

Khomeini showed himself extremely skilful in his use of language. All his audiences of course knew the language of the Koran, and he now began to adapt Koranic words to current usages. One such word was *tagha*, meaning to tyrannize, and he started referring to his opponents as *taghutis* (tyrants). All over the country people could be heard accusing others of being *taghutis* or protesting that they were not a *taghuti*. Another such word of Koranic derivation was *mustazafin*, meaning the poor and humiliated, and it was not hard in the Shah's Iran to find plenty of people this identification would fit.

Another way in which Khomeini showed his tactical skill as a revolutionary was in his exploitation of the pattern of mourning observed by all Shi'is. There are three occasions on which mourners congregate to commemorate the dead: the first is called the *majlis el-a'aza*, which takes place immediately after death, when visitors call at the dead person's home to express their condolences to the family; the second is called the *majlis el-tarhim*, and takes place every Thursday, when friends meet to recall the deceased's merits, and these continue until the fortieth day after death, the *majlis el-arba'in*, which is supposed to be the day on which the soul of the deceased is received into the Kingdom of God. These occasions are naturally celebrated with unusual fervour when the dead is thought to have been a martyr for his religion, and there were to be many such before the Shah's reign was over.

It was known that in the last days of March 1963 Khomeini would speak in his *hawza* on the anniversary of the death of Imam Jaafar es-Sadiq.★ Tension in Qom had been mounting for several days past, and the government had sent reinforcements of troops and police into the city. But when the session in the *hawza* began Khomeini felt the presence in it of hostile elements, probably agents provocateurs introduced by Savak. So he halted the proceedings, explaining to the congregation his reason for doing so. Some of those present began to heckle him. He retorted: 'Unless you stop this disturbance I shall go to the shrine of Fatima the Sinless, and there I shall say what I have to say.' There was silence, but suddenly this was broken by a cry of 'Long live the Shah!' Scuffling broke out, and the session was brought to an end.

Next day the police, shouting 'Long live the Shah!', moved against the seminary where Khomeini taught in considerable strength, with the intention of arresting some of his followers. But they met with resistance; fighting broke out; an estimated twenty-two people were killed and many more arrested. Khomeini left the seminary, and went to his house, where several members of his *hawza* followed him. 'Let them attack me here if they wish,' he said. He then continued the address which had been interrupted the day before. 'Yesterday's attack on our school by military commandos and by army personnel in civilian clothes,' he said, 'reminds me of the Mongol attacks on Iran five hundred years ago. The attackers shouted,"Long live the Shah!" Why? Is this not strange when it is the Shah who is assaulting Moslem shrines and violating the precepts of Islam? Is this what the life of the Shah stands for? Does it stand for attacks on the Koran and Islam?'

The authorities were still reluctant to take the final step of ordering Khomeini's arrest. A new tactic was devised. The senior *mujtahid* in the Shi'a Holy Cities in Iraq, Ayatollah el-Hakim, had been pro-

---

★ Jaafar es-Sadiq, sixth of the twelve imams (AD 700–756), was celebrated for his learning. In an age when the Shi'a leaders lived precarious underground lives he elaborated, even before the disappearance of the twelfth imam over a century later, the doctrine that the imam could have a deputy, who could act for him. This deputy should be of exemplary character, above worldly considerations and a faithful interpreter of the imam. This doctrine was to be further elucidated by Khomeini.

foundly shocked by the news of the rioting and deaths in Qom, and
had sent a telegram to his fellow *mujtahids* there suggesting that, if they
felt Qom had become too dangerous a place for them, they should
move to Kerbala and Najaf. The contents of this telegram naturally
became known to the authorities, so they sent a message to the senior
ayatollah in Qom, Shariatmadari, saying that if anyone wished to go
to Iraq everything would be done to facilitate their departure.
Khomeini's response was another telegram addressed to the Shah:
'With the help of God I shall be true to my responsibilities. If we are to
die, we shall be martyrs: if we are to live, we shall be victorious!' Once
again Khomeini dispatched telegrams to the heads of Moslem and
Arab states, giving them his version of events and appealing for their
support, and though these were stopped by the censor copies were
smuggled out to Najaf and distributed from there.

5 June was the day of the *majlis el-arba'in* for those killed in the attack
on the Faydiyah seminary. By now police and army were present in
Qom in considerable strength, and they tried ineffectually to prevent
the meeting from taking place. Khomeini took the opportunity to
deliver the most violent of his speeches yet, once again apostrophizing
the Shah directly: 'Listen to my advice! Listen to those who have a true
concern for the interests of the people! Listen, you miserable, sick
man! You have now lived forty-five years in this world. Just stop and
consider for a moment what you have done to your country. Learn a
lesson from the fate that befell your father. You accuse us of being
reactionaries, but you are the real black reactionary who has betrayed
us with a so-called "White Revolution".' Then he went on to deal
in no less violent terms with the Shah's reliance on America and
Israel.

This was going too far. The police moved in, and Khomeini was
arrested (he was not yet an Ayatollah al-Uzma, which would have
rendered him immune from arrest). Demonstrations immediately
broke out in Qom and in Tehran, where he was imprisoned. To quote
one newspaper report: 'Tehran yesterday was in a turmoil, as were
also most of the other principal cities of Iran. The streets were filled
with tanks and guns, and were the scene of demonstrations, prompted
by the arrest of Ruhallah Khomeini, which observers described as the
most violent since those at the time of Mossadeq's overthrow. Over a
hundred people are reported dead.' Though these early reports of
casualties proved to be exaggerated, there was no question that the
rioting was on a scale which Iran had not seen for a long time. Three
days after Khomeini's arrest the Prime Minister, Hassan Ali Mansur,

was assassinated at the entrance to the Majlis by a seminarian from Qom.

Khomeini was taken by car to the Turkish frontier and deposited in that desolate region. He managed to find his way across the border, and from Turkey moved to Najaf, where he was eventually joined by his wife and family. While in prison he had received hints that the Shah would be willing to meet him for talks to resolve their differences, provided he was prepared to be reasonable. From exile he now delivered his answer: 'They told me that if I saw the Shah this would solve all problems. But surely they know that the Shah has been rejected by the whole nation. It is being put about that the breast of the Shah is as wide as the sea to embrace all who will return to him. But this is a poisoned sea, and anyone who so much as dips the tip of his finger in it will be poisoned. They tried to get me to meet the Shah so that they could poison my reputation.'

Back in Tehran the Shah used the murder of his Prime Minister to crack down on the opposition. Many were arrested and either sent for trial or otherwise disposed of. Qom was crushed, and now there was a migration of the Shah's opponents in the reverse direction – from Qom to Tehran, where concealment was somewhat easier.

# 8

# THE ABSOLUTE SHAH

THE SHAH had won. Qom and Tehran were pacified; the opposition crushed; Khomeini in exile. Nor was there any need for the Shah to worry about the Majlis. When he promulgated his 'White Revolution' he had appealed direct to the masses over the heads of the politicians by means of a referendum. This was indeed the 'Shah–People Revolution' bypassing the politicians. In future the Majlis was to be a cipher; parliaments, as well as cabinets and political parties, were to be created and liquidated as the Shah pleased. The years of absolutism had begun.

The Shah was helped in the consolidation of his position by events elsewhere. Egypt's defeat in the June war of 1967 crippled the authority of Nasser as leader of the surge of Arab nationalism which the Shah had always feared and resented, and vastly increased the standing of the Shah's crypto-ally, Israel. He could now see no ruler in the area with powers and resources comparable to his own. Even more beneficial from his point of view was Britain's decision to wind up its protectorates in the Gulf and by so doing abandon the position of naval and political paramountcy in these waters which it had exercised for 150 years. Kuwait had become independent in 1961, and in 1968 declared that it would no longer be looking to Britain for protection against external aggression. At the beginning of 1968 the rulers of Bahrein, Qatar and the Trucial Sheikhdoms agreed to federate, and thereby to exchange reliance on the protecting arm of Britain for independence. The only complication about this was the Iranian claim on Bahrein – a claim which the Shah had inherited and felt obliged to take seriously, even if nobody outside Iran did. He called the proposed federation 'a colonialist and imperialist manipulation', but in 1969 a face-saving formula involving a mission of inquiry dispatched by the Secretary-General of the United Nations was devised. Bahrain became independent in August 1971, Qatar following just a month later. In July the six former Trucial Sheikhdoms formed themselves into a new sovereign state to be known as the United Arab Emirates.

With Britain more or less out of the picture, and most of the new states weak in everything except cash, there were now only two major powers in the Gulf – Saudi Arabia and, of course, Iran (Iraq had a narrow sea outlet at the head of the Gulf, but at this period its main preoccupation lay elsewhere). As the Shah saw it, the Gulf was becoming the most important economic and strategic area in the world, and control of it would have to be exercised by a partnership between Iran and Saudi Arabia, with Iran very much the senior partner, both looking to the United States for diplomatic support and for arms. The symbol of this new state of affairs was to be the creation of the Iranian navy. Saudi Arabia did not even have a minesweeper in the Gulf, but Iran acquired destroyers, corvettes, frigates and a naval air arm. By 1975 the Shah was claiming: 'The strength we have now in the Persian Gulf is ten times, twenty times more than the British ever had.'

This remark was typical of the *folie de grandeur* from which the Shah began manifestly to suffer as he settled into his role as absolute ruler of a land of destiny. Everything was to be on a huge scale, to make the world take notice. The first symbolic occasion of the new grandeur was his coronation. The Shah's second wife, Soraya, had borne him no children and had been divorced in 1958. In December 1959 he married Farah Diba, who bore him a son and heir in 1961. Now the time had come for the long-delayed ceremony to take place.

Reza Shah, like Napoleon, had placed the crown on his own head, to make it plain to all that he was beholden to nobody; and as he had acquired the throne through his own exertions this gesture was understandable. His son, on the other hand, had inherited the throne, and he justified his self-crowning action on the grounds that he had held on to the throne he had inherited over twenty-six years of storms and tribulations. 'I have,' he said during the ceremony in Gulistan Palace, which took place on 26 October 1967, his forty-eighth birthday, 'crowned myself because now the Iranian people are living in prosperity and security. I long ago promised myself that I would never be king over a people who were beggars or oppressed. But now that everyone is happy I allow my coronation to take place.' After placing the crown on his own head, the Shah placed smaller crowns on the heads of his wife Farah, who was proclaimed Empress, and on his son. He himself assumed in addition to Shahinshah (King of Kings), the title Aryamehr (Light of the Aryans).

Certainly the coronation was a very splendid occasion. As though none of the crowns in the Imperial Treasury was worthy of the occasion, the Shah ordered new ones to be made by Cartier. There were 3,380 jewels in the crown which he put on his own head and rather fewer in the other two crowns.

The Shah celebrated his thirty years on the throne in 1971, but it was a year later that the climax of his reign was reached. This was in October 1972, when two and a half thousand years of monarchy were commemorated on a truly grandiose scale among the ruins of the former Achaemenian capital, Persepolis. Sixty-eight kings, princes and heads of state attended – the Kings of Norway and Sweden, of Thailand and Denmark, of Belgium and Greece. Prince Philip and Princess Anne came from Britain, the Emperor Haile Selassie and President Senghor of Senegal from Africa, Vice-President Agnew from the United States and President Podgorny from the Soviet Union; King Hussein and Presidents Franjieh of Lebanon and Bourguiba of Tunisia, together with all the Gulf rulers; not to mention the Prime Ministers of France, Italy and Portugal and many more. Besides all these, the Shah had collected a strange assortment of newspaper proprietors and editors, of arms traders and financiers.

I did not attend the actual ceremonies but I was interested to see the setting for this extraordinary occasion, which I must confess I found grotesque almost to the point of obscenity. Persepolis had become a city of tents, one for each country's representative. Inside each silk-lined tent – they were really enormous marquees – was a large living room, bedroom, and kitchen. Catering had been put into the hands of Maxim's, but if any of the guests preferred their national dishes to the luxury foods prepared by Parisian chefs their own cooks were flown in at the Shah's expense. As it was, mountains of caviare and other delicacies were consumed by the bigwigs and their suites and by lesser fry like journalists. The equipment needed to prepare and maintain this jamboree can be imagined. Numerous power stations had to be erected in the desert to serve the refrigerators and air-conditioning units, as well as telephones, television, transport and so forth. The whole three-day affair cost the Iranian taxpayers $120 million, but the Shah was sure it was worth every penny.* He said that he wanted to show the Iranian people that they had friends in the world – as if turning up to consume his caviare was a proof of friendship. But his real cause for satisfaction was more personal. He felt that Persepolis had put the seal of legitimacy on the Pahlevi dynasty. 'The de-

---

* The official estimates of the cost was $40 million, but much of the true expenditure, such as new roads and other communications, deployment of the army, etc., was concealed in other budgets.

scendants of Charlemagne came to Persepolis to pay homage to the son of a corporal,' he told a royal friend in Paris. He said this with a laugh, but he meant it very seriously.

Unfortunately it was not only entertainment that was on a lavish scale in Iran during the late 1960s and early 1970s. This was the time when everybody began to get their fingers into the pie. The Shah was treating Iran as if it was his private property, and first pickings naturally went to his family. Certain unwritten boundaries were observed. The Queen Mother was only interested in real estate – land and buildings. She maintained an impressive office in a building in Takhtitaos Street, which after the Revolution became the office of the Ministry of Revolutionary Affairs. The Shah's brother, Prince Mahmud Reza, concentrated on mining, including cobalt, bauxite and turquoise; he was the principal shareholder in the Firouz Mining Company, the Shaharand Industrial Company and many others. Princess Ashraf was involved in banking, paper mills and lotteries, and so on. Loyal friends were not forgotten. General Zahedi's son, Ardeshir, who had married the Shah's daughter and been made ambassador in Washington, took over a controlling interest in the motor industry, and innumerable former politicians, diplomats, soldiers and businessmen were similarly rewarded, as were officials of the CIA who had proved helpful.

One of the Shah's most loyal servants was Jaafar Sharif Emami. He became Deputy Chief Custodian of the Pahlevi Foundation (the Shah himself being Custodian), a post which he held for sixteen years, and which was a source of enormous influence and profit. The Pahlevi Foundation had been set up in 1958, ostensibly as a charitable organization, funded by the sale of crown lands to the tenants, which directed its income to the furtherance of worthy causes. This it undoubtedly did, supporting clinics and youth clubs and sending thousands of students to study abroad. But beyond that its ramifications in the economic life of the country grew to such an extent that it became to all intents and purposes a separate economic empire within the state. By 1979 its assets were estimated at around $3 billion. Between them, the royal family and the Pahlevi Foundation were thought to control 80 per cent of the cement industry in Iran, 70 per cent of hotels and tourism, 62 per cent of banking and insurance, 40 per cent of the textile industry, 35 per cent of the motor industry, and so on.

The same overlapping of private and public interests was to be seen throughout the whole fabric of the state. Hushang Ansari, for many years Finance Minister, also looked after the Shah's personal financial affairs. His brother, Cyrus Ansari, acted for the Shah when he bought a 25-per-cent interest in the foundation controlling Krupp for a reported DM550 million.

This was a period when the regime seemed to have been seized with a sort of madness. Persepolis had gone to the Shah's head. There he had entertained his guests by parading units of the army dressed in the uniforms of Achaemenian times, and now he was to compensate for his previous sense of insecurity by thinking of himself as the reincarnation of Cyrus and Darius.★ Court ceremonial was greatly elaborated. There was continual bowing and scraping, visitors had to leave the royal presence walking backwards, and similar absurdities. I have found it usually a safe assumption that the more rigid the ceremonial in a court, the more likely the people of the country are to suffer oppression.

I noticed the difference when I talked to the Shah. Previously he had spoken freely, enjoying the give and take of conversation; now he listened courteously but, except when being interviewed, contributed only a few remarks. He preferred to present himself as an enigma; like those wooden Russian dolls, always another one to be found inside when you open them, he kept his thoughts hidden within impenetrable shells of royal reserve. He was consciously turning himself into an oriental monarch – the old Persian kings, the Egyptian pharaohs, and the Byzantine emperors all rolled into one. And these monarchies which he was setting out to imitate had in common not just the magnificent ritual of their courts, but a tradition of absolutism. That too became the hallmark of the Pahlevi monarchy. There was one man and one man alone who could make decisions. All those around the Shah cowered in his presence, for they were all his creatures. The more he grew in stature in his own eyes, the more they seemed to diminish, for without him they were nothing. It was sometimes said that while nobody had dared to tell his father, Reza Shah, a lie, nobody dared to tell the son a truth.

'Now we are the masters, and our former masters are our slaves,' the Shah told a royal personage close to the Pahlevi family. 'Every day they beat a track to our door begging for favours. How can they be of assistance? Do we want arms? Do we want nuclear power stations? We

---

★ The Crown Prince was given Darius as one of his names.

have only to ask, and they will hasten to fulfil our wishes.' This was heady stuff, as was to be expected when the repressed man who was at the head of a repressed nation felt himself liberated on behalf of a nation also liberated. The Shah felt almost literally on top of the world.

It was not simply the coronation and the Persepolis gala which were responsible for this euphoria; there was a third and still more exciting stimulus – the rise in the price of oil. After Persepolis Iran had accumulated debts of $3 billion, but by the end of 1973, little more than a year later, all the debts had been repaid and Iran had become a creditor nation from whom others, like Britain, were happy to borrow. This transformation was due to the quadrupling of the price of oil, which promised to raise Iran's oil revenue from $5 billion a year to the staggering figure of $19 billion.

How had this happened? When, following the October war of 1973, the Arab countries had for the first time used 'the oil weapon' and cut back supplies to the West, Iran had not joined them. Iran was, after all, not an Arab country, and enjoyed a special relationship with the Arabs' enemy, Israel. Yet now it was Iran which was prepared to go much further than any Arab government had suggested in squeezing the West. It was the Shah, the West's most trusted ally in the Middle East, who had made himself spokesman for a move which threatened to cripple western economies for years to come. Was this his own idea, or had someone put him up to it?

At the end of 1973 it obviously required expert understanding of market forces to know how large a rise in oil prices the international economy could stand without an explosion. It was no use quadrupling the price of oil if nobody was going to buy it. Yet the Shah showed such supreme confidence in his decision to go ahead with the rise that he must have taken good advice from somewhere, and acting on the principle of *cui bono* the suspicions of many have turned towards the Americans. It was the American oil companies which still dominated and in effect controlled the oil market, and the dollar was the currency for international oil transactions. Western Europe and Japan had been developing into formidable trading competitors of America, and a staggering rise in the price of their main source of energy would put them in their place. As Henry Kissinger rightly said of the oil price rise, 'This is the end of the Marshall Plan' – one of the Plan's main benefits to war-stricken Europe having been the provision of cheap oil.

America benefited in another way. I wrote at the time: 'We Arabs are being bound to America by golden chains'; and this applied in equal or greater measure to Iran. The United States got the oil and supplied Iran and the Arab countries with consumer goods and arms. America kept the oil countries' money in steadily devalued dollars; they spent the interest on their capital on American goods. America got the profits and the oil producers got the obloquy. It was not a bad arrangement for America.

It was not bad for the Shah either, or so it seemed to him at the time. At his famous press conference in Tehran on 23 December 1973 he took the opportunity to read the West a lecture. It was a lecture delivered more in sorrow than in anger – a stern but just schoolmaster admonishing his feckless pupils. The West, he said, had to learn to live within its means. It must search for other sources of energy than oil. If people in the West want to produce hippies and indulge in leftist talk they should do this at their own expense and not at the expense of other countries like Iran. 'There is degeneration in the West,' he went on. 'We have nothing to learn from them. They want to export their degenerate ideas, which they call democracy, but that is something we cannot accept.'

The Shah began to talk about the future, and how Iran was soon to become the fifth industrial nation in the world. He talked of nuclear power and of arms. There seemed no limit to the dreams he had for his country, and for himself. So far had the Shahinshah, the Aryamehr, outstripped his mentors in the West. Unfortunately for him, as events were soon to demonstrate, he had equally outstripped his own people.

# 9

## POLICEMAN OF THE AREA

FROM THE LOFTY EMINENCE which he now occupied the Shah
surveyed the world and came to the conclusion that the time had come
for certain changes to be made. The first area to demand his attention
was, naturally, his own back yard – the Gulf. Here he could see no
possible rival. Saudi Arabia, though immensely wealthy, was a
country of only four million inhabitants compared with Iran's thirty-
seven million. Iraq posed a possible threat but the Shah felt he could
ignore it for the time being. Apart from these two, the Gulf contained
nothing but a number of petty principalities with which he could deal
easily. True, he had surrendered Iran's claims on Bahrain, but there
were better ways of emphasizing Iran's paramountcy in the Gulf than
nagging away at a territorial claim which was unlikely to be quickly
realized. Instead, by encouraging the migration of Iranians to the Gulf
states, all chronically short of labour – to Kuwait and the United
Arab Emirates as well as to Bahrain – he was helping to produce a
subtle but significant change in the pattern of races in the Gulf. The
best indication of the power and prestige Iranians living on the
southern shore of the Gulf had achieved is that when the Shah paid a
state visit to Kuwait the Iranian community there covered the entire
length of the road from the airport to the palace where he was to stay
with Persian rugs for his Rolls-Royce to drive over. All the rulers of
the Gulf states had come to the Persepolis celebrations and had been
deeply impressed by the magnificence of their reception and the
number and distinction of their fellow guests. They continued to pay
fairly regular visits to the court of Tehran, where they were sure of a
welcome. Some of them, like Sheikh Rashid ibn Said el-Maktum of
Dubai, made no secret of their conviction that it was to Tehran that
they must now look as the true seat of power in the area.

Recognition of this by the Sheikh of Dubai was one thing; recognition by the President of the United States of America was quite
another. Yet this was what the Shah obtained. America was desperately trying to extricate itself from the Vietnamese morass, but the
Nixon administration recognized that when this had been done there
would still be many sensitive areas of the world where America had

vital interests and where some security arrangements would continue to be absolutely necessary. What came to be called the 'Nixon doctrine' advocated that the security of these areas should be arranged around a local power or group of powers which would perform the function of policemen in the area, with American backing and American arms, but without, if possible, any direct American involvement. In the Gulf area Iran was obviously the best qualified candidate to take on this role. It was beyond the human resources of Saudi Arabia; Iraq was still in a disturbed state, and ruled out by its rabid hostility to Israel; as for Egypt, though by expelling Soviet advisers in the summer of 1972 President Sadat had shown where his sympathies lay, he was now preoccupied with preparations for the war to recover Sinai. That left only Iran, which had the manpower, and, more important, the resources for the job. To their delight, many of the American companies involved in aircraft production, electronics and other industries which had prospered during the Vietnam war now found in the Shah a customer eager to purchase their hardware and to pay good money for it.

So when Nixon and Kissinger visited Tehran in May 1972 on their way back from their meetings with Brezhnev in Moscow, they found themselves talking to a man who was already thinking along the same lines as they were. The Shah treated them to an analysis of the situation as he saw it, which was the sort of thing he could do extremely well, speaking with clarity and force. He had always followed current affairs closely, and now was being regularly supplied with the most expert political assessments prepared in American ministries and foundations, many of which were in receipt of Iranian money.

As he later explained, the Shah tried to bring home to his visitors two mains points: first, that the Soviet Union was pressing ahead with the drive towards the warm waters of the Gulf which had been the dream of all the rulers of Russia from Peter the Great onward; second, that, as the Iranians knew to their cost, the Soviets coveted Iran's oil. Nobody kept a closer watch than he on projections for future world oil supply and demand, and the latest intelligence appreciations showed that by 1985 the Soviet economy would have to rely on oil from Iran or from other major suppliers in the Middle East. When it came to discussing Iran's role as the principal anti-Soviet bastion in the area the Shah could point to a number of impressive attributes. In the first place Iran was not an Arab country, and so was not caught up in the Arab-Israel imbroglio; yet it was a Moslem country, and so could give a lead to other Moslem states. Then it was a rich and prosperous country governed by a man who was eager to play the part.

But – and this was something the Shah laid particular stress on – it was a part he was prepared to play only as an equal, not as a subordinate. He had already shown himself irked by some of the forms American involvement in his country's affairs had taken as a result of the 1953 counter-coup and had begun to put a stop to them. He had given up his regular weekly meetings with the head of the CIA station, and had demanded that the CIA should withdraw the officials it had placed after 1953 as consultants and advisers in almost every ministry and in the army. In future he wanted all communications between Tehran and Washington to be channelled through a direct line from the Niavaran Palace to the National Security Council of which Kissinger was head. This was done, but later it was to backfire on the Shah, since it meant that during the last months of his regime the CIA was no longer able to obtain the information which it needed and which might have enabled Washington to obtain a more accurate assessment of what was going on, and so perhaps have even saved the Shah's throne for him.

Perhaps the clearest evidence that the Shah was no longer just a junior partner in the alliance is to be seen in the fact that, just at the time when he was putting checks on American involvement in Iranian affairs, Iran was becoming increasingly involved in domestic American affairs. Now that Iranian money had found its way into so many American businesses, and Iranian contracts had become so profitable, quite a sizeable Iranian lobby had developed in the United States, with ramifications in banking, oil, and armaments. The influential nature of the new Iranian connection was symbolized by two developments: following instructions in a letter written and signed by the Director of the Shah's Private Office, the wife of a leading Republican, Senator Javits, was appointed Public Relations Adviser to the national airline, Iranair; and Iranian money, as documentary evidence was later to prove, was sent direct to the White House to help in Nixon's campaign for re-election.

The Shah lost no time in demonstrating that he was going to take his role as policeman of the Gulf seriously. He had already symbolically stepped into Britain's shoes as protector when, on 1 November 1971, the day before Britain's long-standing guarantees to the Trucial States came to an end, Iranian forces moved in to occupy three small islands at the western approaches to the Straits of Hormuz, Abu Musa and the

Tunbs, long owned by Sharjah and Ras el-Kheimah but claimed by the Shah as Iranian property. Though hardly a major military operation this extension of his authority gave the Shah much satisfaction.

Now, following the understanding with Nixon and Kissinger, his forces undertook a more testing task. For some years there had been a smouldering Marxist-oriented rebellion in Dhufar, the most southerly area of Oman adjoining the Hadhramaut, since 1967 a part of the Marxist People's Republic of South Yemen (formerly Aden Protectorate). In 1972 the new young Sultan of Oman, Qabus ibn Said, who had come to power in July 1970 as the result of a British-inspired coup which ejected his father, began an offensive against the rebels. His armed forces had been strengthened by British and Pakistani officers, NCOs and pilots serving on contract, but by late in 1973 it became known that Iranian troops were actively engaged there also. Exactly when they had arrived nobody could be sure, but it seemed that at least one armoured brigade and one paratroop brigade were involved. Nor did the Shah make any attempt to deny their presence; he was, on the contrary, glad that the world should see that the policeman was on the job.

Another region where the policeman was showing increased activity was Kurdistan. The Congressional Pike Report (US Intelligence Agencies and Activities, 1975) shows that already in August 1971 the head of the Tehran CIA station reported that Mulla Mustafa Barzani had been in contact to ask for help in the struggle he was waging against the central Iraqi government in Baghdad. Although Barzani had himself been the recipient of Soviet aid, and had in fact lived in Moscow between 1945 and 1958, he was now appealing to the United States on the grounds that the Iraqi government had allied itself with the Soviets. The Pike Report reveals that in March 1972 the head of the Tehran station was reporting back to Washington on Barzani's needs and recommending that they should be met.

When Nixon and Kissinger saw the Shah he raised with them the problem of Kurdistan. He explained that in view of his growing commitments in the Gulf he wanted to be sure that Iraq was neutralized. He had therefore assured Barzani that the Americans would come to his (Barzani's) aid, and added that if there was any problem over paying for this aid he was prepared to make himself responsible for it. Nixon told the Shah that he would take up the problem actively on his return to Washington. On 1 June the Iraqi government issued a declaration that all oil operations in the country were to be nationalized. On 16 June Nixon got in touch with the Shah to inform him that he was sending a messenger with a reply to his request concerning the Kurds. The messenger was John Connally, the former Governor of Texas, now a Republican and a lawyer who had many connections with the unholy triumvirate of oil, armaments, and intelligence which was coming to dominate the international scene (and, incidentally, dominates it still). Connally saw the Shah, and the Pike Report shows that the message which he brought was that America was prepared to assist the Kurds as a gesture to an ally (Iran) who felt itself threatened by a traditional enemy (Iraq). The report shows that what the Americans were aiming at was not an outright victory by the Kurds over Baghdad, which would enable them to claim some form of independence – this would have been a grave embarrassment to Iran with its own large Kurdish minority – but to supply enough aid to give the Kurds a considerable nuisance value.

How this could work out in practice was demonstrated in 1974. By February of that year Iraq was showing itself extremely obstructive over the disengagement agreements America was trying to cobble together between Israel, Egypt and Syria in the wake of the October war. When Kissinger was in Cairo during January 1974 he assured the Egyptian negotiators that they need not worry: 'The Shah will take care of Iraq,' he told them. A message from Kissinger went to the Shah, and several days later agency reports carried a message with a Tehran dateline: 'An Iranian military spokesman today stated that many had been killed and eighty-one wounded in a border clash between Iranian and Iraqi forces. The Iraqis were said to have left fourteen dead on the battlefield. An Iraqi communiqué announced heavy losses on both sides, and stated that Iranian forces were massing on the border and units of the Iranian air force had violated Iraqi airspace.'

The story of Iran and the Kurds took another twist in 1975. The Shah was showing signs of disillusionment. The Kurds seemed unable to make profitable use of the aid that had been sent to them; not only had they made little impression on the Baghdad government, but there were rumblings of discontent among the Kurds on the Iranian side of the border, which was the last thing the Shah wanted. So he decided to hold up $25 million worth of arms which America had procured for the Kurds and to get in touch with Sadam Hussein, who had now emerged as the strong man in Iraq. They were both to attend the OPEC conference in Algiers in March 1975, and through the good offices of Houari Boumedienne, the Algerian President, a meeting between the two leaders was arranged at which the Shah agreed to cut off all aid to the Iraqi Kurds. This volte-face took everyone, including the Kurds and Kissinger, by surprise. Kissinger complained to the Shah that he was left with $25 million worth of Soviet arms on his hands (these had been procured by arms dealers in the area from Eastern Europe).

It was while the Shah was riding high that I had another interview with him. We had been in contact on a number of occasions, but this was our first meeting for twenty-five years. I think it is worth giving a good deal of the content of this interview because it not only shows the lines along which the Shah was conducting his policies but is revealing of how the man had changed in a quarter of a century.

My earlier meetings had been in the Marmar Palace in the centre of Tehran, but this was in the much more magnificent Niavaran Palace in Shemran, in which the Shah's office commanded a breathtaking panorama over the whole of the capital spread out below. I noticed that court ceremonial was now more elaborate than I remembered, and though the Shah greeted me warmly there was more reserve in his manner than before. Only once did he hesitate in the answers he gave me; this was when, at the outset of what promised to be a long interview (he told me his time was 'unlimited' and he had instructed the Court Chamberlain that on no account were we to be disturbed), I asked him if I might dispense with using honorifics like 'Your Imperial Majesty' all the time while addressing him. He agreed, but only after a slight pause which showed that this concession went against the grain.

I began the interview by recalling the circumstances in which we had first met – his Prime Minister assassinated, oil nationalized, Mossadeq and the Majlis openly defying him. At once the Shah reminded me of the title of the book I had written then on my return to Cairo, *Iran on a Volcano*. The Shah smiled. 'Iran is not a volcano now,' he said. 'You saw us while we were being tested, but now we have passed our test. In those days everybody was testing me. The British tried to test me through Mossadeq' (it was revealing that he still looked on Mossadeq as Britain's man). 'The Russians tried to test me through Pishevari, and the Americans tried to test me by forcing Ali Amini on me. Mossadeq started out as a good man, but ended up as a bad one. I think Fatimi was Mossadeq's evil genius.' I interposed that while I had been an admirer of Mossadeq, I had regarded Fatimi as a friend. But the Shah insisted: 'Mossadeq was sincere; Fatimi was not sincere.' He added that he knew Fatimi's family were still receiving money in their Isfahan exile from some source.

We did not waste much time going over the past but moved on to the present. I told the Shah that there were three things in particular which had attracted my attention and which I wanted to ask him about. The first concerned arms. 'Every day Iran is buying more and more arms. This year's expenditure on arms is going to be $4 billion. But who is supposed to be the enemy Iran is arming itself against? In my opinion they can't be intended for use against the Soviet Union, because however many arms Iran acquires it can never, owing to their disproportionate strength, be a match for the Soviet Union. My second question concerns Oman. In Oman there are Iranian troops fighting against the rebels in Dhufar side by side with the troops of the Sultan. I make no comment about the rights and wrongs of the rebellion, but surely this constitutes interference by Iran in internal affairs of an Arab country. My third question is about Kurdistan. As I see it, Iran had been the motivating force behind the Kurdish revolt, at any rate in its later stages. Yet after your agreement with Sadam Hussein in Algiers you withdrew all support and the revolt collapsed. Isn't this proof that it was you who were responsible for keeping the revolt going?'

The Shah listened attentively to my questions, never moving except once to adjust his spectacles. 'I will answer your questions one by one,' he said. 'First, about arms. The answer is, yes, we are arming. Yes, our purchases of arms this year will amount to $4 billion. The amount will increase next year and the year after, and will eventually reach $8 billion. The level will be maintained for several years. You ask me what these arms are for. I will tell you. They are there because we want to be very strong in the area in which we live. Do you want us to be weak? Should we be weak because this would make the Arabs happy? No country can adjust its defence policy to allow for the fears of others.' (I could not help feeling at this point that, though the Shah had changed little physically over the years, this was a very different person speaking from the puzzled young man who had talked to me with such openness in 1951 about his father and his sisters and about his determination to build himself a place in the hearts of his people.)

'You ask me who these arms are directed against,' he went on. 'Do you think they are directed against the Arabs? The attitude I adopted over Bahrein should be sufficient to dispose of that idea. Although we consider Bahrein to be Persian we do not wish to acquire territory which can only be held by force. Some people accuse Iran of having designs on the Emirates. But what have they to offer us? Do we want their oil? How much do they get? Two billion, three billion, four billion a year? That, for Iran, is peanuts.

'I will give you an explanation of our defence policy. I live in an area which, as I recall, you yourself in one of your weekly articles called the centre of gravity of the world. I belong in this area; I have a stake in it which I intend to preserve. I have a function in it which I intend to exercise. I have a policy which I intend to pursue. There can be no stake, no function, no policy, which is not backed by military power. The military power is for use against any threat, wherever it comes from. If we are threatened by someone of inferior strength we can deal with it. We can face a threat from an equal. But a threat from a stronger power is another matter. In that case I would regard our forces as simply a lock in the door, which we could hold long enough to give our friends time to come to our aid.

'The Iranian air force ought to be strong enough to protect the whole area from the Persian Gulf to the Sea of Japan. India is going to collapse. India and Pakistan will become natural markets for Iranian industrial projects, but I shall have to protect Pakistan against Indian aggression. I am against any division of Pakistan; India wants that, but I am against it.'

I put in a question about nuclear weapons. 'For the present I don't have any nuclear weapons,' said the Shah. 'They are too costly, and we have no delivery system. But one thing I can assure you, and this is that Iran will not be the last in the area to be a nuclear power.'

Then he moved on to my second question, Oman. 'Yes,' he said, 'some of my forces are fighting in Oman. Yes, we are fighting side by side with Sultan Qabus. The revolution in Dhufar is a communist one, and I am against communism in the area. This is not a matter of belief but of security.' Then he went to his desk and pulled out a map. 'Look,' he said, pointing to the Straits of Hormuz, 'there is my outlet to the world. That is the passageway for Iran's oil – for twenty million dollars' worth a day.' Then, realizing that he was still calculating in terms of the old oil prices: 'What am I saying? It's far more than that – $100 million – $120 million passing every day through that narrow channel. Anyone could interrupt navigation there by simply throwing a stone. Am I expected to allow a communist regime to install itself on the Straits? No! I will never tolerate it! The Straits of Hormuz are Iran's lifeline, so when the Sultan asked me for help I gave it. I told him that I did not want my forces to stay there. The revolution in Dhufar is not a big thing, but it is a spark, and I want to extinguish the spark before it becomes a blaze. My information is that the revolutionaries do not amount to more than five or six hundred.' I interrupted to say that I had recently been in Muscat, and had gained the impression that they were probably more like ten times that number – otherwise, how could the rebellion have gone on so long, and why had he sent such a large force to deal with it?

The Shah said: 'You misunderstand me. The size of the force I sent to Dhufar was not determined by the scale of the rebellion, but by the importance which I attach to the Straits of Hormuz. It is meant to demonstrate my determination never to tolerate a communist regime there. I urged some of my Arab friends to deal with this problem, and they tried, but had no success, so it was left to me to do something. Have I been frank with you?' (This was in answer to a question I had put to the Shah at the beginning of our talk. I had explained that in interviews such as this I always liked to know the degree of frankness with which they would be conducted – fifty per cent? Seventy-five per cent? A hundred per cent? The Shah had opted for a hundred per cent.)

So we came to my third question – Kurdistan. Again the Shah said his answer would have 'a hundred per cent frankness'. 'Certainly we helped the Kurdish revolution,' he said. 'Towards the end we were the only people helping it, and when we withdrew our help it collapsed. For many years the Iraqi government had been annoying us with their hostile propaganda and attempts at sabotage. I saw potentialities in the unrest in Kurdistan, and after thinking over the matter I decided to support it.' I asked the Shah how long it had taken him to reach his decision. 'I thought about it for one hour,' he said. 'Obviously,' he went on, 'I did not wish to reactivate the Kurdish question, since we have a large Kurdish minority in Iran, but I wanted to give the government in Baghdad a slap in the face. When they stopped annoying us, I stopped annoying them. The affair in Kurdistan cost us $300 million. This was a lot of money to spend, but I had to spend it. I am not trying to conceal anything. Iran should never conceal anything. The Shah of Iran does not hide. We tell everyone what we intend to do, and do it.'

Now I moved on to another subject – the cooperation between Savak and the Israeli intelligence service, Mossad. On this subject too the Shah spoke with a frankness which, considering he was talking to an Arab journalist, was quite extraordinary. 'Our cooperation with Israel,' he said, 'is not confined to intelligence. It is much wider than that. I have sent elements from every branch of the army and civil administration for training in Israel.' Perhaps feeling this needed some justification, he went on: 'Let me ask you a question. You were a friend of Gamal Abdel Nasser. Can you tell me why he made a difference in his treatment of Turkey and his treatment of me? From the creation of the state of Israel, Turkey had relations with it at ambassador level. To begin with our relations with Israel were much more limited, but when we increased them – and still not to ambassador level – Nasser became very angry and broke off diplomatic relations with us. Why did he not do the same to Turkey?'

I said, 'Sir, Turkey had established its relationship with Israel before Nasser came to power. His policy was to keep up the siege round Israel, so he was opposed to any country's forming links with Israel. Turkey had turned its back on the Arab world a long time ago, when Atatürk aspired to make it a part of Europe. Our relations with Turkey had been equivocal, but with Iran they had always been strong. Nasser was afraid that if Iran broke the ring round Israel a precedent would be set for other Moslem countries like Indonesia, Malaysia and Pakistan to do the same. It was the same principle as the Hallstein Doctrine in West Germany which laid down that any country recognizing East Germany would find its relations with West Germany automatically broken off.'

'I can't accept your explanation,' said the Shah. 'I think your ambassador in Tehran persuaded Nasser that my regime was about to collapse.★ Anyway, when Nasser became my enemy I acted according to the old principle "the enemy of my enemy is my friend." But now things are different. Did you not know that the Israeli press is now conducting a violent personal attack against me? I told the Israelis who came here to see me that they could not expect to go on occupying Arab territory by force. If they wanted to do that they would have to be a nation of twenty or thirty million instead of their present two or three. Unfortunately they did not listen.'

Talking about Israel led the Shah to talk about America and oil. 'Some people accuse me of being an American puppet,' he said. 'But give me one reason why I should accept such a role. You can have no idea of the number of clashes I have had with the Americans. The last of these was over OPEC. The Americans wanted to break it up from the inside, and tried to do so. The Saudis were terrified, and it was I

---

★ This was far from being the case; the ambassador at the time was quite correctly trying to keep on good terms with the government of the country to which he was accredited.

who had to bear the brunt of the confrontation. I can exercise power on my own. Why should I want to exercise power on behalf of somebody else?'

He continued: 'Now we have great wealth from oil, but the challenge is how to employ the time and wealth at our disposal to build up the strength of the nation. The West is conducting a campaign of hatred against us. They accuse us of being the cause of the inflation from which they suffer. They fail to realize that inflation was not caused by the oil crisis – in 1974 inflation in the West was at the rate of thirty per cent a year, of which the rise in the price of oil accounted for only two per cent. In fact we are still selling our oil too cheaply. In my opinion the price should continue to rise. There should be a balance between the price of oil which we export and the price of the goods which we import from the advanced world. That is only fair. It might encourage the degenerate West to find new sources of energy so that it does not in the end leave Iran with nothing but a lot of empty wells. Oil for us is not income, but capital, and I'm not going to let the advanced world live off our capital.'

I said, 'Now, sir, there is a question I am itching to ask. Isn't it to us Arabs that you are indebted for the conditions which have made possible this increase in the price of oil?' 'That is partly true,' said the Shah. 'You did help to create favourable conditions, so that the price of oil could be brought nearer its proper level, but it is still too cheap.

'I want to build a better country for my son to inherit than the one which I inherited from my father,' the Shah continued. 'When I was his age I heard voices whispering in my ear about the destiny of Iran. I want my son to inherit not dreams but the realization of a dream. The future for my country lies not in the export of crude oil but in petro-chemicals. Iran should become a huge factory for petro-chemicals. If I export oil, I am paid perhaps $20 a barrel for it. But if I export petro-chemicals I get $120 a barrel. I can buy technology. I am not like your Arab compatriots who spend their money on buying apartment buildings in London, Paris and New York. If I invest abroad I invest in technology. My programme is for Iran to produce twelve million tonnes of iron and steel a year. I want the standard of living in Iran in ten years' time to be exactly on a level with that in Europe today. In twenty years' time we shall be ahead of the United States. Most of the Arabs don't understand these ideas of mine, but a few are beginning to appreciate them.'

The Shah asked me how I viewed the world situation, and I explained what I saw as the main changes – the decline in the influence of the West since 1956, the disappearance of the magic of Marxism (the Shah interrupted to say: 'Yes, I have always said that anyone who is not a communist at twenty has no heart, and anyone who is a communist at forty has no head' – he really did seem to think he had invented that cliché), the limitations on American power, new problems like pollution, space, the control of genes and so on. This prompted the Shah to launch into a survey of the world scene, which was the sort of thing he enjoyed doing and did extremely well.

'We have agreed,' he said, 'that the Gulf is going to be the centre of gravity and the centre of conflict for world mastery over the next twenty years. The Indian Ocean is a vacuum where there will be a clash between the two super-powers, and we should play a part in this. I foresee a prolonged period of chaos in the Indian sub-continent. South-East Asia is still in the process of readjustment after the Vietnam war. I had been afraid that Vietnam would make America isolationist, and if that had happened the Americans would, in ten years, have destroyed themselves and the rest of the world with them. So I tried to get them as much involved in the world as possible, and I think that now they are coming out of their shock over Vietnam.

'But American withdrawal from South-East Asia has left a vacuum of power which can only be filled by Japan. To my mind Japan is an enigma. Only the future can show how Japan will respond, but my belief is that Japan must become a military power again; the only question is how and when?

'Now let's look south and west, to the Arab world. The Arabs are completely absorbed by the Arab-Israel conflict. Can't there be a solution to that problem? I have been thinking of a new balance of power in the area, based on a triangle of Iran, Egypt and Algeria. The distance between Tehran and Cairo, and Cairo and Algiers is almost exactly the same. Obviously Iran is not Arab, but I must ask you, is Egypt really Arab? Is Algeria Arab? I know that you will defend your Arabism, but ought we not to be seriously thinking about a new balance based on Islam?' I intervened to say that I certainly did consider both Egypt and Algeria to be Arab. I added that the Shah seemed to be talking exclusively about countries, and not about people.

'Do you want me to gossip?' he asked, but switched all the same to a consideration of personalities. 'I met King Khaled recently for the first time,' he said, 'and he seemed to be a person with good intentions. They tell me that Fahd is the real power and that he can do a lot, but I don't know. This will have to be demonstrated. Sadat is a close friend of mine; my heart is with him. I think of him every morning. I have passed all my tests, but I know how many tests he has still to undergo. Boumedienne is an intelligent man, but his aims are bigger than he is. He plans a big role for Algeria in Africa, and that would be a good thing, provided it was well directed. We should all be thinking about Africa. I have never met Ghadaffi, and I don't think I understand him. Anyway, one Ghadaffi in the Arab world is sufficient.

'In Western Europe, Giscard is a good example of the new leadership which is emerging. Maybe the French have too long a tradition of bureaucracy to dream dreams, but we will supply the visions for them. Another remarkable man is King Juan Carlos. I regret that Franco was so selfish about power that he never gave Juan Carlos any experience of authority while he was still alive. Brezhnev has a strong personality, but one of those personalities which are only useful in periods of transition. Our relations with the Soviet Union are now very good. We have found a reasonable basis for cooperation with them.'

Then the Shah broke off to ask me what I had been doing in Iran – what I had seen. I said something about afforestation and the cultural projects, in both of which I understood the Empress was interested, but apparently the Shah was not particularly keen on sharing the limelight with her, for when my interview was reprinted in *Etelaat* this was one of the passages omitted. I asked the Shah about the Iranian youth – why was it that whenever he went abroad the Iranian students there demonstrated against him? He dismissed this with a snort of indignation. 'All communists,' he said. 'Communists or in the pay of communists.'

'What about the reports on torture by Savak prepared by Amnesty International and printed in the *Sunday Times*?' I asked. 'Communism again,' was the answer. I protested that I knew the *Sunday Times* people; surely he was not saying that they were communists. 'Perhaps not,' he said, 'but I know that $1 million was paid to get that report published.' This charge was ridiculous, but it was the only way the Shah could find – or that others found for him – to defend a very weak case.

On the surface, the transformation that twenty-five years had brought in the Shah was truly amazing. The anxious young man had become the self-confident autocrat; the frightened prince picking his way through the political minefield had become the elder statesman with thirty-five years of rule behind him; the pupil of the Americans was now dealing with them on equal terms, his ambitions bigger than theirs, his global conceptions more far-reaching. Only in two respects had there been little change: the Shah still considered the main threat to him to be communism and communists, and he still mistrusted the politicians of his own country.

One very curious application of the Shah's role as an international policeman was already in hand when he spoke to me, though in view of its highly secret nature he not surprisingly did not mention it. It concerned Africa, the Saudi Arabians, France, and the new complex of oil, arms and intelligence which had by now infected Iran as well as many of the Arab countries.

Everybody now had their eyes on Africa. Ever since Reza Shah's exile in South Africa the Shah and others of his family had been interested in that country, either for sentimental or more hard-headed reasons, and they now had big investments there. The Shah was the biggest shareholder in the Transvaal Development Company. Like the South Africans, with whom he had these close links, the Shah was extremely worried by the spread of communism in Africa, by Russian and Cuban military intervention in Ethiopia and Angola, and by the growth of Marxist-oriented national liberation movements elsewhere. The Saudis, who preferred a Riyadh–Tehran–Cairo axis to the Tehran–Cairo–Algiers axis propounded by the Shah, were equally concerned over developments in Africa.

Both the Shah and the Saudis were disappointed in the United States. They had little confidence in President Ford; but they had hopes of President Giscard. So had President Sadat, who had expelled all his Russian advisers in July 1972 and was now as staunchly anti-communist as the Shah and the Saudis. A French connection was developing whereby Egypt was to buy arms from France, including Mirages 2000, with Saudi money. France's interests in Africa were obvious. The French maintained a military presence in some of their former colonies, especially the Congo and Chad, and French industry had an enormous stake in the companies dealing with uranium, cobalt, copper, diamonds, gold and other minerals. Needless to say, the oil companies watched what was happening in Africa with as much anxious interest as governments.

Thus the outline for a new anti-communist alliance was beginning to take shape. Its members were determined to be their own masters, and not the agents of America, but this desire for independence in no way displeased Washington. Kissinger was more than happy to see his aims in Africa implemented by proxy; in fact this could solve a lot of problems for him. When he had tried to intervene openly in Angola he had been baulked by Congress, but here was a syndicate over which Congress had no control, and one which, moreover, was prepared to be self-financing. Also aware of the existence of the new alliance, and happy that it should exist, were David Rockefeller and the Chase Manhattan Bank, with its heavy African investments.

So was born what, following its inaugural meeting in Saudi Arabia, came to be known as the Safari Club – a name chosen because it seemed to the participants to have a suitable whiff of Africa and adventure. It was the brain-child of a remarkable man, Comte Claude Alexandre de Marenches, head of the French Sécurité d'État et Contre-Espionage (SDECE). De Marenches, a commanding personality, tall, speaking excellent English, had been in the wartime Resistance. His position brought him into contact with all those who came to Paris to buy arms, or sell oil, or coordinate intelligence, or, as was frequently the case, for a combination of all three purposes. It was his business to ensure these people's safety and, if necessary, their anonymity, and of course to know exactly what they were up to. He had for some time been extremely concerned about the vulnerability of the shipping lanes which brought oil from the Middle East to Europe, and his office was decorated with maps showing thickening lines representing the volume of tanker cargoes round the Horn of Africa and the Cape. It was his idea that all those interested in checking the spread of communism in Africa should combine for action. Five governments were persuaded by the Comte's arguments – those of France, Iran, Saudi Arabia, Egypt and Morocco. Algeria had originally been canvassed, but had dropped out.

An agreement between the five governments was drawn up and duly signed, Sheikh Kamal Adhem, Director of Intelligence, signing for Saudi Arabia, General Nassiri, head of Savak, for Iran, the Director of Intelligence for Egypt, Ahmed Duleimi, Director of Intelligence, for Morocco, and Comte de Marenches himself for France. A copy of the agreement was found in Savak archives after the Revolution.

The agreement started off by stating: 'Recent events in Angola and other parts of Africa have demonstrated the continent's role as a theatre for revolutionary wars prompted and conducted by the Soviet Union, which utilizes individuals or organizations sympathetic to, or controlled by, Marxist ideology.' Soviet aims in Africa were defined as being, first, control over the continent's raw materials 'and thus over the industry and economic life of Europe and the Third World';

second, control over the sea routes round Africa; and third, the manipulation of client states.

The agreement then moved on to consider ways of combating this threat. The enterprise would have to be 'global in conception', with an Operational Centre equipped to evaluate what was going on in Africa, identify the danger spots, and make recommendations for dealing with them. The Centre would be divided into three sections – a secretariat to run routine matters; a planning section; and an operations section. Cairo was chosen as the site for the Centre 'for obvious reasons', and the Egyptian authorities were requested to prepare suitable office and living accommodation. France was to supply the technical equipment for communications and security. The chair was to be held for one year by the representative of each member country in turn. A timetable was agreed, which would see the Centre established by 1 September 1976 and its staff moving in two weeks later.

Several meetings of the Safari Club were held, in Saudi Arabia and Paris as well as at the Centre in Cairo. A great deal of money was spent in acquiring premises, setting up 'cover' companies, installing direct 'hot lines' and other sensitive equipment, and so forth.

The Club's first successful operation was in the Congo. When General Bomba threatened to take over Katanga, the mining companies there and President Mobutu were greatly alarmed and appealed to the Club for help. They did not appeal in vain. Moroccan and Egyptian forces came to the rescue, and Mobutu owes his continued prosperity to the Safari Club.

But the Congo was a comparatively minor operation in scale and importance. A much bigger target soon presented itself – Somalia. Siad Barre, who had become President of Somalia in October 1969, made no secret of his ambition to reunite the scattered territories where Somalis formed a majority of the inhabitants. These included, besides the former British, Italian and French Somalilands, a sizeable chunk of Kenya and the Ethiopian province of Ogaden. He found that the Russians were prepared to help him in his ambitions, and though in exchange he gave them no more concessions than he had to, the Russian presence in Somalia thoroughly alarmed the Americans. Whenever Kissinger passed through Cairo he used to produce a satellite photograph of Berbera, showing what he claimed to be a Russian submarine base. (There was in fact no such base, though the Russians had been granted certain naval facilities.) All the members of the Club were alarmed, and each time Siad Barre approached them for aid he was met with the accusation that he was no more than a puppet of the Soviets.

Then, in the summer of 1974, the revolution took place in Ethiopia and changed the whole picture. From the point of view of control of the Horn of Africa, Ethiopia was obviously a much more attractive proposition than Somalia, and Mengistu Haile Miriam a more promising protégé than Siad Barre. The Soviets began to rush military and economic aid to the Mengistu regime, and just when his forces had seemed on the point of completing the liberation of the Ogaden, Siad Barre found himself deserted by his Russian backers. But the Safari Club was prepared to step into the breach. Its members told Siad Barre that if he would get rid of the Russians they would supply the arms he needed. The Shah was particularly enthusiastic; his letters to Siad Barre were full of encouragement. Egypt sold Somalia $75 million worth of now unwanted Soviet arms, paid for by Saudi Arabia. So Siad Barre duly expelled the Russians, abandoned all the pseudo-Marxist jargon with which he had dressed up his government, and continued his help for the Ogaden insurgents.

But both he and the Safari Club found that they were now operating in a different league. They were caught up in the super-power rivalries in the Indian Ocean, in which control of the Horn of Africa was one of the main prizes. The Russian airlift to Ethiopia increased in scale; the former Russian adviser to the Somali forces turned up in Addis Ababa as adviser to the Ethiopians. Siad Barre hoped that, after he had abandoned his Russian alliance, he might expect help from the Americans. In his election campaign President Carter had spoken of facing up to the Russians in Somalia, and after he came to office he had said that America would supply Somalia with arms. But Russian and Cuban intervention was much more effective than anything on the other side. For Siad Barre the Ogaden had become a trap. His troops were desperately short of arms, particularly anti-tank guns. He summoned the Egyptian Ambassador and told him 'My neck is in danger,' but there was little that Egypt could do. The Saudis said they were unable to help. Only the Shah continued to be optimistic. He sent Siad Barre a written message, assuring him that he knew the Americans would come to his aid. At a CENTO meeting in May 1977 the Shah pressed the Secretary of State, Cyrus Vance, to provide the arms needed to save Siad Barre from disaster. He himself did what he could, sending some German mortars acquired through Turkey, as well as some anti-tank weapons, which, however, when they arrived proved to be of Israeli origin, so that the Somali troops refused to handle them.

Then the Shah's attitude changed. He summoned the Somali Ambassador three times in a month and told him that Siad Barre would have to get out of the Ogaden. 'I've had three messages from President Carter,' he said. 'You Somalis are threatening to upset the balance of world power. If you get out of the Ogaden we will see that you get all the aid you want, but it will be economic aid, not military. You must forget about the Ogaden.' Not surprisingly Siad Barre came to the conclusion that he had been the victim of a piece of horse-trading between the super-powers, whereby the Russians kept out of the Rhodesian problem provided the Americans held off the Ogaden.

Be that as it may, the Somalia story demonstrated their limitations to the members of the Safari Club. A policeman on the beat has a certain authority in his area, but above him are police inspectors and police superintendents, who have more, and who can give orders to the policeman on the beat which have to be obeyed.

One curious aspect of the Club was that, although all its members pretended to each other that they were keeping their activities secret from the CIA, in fact all of them were privately briefing the CIA as to what was going on. More than that, General Nassiri later admitted that not only was he keeping the Americans informed, but the Israelis also. On one occasion he was responsible for an even wider distribution of reports on the Club's activities. After one Club meeting in Casablanca he was travelling to Cannes to meet his wife, but left his briefcase, containing all the secret documents, in the airport at Casablanca. It was never seen again, but presumably fell into interested hands. It was subsequently discovered that one of the Comte de Marenches's assistants was a Soviet agent, who had been passing information to Moscow. He was liquidated, but not before the damage had been done. In fact there was a strong element of *opéra bouffe* about the Club's activities.

In a way, however, the Club could claim responsibility for President Sadat's initiative which took him to Jerusalem in November 1977. The first letter suggesting a meeting came from Rabin when he was still Israeli Prime Minister and was carried to Sadat by Ahmed Duleimi, the Moroccan representative in the Club, and it was under the auspices of King Hassan that an initial meeting took place in Morocco between Moshe Dayan and an Egyptian Deputy Prime Minister. So that when Itzhak Rabin later claimed that the breakthrough with Egypt had started before Mr Begin came to power he was speaking no more than the truth.

# 10

# THE REVOLUTION
# RETURNS TO TEHRAN

FOR TEN YEARS, from 1953 to 1963, Qom had been the centre of opposition to the Shah's regime, but after the arrest and deportation of Khomeini the army and Savak had done an effective cleaning-up operation in the city. A week after Khomeini's arrest the Shah, in an interview with a foreign journalist, could claim that he felt his position to be 'stronger than ever' since 'the people now see where the forces of reaction lie, and the army fully supports my revolution from the throne.' If the mullahs (reaction) were discredited, and the army was loyal, what had the Shah to fear?

His confidence might have been justified if Iran had been allowed to remain static, but his own policies ensured that it was not. On the contrary it was, in the coming years, to be the scene of a deliberately planned convulsion on a vast scale which, had he been a more careful and a more humble student of history, the Shah might have realized was building up all the ingredients for an explosion.

It has been explained* how his coronation and the ceremonies at Persepolis celebrating 2,500 years of the Persian monarchy seemed to go to the Shah's head, and that a change came over him and over the whole character of the regime. At the beginning of his reign there had been a tendency to treat the Shah as a playboy whose ambitions could be satisfied with a supply of fast cars and beautiful women. I recall Eric Johnson, President of the American Motion Picture Corporation and for a time President Eisenhower's special envoy in the Middle East, explaining how, when in 1954 the Shah was on a visit to America, the moguls of the film industry decided that the most suitable way to entertain him and his Empress would be to organize a banquet in one of the smartest hotels in Los Angeles at which the Shah would be dined in one ballroom, alone but surrounded by all the most gorgeous female stars of Hollywood, while in a neighbouring room the Empress Soraya would be alone with all the leading male stars. This

---

* Chapter 8.

was done. But by the early 1970s the playboy Shah had developed into a much more serious – and a much more dangerous – personage.

All power was concentrated in the hands of the absolute Shah. Even in the days of the Qajars Persia had been notorious as a country where the bureaucracy was grossly overstaffed and inefficient as well as corrupt, and in spite of attempts to improve matters by modernization and anti-corruption drives nothing had really changed. In fact matters had grown worse. The Qajars lacked the means and the will to become dictators; the Shah lacked neither. Everything had to be referred to Tehran, and every decision of any importance had to land up on the desk of the one man who could give a ruling. The only people who had any share in power were members of the Shah's family and the small group of lucky ones who surrounded the imperial court. What is more, each member of the royal family had his or her own satellite court, and his or her own creatures in the ministries, in Savak, in the Central Bank, and in the armed forces. There was no love lost between them in the scramble for power and influence. The younger brothers of the Shah and their families, while enjoying to the full the favours their position brought them, felt particularly hard done by when the birth of the Crown Prince in 1961 seemed to destroy the hopes they had nourished of one day succeeding to the throne.

The scramble at the top was as much for money as for power. With the increase of wealth in the country went an increase in corruption and display. This was the time when almost every day western newspapers were reporting the acquisition by the Shah or one of his relatives or by some 'prominent Iranian' of new properties – houses in the San Fernando Valley or Los Angeles, flats in Paris, apartments in New York, mansions in London and on the Riviera. Over 3,000 flats were acquired by Iranians during this period in Geneva alone. The Shah set the pace with his estate in Surrey and with the Villa Suvretta in St Moritz, for which he paid $10 million. Although only occupied for a few weeks in the year his foreign homes had to be always ready to receive him; at the Villa Suvretta the caretaker, in charge of a full-time staff, was a Qajar princess.

The Shah did nothing to discourage the orgy of plunder in which his relations and favourites were indulging – in fact he orchestrated it. It was his office which arranged the distribution of profitable agencies for western and Japanese firms. It was he who received from the National Iranian Oil Company a contribution of $1 billion, theoretically 'to promote the security, prestige and greatness of Iran.' His office arranged the distribution of moneys abroad. I have, for example, myself seen in Tehran three royal orders, each allocating $200,000 to Bishop Abel Muzorewa,* and huge sums were disbursed among politicians and political parties in America and Europe as well as in Africa. The same office arranged appropriately lavish gifts for visiting foreigners and for payments to suitable foreign journalists.

All restraint had gone. Ostentation was the order of the day, just as it had been at Persepolis. Small wonder that tales of the fortunes to be made lured people from all over the country to the capital, and when they discovered that the streets of Tehran were not in fact paved with gold all they could do was squat in makeshift houses on the periphery, picking up such casual work as they could find, a natural reservoir of support for Khomeini's revolutionary message as soon as it should reach them. The capital was afflicted by a cancerous growth. Before the war Tehran had been a city of about half a million inhabitants. By 1970 it had swelled to more than six times that size and was still expanding at a rate of about 6 per cent a year. About 60 per cent of all the students in Iran were to be found in the capital and 50 per cent of all the doctors. Nearly half the building permits issued related to Tehran, with the result that it quickly outstripped its never very adequate services. The streets become hopelessly choked with traffic; sewage had always depended largely on the street water-conduits (jubs) which were also for the majority the only source of water for drinking and washing. All the foreign companies with big commercial interests in Iran felt it a matter of prestige to construct their own skyscraper office blocks. To the south of the city the oil refineries and petro-chemical concerns sucked in more unemployed people from the countryside.

But the two places in Tehran to which the attention of every visitor was directed were strangely irrelevant to the needs of the capital. One was the Treasury housing the Crown Jewels. These fabulous treasures from the Persia of the Safavids and from India included the famous Takht-i-Taos, the Peacock Throne, of solid gold encrusted with diamonds and other precious stones. The most elaborate of modern electronic equipment was installed to protect them. If the glass enclosing them was so much as touched, bells began to ring, and if the bells continued for more than a few seconds all doors in the building automatically closed and hidden machine-guns opened fire on anyone

---

* These were, in fact, only a few among the hundreds of orders that were shown to me, but as they were quoted in an article I subsequently wrote for the *Sunday Times* and were admitted by the recipient, they can be referred to here without fear of the libel charges which might follow mention of some of the others.

approaching the entrances. The other attraction was the Shahyad Monument, which was designed, largely through the initiative of the Empress, to immortalize the memory of the Shah – but at a cost of $200 million. It was, admittedly, a magnificent conception, beautifully executed. Inside, lifts conveyed the visitor to restaurants and museums, while a moving panorama displayed the history of Iran from the time of Cyrus the Great to the Pahlevi dynasty – but with the early Islamic period, or anything which might connect Iran with the Arab world, pointedly ignored.

Another preoccupation of the Empress, no doubt a worthy one but equally irrelevant to the real needs of the people of Tehran, was the recovery of works of Iranian art which had gone abroad. In her pursuit of these lost treasures money was no object, as when she purchased for a large sum from the family of Julian Amery paintings dating from Qajar days. She also acquired for the nation a collection of impressionist paintings which for most Iranians were alien and incomprehensible.

Although these pet projects accounted for only a small fraction of the money being spent, they were there for all to see, and so for all to criticize. The Shah was convinced that all criticism would be silenced as affluence spread. In August 1974 expenditure under the Fifth Five-Year Plan, which was to run from March 1973 to March 1978, was doubled, from $36.84 billion to $69.59 billion, this phenomenal increase being made possible by the great increase in oil revenues following the 1973 surge in the price of oil. The consequences of this lavish expenditure were not so much to catapult Iran into the front rank of industrial nations as a dangerous over-heating of the economy. Inflation during 1975 was admitted by the Shah to be over 20 per cent, but the true figure was nearer double this. The ports were unable to cope with the flow of imports; factories lacked technicians and raw materials; the country was relying on uprooted labour as well as imported technology. And those in charge, with their eyes on an illusory future, were increasingly out of touch with the realities of the situation.

The Shah, as has been seen, was absorbed with his role as policeman of the Gulf, an equal partner with the Americans in the struggle against communism. He was spending $4 billion a year on arms, and was boasting that eventually that figure would be doubled. The armed forces were being pampered. Every officer from the rank of colonel upwards and his wife were given a free trip to Europe each year, as well as a free car and other perquisites.

Under the Shah was the Prime Minister, Amir Abbas Hoveyda, a man not corrupt but just as much cut off as his royal master from the real world around him. There he sat in his enormous office, always courteous, always affable, and always with a carnation in his button-hole.★

No less charming as a person, and no less reliable as an instrument of the Shah's will, was General Nematollah Nassiri, head of Savak from 1965 until June 1978, when as one of the belated gestures of appeasement he was removed from office and sent as ambassador to Pakistan. Nassiri's prisons were full. Amnesty International in 1976 put the number of political prisoners in Iran at 7,500; other estimates ran anywhere up to 100,000. The Shah himself never admitted to more than about 3,000, but in 1975 official figures from the Ministry of Interior gave the number of young urban guerrillas, male and female, who had been shot following trial by secret courts as 174. Nor was there any secret of the fact that Savak relied very largely for its effectiveness on the use of murder and torture. (Its record in these fields is now the subject of a permanent exhibition in Tehran, to which all foreign visitors are taken.)

Savak also controlled a company which had a monopoly over the manufacture of locks and keys. When Bazargan, as first Prime Minister after the Revolution, was taken over the headquarters of Savak he was shown keys which fitted the doors of every foreign embassy in Tehran, as well as the safes in those embassies. He was astonished at the variety and quantity of electronic equipment stored there. It was, he said, like something out of *Alice in Wonderland* – silent guns, gas guns, bugging devices, as well as all the latest technological inventions designed for the torture of man.

One of the films made by Savak, which is now in the possession of the Ministry of Foreign Affairs and which was shown to me while I was in Tehran, demonstrates Savak's methods. It shows the interrogation of a young woman. First she was stripped naked; then a Savak officer began burning her round the nipples with a lighted cigarette until she screamed, broke down and began to give the desired information. I asked why this particular horror had been filmed, and was told that the interrogator had had the reputation of being one of the best at his job, so a film of him in action had been made to help in the training of other Savak officials. The film had been given to the CIA, which had had copies made for distribution to Taiwan, the Philippines

---

★ Hoveyda enjoyed demonstrating how it was he kept his carnation fresh – beneath the lapel of his jacket was a small golden pot of water in which the stem of the flower was immersed.

and Indonesia – part of America's technical assistance to its friends.

Cooperation between Savak and other intelligence services, including the French and Israeli as well as the CIA, cost the Shah a great deal of money but paid good dividends. Among the material found after the Revolution at Savak headquarters, in the Palace and in some of the Iranian embassies abroad were a photostat copy of a secret report on the state of the Iraqi army by the Chief of Staff for President Ahmed Hassan el-Bakr, prepared only three months before the Shah's downfall, and a taped discussion between Ghadaffi and George Habbash about the plans of the PFLP. This took place in a tent in the desert, and ironically enough the tape starts with Ghadaffi saying he has chosen this place for their meeting because he wants to be absolutely certain of security. Also found were lists of undercover agents operating in the Arab world belonging to almost all intelligence agencies. Apparently it was the habit of Savak agents to tape all their meetings with agents from other services, and the wealth of gossip and scandal available to the Shah was almost infinite.


But the most remarkable thing about Iran during the boom years of the 1970s was the total absence of any attempt to involve the people in any way in any form of political representation. The Shah gave the orders; his ministers and Savak carried them out. Other members of the royal family could give orders too, sometimes telephoning direct to ministers, and as their orders often proved contradictory there was a plea from the Cabinet that at least the royals should try to coordinate their demands. But open any newspaper, and it would be obvious that there was really only one man with whose activities its readers were supposed to be concerned – the Shah, whose portrait, with those of his wife and children, greeted them day after day.

In the mid-1950s the Shah had tried to follow the example of Kemal Atatürk by creating an 'official opposition' in the Majlis, but this artificial two-party system had never functioned properly, and in March 1975 he decreed that only a single political party, to be called Rastakhiz (Renaissance) would be allowed to operate, though it was in theory to be divided into two competing wings. But since all deputies, whichever wing they belonged to, were creatures of the Shah's will – as were the Prime Minister, and all the ministers and the whole conception of the party – there was never any real debate in the Majlis, or in the country, let alone the slightest hint of criticism of official policy.

The only real political life in the country had been driven underground. The two terrorist organizations, the Mujahiddin Khalk and the Fedayin Khalk, one Islamic in inspiration, the other Marxist, continued their precarious existence. The Communist Party was active particularly among the students and in large industrial centres like Abadan. Savak had the responsibility for dealing with labour unrest which was 'political', and was the judge of what constituted 'political'. Increasing centralization caused unrest among the minorities, in Kurdistan, Azerbaijan and Baluchistan. Even the pampered armed forces were not immune, jealous of the gigantic sums being spent on armaments and on a prestige navy, many of whose officers seemed more interested in feathering their nests than going to sea.

The more prominent critics of the regime faced a choice between going into hiding or self-imposed exile. They also risked assassination at the hands of Savak (Dr Ali Shariati, a distinguished Islamic scholar, and in a sense the secular leader of the Revolution, died in London, and it is generally believed in Iran that his death was arranged by Savak). Because they were freer to express themselves – though they and their families were still in danger of retaliation from Savak – the thousands of Iranian students abroad became more open in their opposition. Students in Paris formed their own student committee, which was strongly anti-government. There were demonstrations in New York and Boston.

So in the mid-seventies there was an official Tehran, which was presented to the outside world – busy, go-ahead, technologically-minded, under the leadership of a far-seeing and benevolent autocrat – and an unofficial Tehran, which was seething with revolt. Significant of the way in which the true facts of the situation were concealed even from those whose business it most was to be aware of them is the confession made by the Empress Farah in exile that it was not until May 1978 that she first heard the name of the great enemy of her family. 'For heaven's sake, who is this Khomeini?' she asked, after his name had cropped up. It might have been Marie Antoinette speaking.

On the surface it seemed as though the Revolution had left nothing but ashes, but occasionally the ashes would be stirred, and it could be seen that there was still something smouldering. Anybody who cared to probe beneath the surface would have seen what was going on, but most people, including western diplomats and journalists, preferred to accept the optimistic version offered them. Pressure on them to conceal the truth was very strong. They could not help realizing that this was a corrupt society, where political and personal freedom had been

suppressed, but they accepted that this was the price that had to be paid
for progress and that in any case freedom on the western model was
alien to the Persian way of doing things.

It was Lenin who said that revolutions are not created by individuals, but that it is the task of the revolutionary to judge when the tide is
flowing in revolutionary channels and then guide it. That tide was
now flowing in Iran. The whole social fabric of the country had been
disrupted. Envy, rather than stability, had been the dowry wealth
brought with it. Each section of the community felt that those above
them were getting more out of the bonanza than they were
themselves. And Iranians of every class felt, with some justification,
that it was the foreigners who were doing best of all. There were by
now between fifty and sixty thousand American experts and businessmen in the country, well paid, well fed and well housed, as well as
other thousands of Germans, British and Japanese, similarly provided
for. When in 1975 two American technicians attached to the air force
were murdered in Tehran, those in authority might have seen the
writing on the wall. They did not, but away in Qom people began to
realize that things were happening again in the capital, that the Revolution had in fact moved to Tehran, and that it was there that their
activities should now be concentrated.

# II

# THE RESURGENCE
# OF ISLAM

THE ARABS' DEFEAT in the June war of 1967 produced shock waves which extended far beyond the countries which had actually been involved in the fighting. How had it happened? It may be that they had not in their hearts expected to win a war – that the Arabs, like the outside world, had come subconsciously to accept the idea of Israel's military superiority. But a defeat on this disastrous scale – that was something which had never been foreseen. So everybody blamed everybody else. None of the ideas which had hitherto gained general acceptance had authority any longer. Arab unity, non-alignment, support for national liberation movements, the whole package of progressive ideas which, with themselves as their standard-bearers, Arabs had believed were going to emancipate the rest of the world now gave way to disillusion. The revolutionary regimes in Egypt and Syria had failed in the prime duty of any government – they had failed to protect the frontiers of the state.

Nasser survived, his personal popularity undiminished, his words still listened to with attention and respect. He was able to nurse Egypt through its convalescence, to rebuild the armed forces and move to the war of attrition against Israel. But in September 1970, at a critical juncture for Egypt and the Arab world, Nasser died. Sadat succeeded him. To begin with, his policy of greater liberalism at home and, above all, his successful preparation for the October war of 1973 won him respect. But the generation which had grown up with ideals of Arab socialism and Arab unity watched later developments in Egypt with growing anxiety, the final disillusion being Sadat's journey to Jerusalem in November 1977.

In place of the old ideals came the new concept of riches. The Arabs might have lost the military battle in 1967 but they could win the material battle. Oil money was going to solve everything. The Arabs were going to become the sixth power in the world. Iran enjoyed the same wealth and shared the same hopes. There was nothing that money could not buy. There was plenty for everybody – even a revolutionary movement, like the Palestinians', could command all the material resources it needed.

But it soon became apparent that things were not going to work out like that. The Arabs found that money was not the answer. Most of it remained locked up in foreign banks. They could buy expensive armaments from America and Europe, but who could be sure that these would afford any protection against the only real enemy, which was still Israel? As people contemplated the new elite among the Arabs – the arms dealers, the contractors, the wheeler-dealers – and as they became aware of the Arab image that was being fostered in the rest of the world – the waste, the vulgarity, the immorality and the gamblers and playboys – they turned away in humiliation and disgust.

They turned away too from foreign idols. All the indications at this time were that western capitalism was in a state of disintegration. People read daily of growing drug addiction, of hippies and 'flower-people', of sexual promiscuity and the collapse of what Arabs still regarded as the basic unit of society, the family. They read of Watergate and the activities of the CIA, of kidnappings and riots. It ceased to be a sign of emancipation to wear blue jeans, open a Wimpy stall in Cairo or drink Coca-Cola. Nor did Moscow and communism look any more attractive than the West. Revelations about Stalin's rule had destroyed the credibility of communism as a political system; the invasion of Czechoslovakia destroyed Russia's credibility as a benevolent protector of smaller nations.

In the turmoil which followed the June war of 1967 all the people of the Middle East had to rethink a whole series of fundamentals. Before, the lines had seemed so clear-cut, the choices so easy. There was the clash between imperialism and nationalism – everybody knew where they stood as far as that was concerned. There was the conflict between the two super-powers, America and Russia, for position and influence in the Middle East, and everybody thought they understood how to manoeuvre in their own interest between the two. There was the continuing Arab-Israel battle, and nobody had any doubts about that. There was the social division between rich and poor, and everybody agreed that this would have to be remedied.

But as the situation developed the clear lines became blurred, the choices more difficult. Who were now the progressives in the Arab world and who the reactionaries? Egypt, once the leading progressive Arab country, was becoming more and more closely associated with the United States, still looked on by many as the leading neocolonialist power. With the Russians virtually excluded from the Middle East how was it possible to keep a balance between the super-powers? In the state the Arab-Israel conflict had reached, how could anyone talk of war or peace? All the ideals which had been cherished appeared to be illusions, all the old certainties to be lies. How, in this world, was it going to be possible to preserve one's sanity? Was there anything left in which to believe?

For many the only answer was religion. The great debate between religion and secularism, between modernization and tradition, between nationalism and pan-Islam, which had begun to convulse the peoples of the Ottoman and Persian Empires and North Africa a hundred years before was, after all, not so far in the past. As always happens in history, when forward movement becomes impossible people begin to look towards the past, and it was to religion that Egyptians turned for consolation after the military defeat. So it was that the troops who stormed the Bar-Lev Line at the beginning of the October war did so shouting 'Allahu Akbar!', while leaflets distributed to them by the army information services assured them that 'one of the good men' had had a dream in which he saw the Prophet Mohammed pointing towards the east, taking the Sheikh of el-Azhar by the hand, and saying to him 'Come with me to Sinai.' Egypt's Copts were affected by the same mood. It was in April 1968 that huge crowds of Christians and Moslems were attracted to a church in the Zeitoun district of Cairo where the Virgin was reported to have appeared.

The great strength of Islam is that it provides a law, a rule for life which appeals to the heart as much as to the intelligence. It governs a man's relationship with his fellow man, with his wife and family, and with the whole universe. It does not require a sophisticated understanding, since it is a belief which has been handed down over generations and whose language and forms are as natural to the Moslem of the Arab world as the air he breathes. Even liberal thinkers have often ended by returning to the religion of their childhood. Thus Taha Hussein, the distinguished writer and educationalist, whose early book on pre-Islamic poetry had provoked a storm of protest from the orthodox, turned to writing about the Prophet and the early days of Islam. Other Egyptian literary figures such as Mohammed Hussein Heikal and Abbas el-Akkad, who had been greatly influenced by western writers like Bergson, Shaw and Wells, became increasingly concerned with Islamic themes. Even communist novelists started to tackle sympathetically Islamic subjects.

All this should not be the occasion for surprise. While the western achievements appeared to Arabs and Iranians to be represented by weapons of mass destruction and instruments of torture, Islam offered a positive good. The West supplied the machinery of suppression; Islam by contrast put the emphasis on the individual, on the dignity of man. For Islam is the religion of the individual human being; the social content is built into the message of Islam. It is significant that when a Moslem achieves independent manhood he aims to provide himself with two things – a home and a grave. The home is the refuge of his body while he is alive; the grave the recipient of his body after death.

Of course religion was used by governments for their own political purposes; in Sunni countries particularly, religion has always been under the control of the state. So in countries like Saudi Arabia the puritan tradition was appealed to both as a guide for everyday life and to spearhead resistance to communism, or indeed to any progressive ideas. In Egypt the religious authorities were called upon first to say that the war against Israel was a holy one, and later that it was a sacred duty to make peace with Israel. It was time-serving of this sort that prompted Khomeini's sneers about the '*fuqaha* of the Sultan'. And there were initially double standards. The same societies which sanctioned chopping off the hand of a man who had stolen the equivalent of £10 made no protest when someone supposed to be buying arms to defend the state diverted millions of dollars into his own pocket.

But one way and another the revised interest in religion in all Islamic countries and in all classes was having its political effects. The Moslem Brotherhood grew in numbers and influence, and in Syria took up arms against the Baathist regime of Hafez el-Assad. A new organization called the Moslem Communities (El-Gamaat el-Islamiyah) became the most powerful body in the universities of Cairo and Alexandria, and on the occasion of the 1979 Bairam feast could bring 300,000 young men into Abdin Square for prayers. Obscure thinkers like Abu el-Ala el-Mawdudi in Pakistan preached a doctrine which was widely listened to. For the basis of all fundamentalist Islamic movements is simple: in Islam there can be only one who rules, and that is God. The law of Islam is the law of God (el-Hakimiyatu li-llah). The only function of the temporal ruler is to obey the law of God; it is not his business to alter or elaborate this law.

Many of those who were searching for solutions to their personal or national problems found therefore that they could not do without religion. It was significant that in Egypt, the main publishing centre of the Arab world, religious books accounted for half the total sales of books of every description. People went back to the writings of an older generation. The works of Mohammed Abduh (1849–1905), for example, were reprinted over and over again both in Cairo and Beirut. So were the works of those later writers like Abbas el-Akkad, Taha Hussein and Mohammed Hussein Heikal whose interest in western cultures had, as has been said, given place to fascination with the early history of Islam.

For Iranians much the most important influence (apart from Khomeini himself) was the man who became the philosopher of the Revolution, Dr Ali Shariati. When I was having my discussion with the students inside the American Embassy in Tehran I found that any one of them would, in the space of a few minutes, quote Khomeini at me five times and Dr Shariati at least three times. Shariati was a prolific writer, with more than a hundred books to his credit. Part of his teaching, which had a profound effect on Iranian youth, was that every man is in four prisons. First he is in the prison imposed on him by history and geography; from this he can liberate himself through science and technology. Next he is in the prison of historical necessity, and from this he can free himself by an understanding of how historical forces operate. The third prison is the social and class structure; only a revolutionary ideology can provide the way of escape from that. The fourth prison is the self. Each individual is compounded of divine and satanic elements, of good and evil; each individual must choose between them. Shariati admitted that his ideas were an amalgam of Islam and Marxism, of Sartre's Existentialism and the Sufism of el-Hallaj,★ with a dash of Pascalian humanism.

Islam is a very big sea, but which star should one choose to steer by? Who is to be the navigator? Some Egyptian jurists in the present century, such as Abdel Razzaq Sanhuri, felt the need to look outside the dominant Hanafi and Shafi'i schools of law, which seemed to them since Ottoman times to have closed the way to innovative thought by denying the possibility of *ijtihad* (interpretation). So they turned with interest to the Shi'is, who believed that, in the absence of the imam,

---

★ Hallaj, a Persian mystic, was brutally executed by the Abbasid authorities in Baghdad in AD 922 and is regarded by many Persians as a martyr.

who was the proper authority, they could take the task of *ijtihad* on themselves. These jurists noted that, because of the suppression under which Shi'ism had usually had to live from the earliest days, it retained a tradition of being opposed to the temporal authorities, and so was more receptive to revolutionary ideas than were the Sunnis, usually allies or subordinates of the state. So people like Sanhuri were prepared to borrow ideas from Shi'ism, arguing that it did, after all, represent an important part of the legacy of Islam. The Sheikh of el-Azhar during the Nasser period, Sheikh Mahmud Shaltut, who had many progressive ideas, activated a committee in el-Azhar which was charged with lessening the differences between the various divisions in Islam. In Khomeini's eyes this made him the last good Sheikh of el-Azhar.

The crisis facing the Moslem world was both a moral one and an institutional one. Both individuals and governments were trying to find the authority which would enable them to chart a purposeful course. For individuals, as has been seen, this increasingly often meant a rediscovery of religion; for governments it meant a continued search for legitimacy. If they are to survive, states need a nucleus round which the citizens can gather and to which they can transfer their loyalty. This nucleus may be an individual, a family, a tribe, a sect, or a historical function. In the Arab world these nuclei have often had a religious connotation. Thus the Saudi royal family derives its legitimacy from its position as custodian of the Holy Places; the Hashemites in Iraq and Jordan, and the Senussis in Libya, had an authority which was part political and part religious, as has the Moroccan ruling house; and there is a strong religious element in the ruling houses of many of the Gulf states. But in most Arab countries the nucleus is one man, and his legitimacy depends on his success as a leader. The legitimacy of Nasser derived from his great achievements at home and abroad, culminating in the nationalization of the Suez Canal, though after the defeat of 1967 some of his legitimacy was for a time in jeopardy. The legitimacy of Sadat derives from the October war; of President Assad of Syria from his participation in the same war. Ghadaffi in Libya and Boumedienne in Algeria have been other examples where the legitimacy of Arab states became vested in the achievements of one man. The same was true of Iran, and in spite of the Revolution it is still true, though the man has changed. Nowhere has the state fabric developed into the constitutional-legal stage enjoyed by many countries in the West.

These individual rulers are not supported by any effective political organization. What they have are the instruments of power and the machinery of control: the police, the radio and television. President Sadat and other rulers sometimes refer to the press as the 'fourth estate'. But there are no second or third estates – and the first estate is one man, and one man alone.

Of course modern technology puts a formidable weapon of control in the hands of one man, however slender his real base of power. But in Islamic countries there is one institution which his power is unable to reach, and that is the mosque. This cannot be tampered with, because to do so would be to affront the deepest and most cherished convictions of the people. The mosque provides a place where people can congregate which is outside the reach of even the most efficient secret police. People will defend their mosques at the cost of their lives. Religion provides a fence of security round the lives of ordinary people, and the mosque and the Koran are its symbols.

As far as the state authorities are concerned, religion is a double-edged weapon. It can be used, as it has been in Saudi Arabia, Egypt and elsewhere, in the campaign against communism or against Nasserism. The state, fulfilling its traditional role in Sunni countries, can build mosques and flood the radio and television with Koran readings and lectures by the most obscurantist divines, but the forces thus encouraged are difficult to control. The beliefs and customs of Moslems have changed little over the centuries. When, as in recent years, people's thoughts turn increasingly towards religion, new and often primitive cults and societies inevitably spring up, with their own allegiances and fanaticisms. So it is that in Saudi Arabia and Egypt the state has had to face violence and terror from religious dissidents.

In Iran, where religion had always escaped control by the state, and where most of the forces responsible for the resurgence of Islam in Arab countries were also at work, even the loyal 'ulamas of the Sultan' were becoming disaffected. The reason was economic. The ulamas, as has been seen, were not paid by the state, as in Sunni countries, but depended for their maintenance on private subscriptions. But now the bazaar, from where these subscriptions used to come, was being squeezed by the rapacity of members of the royal family and by foreign multi-nationals. Add to this the jealousy which the petit bourgeoisie felt towards the higher bourgeoisie, the disenchantment of students and workers and the rumblings among the minorities and in the armed forces, and it could be seen that a revolutionary situation was developing. One incident can stand for many. There was a strike in some of the oil refineries outside Tehran, and as usual in these circumstances it was the responsibility of one of the Shi'a clergy, a hojat al-Islam or an ayatollah, to collect and distribute the funds needed to keep the strikers and their families going. One of those who contributed most to the strike fund in this instance was a large Tehran contractor. When asked why he should do this, his answer was simply 'I'm fed up. I want to be free.' He was later to contribute millions of rials to the Revolution and to Khomeini.

The resurgence of Islam has affected countries where the government is entirely non-Islamic. In Iran's northern neighbour, the Soviet Union, people of Moslem origin number 40 million, or 15 per cent of the total population. The men in the Kremlin already had cause for worry in the demographic implications of this fact, for the 1979 census showed that whereas the population in the rest of the Soviet Union had over the past nine years increased by 6 per cent, in the Moslem republics the rate of increase had been 31 per cent. This was in part a result of the policy of encouraging a higher birthrate to make up for the appalling losses in the war – a policy which was modified when it was found that most of those winning prizes for large families came from the Moslem regions. This rapid growth in the Moslem population was acknowledged – and indeed given an official welcome – by Brezhnev, who said it reflected the great strides in economic development taken in areas which in Tsarist times had been regarded as incurably backward.

But the Revolution in Iran raised much more serious problems. Instead of being Moslem in name only, these southern provinces of the Soviet Union, many of them bordering on Iran and sharing ethnic links with those across the border, began to be increasingly Moslem in practice. Mosques were more frequented. Certain Sufi groups, notably the Naqshabandiyeh, the Shadhiliyeh, and the Qadiriyeh, were starting up again, to such an extent that Moscow asked friendly Moslem governments for more information regarding them.

In many other ways the Iranian Revolution was profoundly disturbing the Soviets. They had learned to live with the Shah, selling him arms, buying his gas, and so on. Now they had to start again. It was true that the new regime's main quarrel seemed to be with the other super-power, America, but that would not necessarily last. Ultimately common interests would probably bring Iran and America together again, just as ancient differences would probably continue to keep Iran and Russia apart. Meanwhile it was disconcerting to find that the peoples of the Asian republics, who had always been pointed to as an example of communism's success in dealing with minority races, seemed to see their identity lying more with their fellow Moslems to the south than with their fellow communists to the north.

# 12

# KHOMEINI LEADS

IN IRAN the stage was set for the emergence of a man who would apply a match to all this combustible material and set off the explosion. He would have to be a man of religion, and he could hardly be an unknown figure emerging from the desert. Such a man was at hand in the person of the Ayatollah Ruhallah Khomeini.

Khomeini was born Ruhallah Musawi in 1902 on 20th Jumad, which is also the birthday of Fatima, the daughter of the Prophet Mohammed who became the wife of Ali and the mother of Hassan and Hussein – a most auspicious date. He was born in Khomein, a village about eighty miles south-west of Qom, where his father, Mustafa Musawi, was a mullah. (Ayatollahs always take the name of the town or village from which they come.) Only a few months after Ruhallah's birth his father was shot in the head and killed by the agents of some rich landowners, as a consequence of having championed the cause of some of their tenant farmers.*

The young Musawi's mother died in 1918, so he went to live with his elder brother, Basendidah Musawi, who was already a mullah, and who is still alive today. Ruhallah enrolled in the *hawza* of a well-known mullah in the town of Arak, about thirty miles north of Khomein, the Ayatollah Abdel Karim el-Ha'iri. In 1922 el-Ha'iri decided to move his *hawza* to Qom, and all his pupils, including young Ruhallah Musawi, went with him. This was the future Ayatollah's first sight of the city to which his fortunes were to be so closely linked.

There being nowhere for the young and impecunious student to live, he lodged in the mosque where the sessions of the *hawza* were held, spreading his *doshak* (blanket) on the floor. (He has always continued to sleep on a *doshak* and not in a bed.) In due course he completed the first stage of his studies, taking the degree known as

---

\* It has sometimes been alleged that Reza Shah, who was then a private soldier in the Cossack Brigade, had something to do with the murder of Mustafa Musawi. This would make a neat pattern – the father killing Khomeini's father and the son killing his son (Savak was responsible for the death of Mustafa Khomeini in 1977). I asked Khomeini about this, but he said there was absolutely no truth in it.

*Mahallet es-sutuh el-aliyah* ('the high roofs'), and began to assist his master, specializing in Islamic philosophy and logic. He also started a course on ethics (*akhlaq*), but Reza Shah's police put a stop to this on the ground that political matters were getting mixed up in it.

Ruhallah Musawi had a friend in the Ha'iri *hawza* called Mohammed el-Thaqafi, a Shi'i from Taif in the Hejaz. He was an older man, already married and with a daughter called Khadijah, the name of the Prophet's first wife. When she was fourteen and Ruhallah was twenty-five he asked his friend for his daughter's hand in marriage. They had never met, but she had caught a glimpse of Ruhallah one day when he came to visit their home. When she heard of the marriage proposal she protested. She had no wish to marry a mullah, her ambition being to marry a government official and go to live in Tehran. But, as she tells the story, the night after she had rejected the proposal she had a dream, in which she saw with great clearness the figures of the Prophet Mohammed, Ali, and Fatima. There was an elderly woman there also, who pointed to the other three and said 'None of these like you.' She asked why, and was told 'Because you have refused their son, Ruhallah.' The next morning she told her father that she agreed to the marriage.

So they were married. Their first three children, a boy called Ali, and two girls called Latifa and Karima, all died. Then they had two more sons and three daughters – one son, Mustafa, was murdered by Savak in 1977; the other, Seyyid Ahmed Khomeini, is his father's chief assistant. Mustafa left a son, Hussein, a great favourite of his grandfather and one of his aides, and a daughter, Miriam. Khomeini's three daughters all married mullahs, who have usually served in some capacity on Khomeini's staff. Farida is married to Ayatollah Aradi; Sadiqa to Hojat al-Islam Ishraki, who was with Khomeini in France, and Fatima to Ayatollah Bargroudi, son of the former Ayatollah al-Uzma whom the Shah wished to replace by one of the religious leaders in Najaf. Khomeini now has thirteen grandchildren, eight boys and five girls.

Khomeini's wife is a woman of great strength of character, energy and charm. When he was deported from Qom in 1963 and dumped on the Turkish frontier, Khomeini told her not to try to follow him, but she ignored his instructions and made her way to Najaf. She accompanied him from Najaf to France, and though he went direct to his suburban house of exile in Neauphle-le-Château, and never set foot in Paris, she made several visits to the capital, saw all the sights and was interested in everything she saw.

It is still Khadijah who cooks the Ayatollah's food for him. His routine is regular and his menu simple. He wakes at about 5 a.m. for the dawn prayer, then goes back to sleep again. His breakfast, consisting of bread and a saucer of honey, is placed by Khadijah for him beside his *doshak*. At 11 a.m. he has a little fruit juice, usually orange juice, and at noon a little rice and boiled meat, which he eats with a spoon – the only utensil he ever uses. He is particularly fond of the yellow Persian water-melons. After his midday meal he has a nap, then wakes for the afternoon prayer and continues dealing with business and meeting people until after midnight. Khomeini does not smoke, and never uses the telephone, though while he was in France he once made an exception to this rule when he heard that his brother, Basandidah, was very ill and he wished to hear his voice. The elder brother now occupies the small house in a side street which used to be the Ayatollah's home until he attained power. Now he has moved to a new residence, one of a group of four houses, all single-storey, grouped on either side of a street. One pair contains the offices of his secretary and personal mullah, his security guards, and so on. Across the street one house contains a section of revolutionary guards and the other is the Ayatollah's own home. Inside there is a reception room, about 16 feet by 24, with an undistinguished blue carpet on the floor and spotlights cluttering the ceiling. It looks like a makeshift television studio. This leads into three tiny private rooms and a minute kitchen. One of these rooms is for Khomeini's wife, one for any member of the family who wishes to make use of it, and the final one is Khomeini's own bedroom. From what I could see, all his worldly possessions there consisted of his *doshak* and a trunk containing his clothes.

As a *faqih*, a canon lawyer who has made his own contribution to jurisprudence (*fiqh*), Khomeini is the author of several books, the most important of which are *The Liberation of the Means* and *Islamic Government*. He has a good brain, but his ideas are simple. He sees Islam as a whole, as a unity, and often speaks of it as an international force. He denounces any government in the Moslem world which deviates from the rules of the Koran as *shirk* (heretical) and its ruler as *taghuti* (a tyrant).

Khomeini sees Islam as being one-eighth a matter of prayers and ceremonies and seven-eighths a matter of principles and organization, these latter being designed to bring men to an understanding of justice. He believes that the necessary return to Islam involves two stages: first *takhliya*, which means getting rid of obsolete ideas and practices, and secondly *tahliya*, which is a sweetening process, the adding of new things. Among the ideas which had to be swept away by *takhliya* was *tuqi'a* (the practice of disguise or deception which had been a necessary system of protection for Shi'is in the days of persecution under the Umayyads but which, Khomeini insists, had developed into a bad habit for which the excuse no longer exists). Khomeini tells his disciples that the second stage, *tahliya*, will be harder than the first, *takhliya*, because it involves change and innovation. But the new things, the answers to new situations, will have to be reached by *ijtihad*, the formation of opinion by the *fuqaha*.

Khomeini believes that the imams are created from the light of God and have a rank which cannot be attained by temporal monarchs or even by angels. The *fuqaha* (plural of *faqih*) are the representatives of the imams, and since they know more of the law than anybody else they alone are capable of acting for the imam in his absence. They can act both as the interpreter and executor of the law: 'The ink of the pens of the *fuqaha* is as sacred as the blood of the martyrs.'

In these days, when the problems confronting a ruler seem to have developed so far beyond anything which faced rulers thirteen hundred or a thousand years ago, leaving everything to the *fuqaha* may sound a little naive. When I saw Khomeini in Paris I asked how a *faqih* would deal with, say, the problems of economics or of space. His answer was quite shrewd. 'What does King Khaled know about space?' he said. 'What do these military men who have seized power in the Arab world know about economics? A *faqih* at least understands the laws of God, but these people do not understand the laws of man or the laws of God.'

Khomeini dismisses critics who say that religious men should keep out of politics. Did the Prophet Mohammed keep out of politics, he asks. If he had been no more than the messenger of God he would have delivered God's book, the Koran, to men and then disappeared. But he was told by God to fight and to plan. He organized society and acted as judge in the community. He commanded armies in battle, dispatched ambassadors, signed treaties. To say that religion can be separated from the business of government is nonsense. This, says Khomeini, is what the imperialists want. They want to persuade us that religion is just a matter of theology. He claims that when the British entered Iraq during the First World War they banned all demonstrations. Then one day someone reported to the General Officer Commanding that people were shouting from the minaret of one of the mosques. 'If that is all they are doing,' the General said, 'they can go on shouting till the end of the world. Let them stay in their mosques and shout from the minarets.'

Khomeini also claims, as he told me in one of our discussions, that after his arrest in 1963, while he was in prison in Tehran, someone came to him friom the Palace and asked him why he bothered with politics: 'Politics is all a matter of treachery, lies and hypocrisy,' said the envoy. 'You had better leave it to us.' Khomeini says his answer was that that might be a true description of their sort of politics but it did not describe Islamic politics. He said that after this interview the man from the Palace sent a statement to the newspapers to the effect that Khomeini agreed that religion and politics should be kept separate, with politics being left to the politicians. When he got to Najaf he denounced this statement as a lie: 'It is the man who published this lie who ought to have been sent into exile, not me.'

Khomeini's speeches and writings are bound to have a strange sound in foreign ears because part of his genius lies in the use he makes of phrases from the Koran. These have an immediate relevance to Moslems but need a good deal of explanation for non-Moslems. I have already mentioned his use of the words *taghuti* (tyrants) and *mustazafin* (the humiliated). He used other Koranic words to contrast the *mustaqbirin*, the vain and arrogant, with the *mahrumin*, the deprived. When officials of the Shah's regime went on trial, and were accused of being 'soldiers of Satan', some western newspapers found the expression slightly ridiculous, but again it had a familiar sound to Moslems.

To give an example of how far-reaching Khomeini's influence became, I recall a meeting in Tehran with a Qajar princess who was married to a former ambassador. She had lost her voice completely and I enquired how this had happened. She said that she had spent a quarter of an hour the evening before shouting protests against the Security Council, 'because the Imam asked us to.' She defended her action by saying, 'I'm not a *taghuti*, I'm a *mustazaf*.' This from someone who had seen all her lands and a palace outside Tehran confiscated as a result of the Revolution.

Khomeini is in the true Shi'a populist tradition. He often repeats what is claimed to have been the testament Ali left to his sons, Hassan and Hussein: 'Be always the protectors of the oppressed and the enemy of the oppressor.' This he believes to have been in fact the testament which Ali bequeathed not simply to his sons but to all imams and to the *fuqaha* who represent them. It is an instruction which the *fuqaha* can carry out because they are beholden to nobody, financially independent, without ulterior motives or any of the preoccupations of monarchs who have to keep up their state, provide for their countries, and preserve the throne for their heirs.

In many respects Khomeini's ideas are extremely progressive. In his book *Islamic Government* he discusses subjects such as imperialism, exploitation, and the influence of America in very modern terms, while he introduces the book with an appropriate verse from the Koran: 'If kings enter a village, they will despoil it, loot it, and turn its honourable inhabitants into slaves.' In this book, as elsewhere, he emphasizes his main themes – hostility to the United States, which he regards as Iran's arch-enemy, and hatred for Zionism and Israel. One of his *fetwas* was that it was right that some of the money due to the imam should go to the Palestinians; this of course pleased the Arabs.

It was characteristic of Khomeini, and one of the reasons for the growth of his reputation, that his interests extended far beyond the confines of Iran; he was never parochial. He tried to address people not just as a Shi'a ayatollah, not just as a Persian, but as a Moslem leader who could speak with authority to all Moslems. Islam, he said, made a man free in all that he does – in his person, in his reputation, in his work; in where he lives and what he eats, provided that he does nothing that is contrary to Islamic law, to the *Sharia*.

These were the principal ideas which Khomeini took with him to Najaf when he was driven out of Qom. Although he had been obliged to abandon his *hawza* he still regarded himself as a part of it, and from Najaf he used to send every week to his pupils a lesson he had recorded on cassette. These pupils would congregate to listen to his voice, and gradually others from outside the *hawza* came to listen too. Soon the message on the cassettes moved away from theology and became increasingly political. The cassettes were transcribed, the message on them copied and circulated outside Qom, in Tehran and all over the country. These taped messages became known as *i'ilamiyahs*, communiqués, or, literally, 'I-am-informing-you'. As someone said, what was happening was a revolution for democracy, against autocracy, led by theocracy, made possible by xerocracy. Or, as one foreign ambassador observed, the right man had appeared at the right historical moment, saying the right things.

From his place of exile in Najaf, Khomeini began to be the focus of attention for all those opposed to the Shah's regime, outside as well as inside the country. Some of those who were later to hold leading posts in post-Revolution governments, such as Ibrahim Yazdi and Sadeq Qotbzadeh, abandoned their studies in America and came to Najaf to offer their services to the Ayatollah. Dissident politicians in Tehran, like Mehdi Bazargan, made contact with him.

In 1974, while Khomeini was still in Najaf and at a time when relations between Tehran and Baghdad were particularly tense, the Iraqi President, Ahmed Hassan el-Bakr, sent his son-in-law to see Khomeini, asking for his support in the campaign against the Shah. This Khomeini refused to give. He did not feel that the time was ripe for an open campaign, and quoted the Prophet: 'There is a right time for everything.' The Iraqis accused him of being afraid, but this was unjust; he knew the time for an assault on the Shah's regime would come, but he intended to choose the time himself and not to act in cooperation with anybody else.

By 1977 the quarrel between Tehran and Baghdad had been patched up, and as Khomeini's activities were causing a great deal of concern to the Shah and Savak, an approach was made by the Shah to Sadam Hussein, the Iraqi leader. The Shah pointed out that, according to their agreement of March 1975, Iraq and Iran had undertaken not to interfere in each other's internal affairs, and Khomeini's activities were clearly contrary to this undertaking. So Saadun Shakir, the Director of Intelligence (later Minister of the Interior), was sent to Khomeini to tell him that the Shah had invoked the 1975 agreement and therefore he would either have to stop his agitation or leave the country. After some discussion Khomeini said he preferred to leave. When the Shah heard of this decision he changed his mind: Khomeini, he realized, would be more of a danger outside Iraq than inside. So he asked the Iraqis not to expel Khomeini but to prevent him from carrying on his campaign against the Shah. Sadam Hussein replied that this would mean placing Khomeini under arrest, and that was something he could not do.

Before the expulsion of Khomeini took place he suffered a personal tragedy. His elder son, Mustafa, had been acting as one of the principal couriers between the Ayatollah and his supporters inside Iran. In September 1977 he fell into a Savak ambush and was killed. (It was clear that his killing was the work of Savak, since it was immediately followed by a wave of arrests of people whose names must have been traced through the correspondence he was carrying.) Some people have tried to present the whole Iranian Revolution, or at any rate Khomeini's part in it, as essentially an act of personal revenge for Mustafa's assassination, but this is not true. The revolutionary forces had already reached an almost irresistible momentum by the time Mustafa was killed.

Mourning for Mustafa was made the occasion for demonstrations of devotion to Khomeini and hostility to the Shah. Thousands tried to go to Najaf to join the *majlis el-a'aza* and commiserate with the father, but were turned back by the police. They retaliated by holding their own *majlis el-a'aza* in Tehran, Qom, Tabriz and Isfahan. Every Thursday the *majlis el-tarhim* for Mustafa was similarly celebrated with great emotion. But at the beginning of November, on the occasion of the *majlis el-arba'in*, the final day of mourning, Khomeini told his followers: 'We have shed enough tears. We have remembered my son's death many times. You have offered your condolences to us and to the Imam many times. But from now on I am not going to accept any more condolences. What is needed now is action.' In the final *i'ilamiyah* sent from Najaf, Khomeini gave four instructions to his supporters. They were: to boycott all government institutions, since the government had no claim to be an Islamic one; to withdraw any form of cooperation with the government; not to cooperate in any activity which might benefit the government; and to initiate new Islamic institutions in every field – economic, financial, judicial, cultural, and so on. The *fetwas* of the ulamas are as sacred as the blood of the martyrs. The second act of the Revolution had begun.

# 13
# FACING THE ARMY

ON 6 OCTOBER 1977 Khomeini flew to France and settled in the small house at Neauphle-le-Château, twenty miles west of Paris, which was to be his headquarters until his final return to Iran. It was here that in December I had my first meeting with him.

Outside the villa in which he was living was a parking lot on which had been erected two marquees, one for the assemblies in which the Ayatollah addressed his followers daily after the evening prayers, and the other a place where food was served for members of his entourage. On the day I arrived I found people there who had come from all over the world – students from the Sorbonne, graduates from Harvard, Yale, Berkeley and other American universities, many from leading families in Iranian society and public life. Also present most of the time were members of the Paris Committee of Iranian Students, headed by Abolhassan Beni-Sadr. The Committee had arranged for Khomeini's journey and rented the villa on his behalf. Some of these followers acted as a bodyguard, having reason to fear that Savak or the CIA might try desperate remedies to get rid of this turbulent priest. They had a permit from the French police to carry a limited number of weapons, including two machine-guns, but their Palestinian friends sent them more.

I was met by Ayatollah Hussein Muntazari, the second most important Iranian divine and the man who would have had to take over from Khomeini if anything had happened to him. He took me to see Khomeini in his villa, who, after we had been talking for some time, asked me if I would care to attend the evening prayers and sermon. When I said that I would, he instructed his grandson Hussein to take me across to the marquee. Soon Khomeini entered and began to address his followers.

He started talking in a low key, but I have never heard a voice which was so quiet and yet so moving. It seemed to caress the ears of his hearers in gentle waves, producing in them a state almost of intoxication. At first Hussein translated his message into Arabic for me, but some of those near us begged us to be quiet, and in any case I preferred to watch the effect of his words on the audience rather than be told their exact meaning. It was a most extraordinary scene. Here was the

Imam, with his long grey beard and the black mourning turban of the Shi'is, a figure who might have stepped straight out of the seventh century. Yet all these people, representatives from the intellectual and social elite of Iran, were listening to him in absolute silence, hanging in rapt attention on every word that fell from his lips.

What most impressed me, when the chance came to talk alone to Khomeini, was his ability to grasp the essentials of a situation. When I saw him, he had already been clear in his own mind for the best part of a year that the stage in Iran was set for a revolution, but he knew that there were no political forces and no individuals inside the country capable of leading it. The remnants of the old political parties, and the new groupings like Mujahiddin Khalk and Fedayin Khalk, had been living too long in a state of siege to see the position clearly, and some of them had compromised with the regime. So had some of the religious leaders, but Khomeini was absolutely certain that the motive force of the revolution was going to be religion, and that this meant he was the man who was destined to lead it.

Khomeini knew well the effect the circulation of his *i'ilamiyahs* was having in the country. The response to them was obvious, and he could be sure of the allegiance of the people. The problem was not how to sway opinion but how to overcome the forces of repression at the disposal of the Shah. He was not particularly worried by Savak – it might have 50,000 agents, but what could 50,000 do against thirty-five million? Long before he left Najaf Khomeini had come to the conclusion that the real problem was the army.

The Shah's army numbered 700,000, and somehow it had to be neutralized. Underground groups like the Mujahiddin Khalk and the Fedayin Khalk talked of armed resistance, and so too did some members of Khomeini's staff. Ibrahim Yazdi was later to describe to me the atmosphere at Neauphle-le-Château in those days. He explained how he and those like him who had been educated in the West used to work in the ways they had been taught, preparing position papers which they would present at the Ayatollah's daily *majlis* for his approval. Many of these papers dealt with the necessity for armed struggle, and their authors would try to back up their written arguments with spoken appeals. Khomeini would let them have their say, but would then intervene: 'No, you cannot confront the army. Arms cannot be fought with arms. The only way to fight the army is to disarm it.' He explained that somehow the chains which bound members of the armed forces to the Shah – their oath of loyalty, their habits of obedience – had to be broken.

This was easier said than done. In the officer corps the Shah had created a large elite class, highly paid and privileged and owing everything to him. Other ranks usually served in units far removed from their homes – thus Azerbaijanis would serve in Tehran, Tehranis in Azerbaijan, and so forth. This meant that there was little in common between the troops and the people round them, who could be alien in race and often in language too. Key sections of the army were manned by members of minority groups who were unlikely to respond to the Ayatollah's appeals.*

So from the beginning of 1977 an increasing number of Khomeini's i'ilamiyahs had been directed at the armed forces. The message was simple: they must stop serving the Shah; the Shah was the devil, the taghuti incarnate. They were the mustazafin, the soldiers of God. They must not fire on their fellow Moslems, because every bullet in the breast of a Moslem was a bullet in the Koran. They must go back to the villages, to their families, to their lands, they must go back to the mosque and to God.

By the middle of 1977 cases of desertion from the army began to be reported. Oddly enough, from documents which were found after the Revolution, it seems that the Israeli mission in Tehran was the first to take serious notice of what was happening. Its warnings were passed on to the Shah, who discounted them, maintaining that they were prompted by the Israelis' pique at Iran's cooperation with the Arab governments in OPEC and the Shah's improved relations with Saudi Arabia and Egypt.

But by the autumn of 1977 Khomeini's verbal assaults on the army had redoubled. He had already called on the soldiers to desert; now he urged them to take their arms with them. 'Leave in small numbers,' were his instructions; 'singly, or in twos and threes. You are the soldiers of God. Take your weapons with you, for they are God's weapons.'

Counter-attack by the Shah's forces took many forms. Mention should be made here of one rather unpleasant incident because it demonstrated Savak's use of what I call censorship by commission as well as by omission. In November 1977 Farhad Massoudi, the editor of the leading Tehran daily, Etelaat, had delivered to him an article attacking Khomeini. It was a particularly vicious personal attack, accusing the Ayatollah of corruption, of being a homosexual, and so on. Massoudi knew of the authorities' habit of sending to the news-

---

* Communications were largely run by Bahais. See p. 69.

papers ready-made articles for publication, always neatly tailored to the style of each paper and its writers, but he was so shocked when he read this particular article that he got in touch with the Minister of Information and lodged a complaint. 'If we print this,' he said, 'there is bound to be an attack on our office tomorrow.' The Minister confessed that he had not read the offending article; he had, he said, simply received the sealed envelope direct from the Palace, marked for onward transmission to *Etelaat*. But he promised to get in touch with the Palace. This he did, only to be told that publication was absolutely essential. When Massoudi protested about the inevitable reaction this would provoke, he was told, 'Never mind, I'll tell the Minister of Interior to send you some protection.' The expected attack duly took place, and all the windows in the front of the office were smashed by the indignant crowd. Later Massoudi learned that the article had been prepared in the Information Department of Savak.

That same November the Shah paid a visit to the United States, where he was received with every mark of respect at the White House, the occasion marred only by hostile demonstrations by Iranian students. On New Year's Day it was the turn of President Carter to be the Shah's guest in Tehran, and it was on this occasion that he publicly told his host: 'Iran is an oasis of stability in a sea of trouble, and I am sure that the reason for this is the just, the great, and the inspired leadership of your majesty.'

On 1 January 1978 an entire anti-aircraft battalion, about 500 soldiers in all, which had been stationed in the Meshed area, deserted with their arms. Disturbances spread in all parts of the country; Khomeini's tactics were to increase the number of strikes and demonstrations. These would tie down the energies of the police and Savak, and so make necessary the involvement of the army. And although the army was not yet directly involved, Khomeini's *i'ilamiyahs* were preparing the people for the inevitable day when that would happen. He told his followers that in no circumstances were they to clash with the armed forces; even though the army might appear loyal to the Shah, it must never be forgotten that it was made up of men who were their brothers. Appearances were deceptive – in spite of their uniforms, the soldiers were part of the people, and shared the same feelings as the rest of the people. All that was needed was one blow which would break their link with the Shah. 'Do not attack the army in its breast, but in its heart,' was his message. 'You must appeal to the soldiers' hearts even if they fire on you and kill you. Let them kill five thousand, ten thousand, twenty thousand – they are our brothers and we will welcome them. We will prove that blood is more powerful than the sword.'

In one of the *i'ilamiyahs* circulated at this time Khomeini talked about the martyrs, who form so important an element in Shi'a tradition. 'It is sometimes said that the hero is the essence of history. But those who say it are wrong. It is the martyr who is the essence of history, the motivating spirit of history. So bare your breasts to the army, for the Shah is going to make use of the army and the army is going to obey him. We know that the soldiers are confused, not knowing how to act, but they will be obliged to obey their orders. How can they refuse to obey orders when they are bound by army discipline? But one day they will liberate themselves from the discipline of the Devil and come to the discipline of God. If the order is given to them to fire on you, bare your breasts. Your blood, and the love which you show them as you are dying, will convince them. The blood of each martyr is a bell which will awaken a thousand of the living.'

Then Khomeini used the word often found in Sufism, *wujdan*, meaning the inner consciousness, the conscience which is deep in a man's heart. 'You must appeal to the *wujdan* of the army,' he said. In spite of the size of the army, and the care which had been lavished on it, he realized its vulnerability. It was top-heavy with the latest inventions of American technology, and whatever else these may have been suitable for they would be of little use against a resolute nation. If he could separate the men from the officers he would reduce the army to a phantom. He would have effectively disarmed the Shah's army before the final battle with the Shah took place.

# 14
# THE FALL OF THE SHAH

IT TOOK A LONG TIME for the Shah and those around him to appreciate the change in the atmosphere which had become obvious to almost everybody else. The first sign that he felt some alteration of course might be necessary did not come until the end of July 1977, when he appointed a new Prime Minister, Jamshid Amouzegar, leader of one of the two wings into which the sole political party, Rastakhiz, was divided. Amouzegar's predecessor, Amir Abbas Hoveyda, had been in office for an unprecedented twelve years. Talking to him one received the impression of a thoroughly decent man – courteous in manner, elegant in dress, a diplomat, one would have said, of the old school. When Hoveyda talked about 'the Plan' it was clear that he had the facts and figures at his fingertips. But it was equally clear that he was no politician, that he knew little of what 'the Plan' meant in terms of people or of what was going on in the country. Even the nicest bureaucrat cannot be changed into a politician simply by keeping him in power. Amouzegar was by training an engineer. He had been Minister of Interior, a post which then carried responsibility for oil affairs, and when oil was made a separate portfolio he was put in charge. He gave the impression of having an organized mind, and of being keen to bring some order into the country's affairs, but he seemed no more a politician than his predecessor.

The changeover at the top did nothing to improve the situation. Demonstrations were continuing; there were desertions in the army; Khomeini's i'ilamiyahs were circulating everywhere, and he was now calling for the formation of Komitays – 'Let every mosque be made a Komitay for the revolution' (for the police and Savak were unable to penetrate the mosques). Yet the change was difficult to analyse – it was a sense of danger, but of a danger which was hard to define, and harder still to counter.

In February there had been some talk of the Shah's taking a skiing vacation in St Moritz, and the Villa Suvretta was prepared to receive him, but this had had to be cancelled. Now the idea of a vacation was revived. It could fairly be pleaded that the Shah was in need of one, and the Palace staff had been under severe strain for several months and were clearly tired. If the Shah took a rest, they would rest too. The key man in the Palace was General Afshar Amini, the Director of the Shah's Personal Office, and to all intents and purposes his Chief of Political Staff. A tireless worker, he was the Shah's link with Savak and the armed forces, the distributor of gifts and favours, the essential coordinator of the many strands of the new absolutism, and so in Khomeini's eyes almost as culpable a *taghuti* as the Shah himself. Perhaps around the end of May or early June General Amini became one of those who began to think there might be a lot to be said in favour of the Shah's going abroad. With the royal family out of the country and the universities and schools on holiday, things might be expected to cool down; anyway, it would give everyone a chance to reflect on what should be done next.

So far from cooling down, however, high summer brought an intensification of the struggle. On 17 June there were huge anti-government demonstrations, with a particularly large one in Qom. Although in Najaf Khomeini was already calling for the deposition of the Shah, the demonstrators' demands were only for fresh elections and for the application of the 1906 constitution. Elections were not due until 1979, but there began to be hints from the government side that they might be brought forward. Documents which came to light after the Revolution show that the idea was to replace the Amouzegar government with one headed by some experienced politician, which would hold the fort for six months or a year while preparations for new elections were made.

But in fact it seems that almost everybody had his or her own idea of what should be done. There were three principal personages in the Palace – the Shah, the Empress, and General Afshar. Outside were influential figures like Princess Ashraf, Ardeshir Zahedi, the Ambassador in Washington, and the many politicians and businessmen who had done well under the regime.

The Empress Farah was in a good position to form her own judgement. She regularly saw members of her family and had her own circle of friends. Many people, including court officials and even army and Savak generals, felt they had a better chance of getting their point of view listened to if they spoke to her than if they made a direct approach to the Shah.* The Shah himself had by now become almost com-

---

* General Muqadimi, deputy head of Savak, gave the Empress a thirty-page report on conditions in the country which he wanted her to show to the Shah. Having read the report, the Empress became a strong advocate for the General to be appointed head of Savak.

pletely unresponsive. There were many forms of silence in this complex and moody man – the silence of the inscrutable autocrat, who would listen but would only speak to give orders; the silence of the melancholy father of his people, who viewed the world and its follies with an eye clear of illusion; and now the silence of frustration, of a man trapped and bewildered. The Shah spent hours staring out of the window of his office, and answered those who spoke to him with grunts rather than with words. It was impossible to tell whether he paid any attention to what was said to him or to gain any clue as to what was going on in his mind.★

The Empress, on the other hand, had become even more preoccupied than the Shah with the need to keep the throne for her son, the Crown Prince. She was a proud and intelligent woman. Sometimes, angered by her husband's continuing random infidelities, she contemplated leaving him, as she did again during their Mexico exile. But she knew well that her marriage had never been intended as a love match. As she once said to Jaafar Sherif Emami in a moment of bitterness, 'I was only valuable to them because I got pregnant. I was a good cow.' But her pride kept her loyal.

Two outside parties very much concerned with everything that was going on were the Americans and the Israelis. By now the CIA had grown to such an extent that its officials had overflowed the Embassy compound and were to be found installed in a number of subsidiary buildings, supposedly devoted to such purposes as aid, communications and so forth. Many CIA officials had been brought into the country over recent years in various cover positions, as diplomats, advisers, and businessmen. But as the crisis deepened they began to spend less time on their cover occupations and more on their real tasks. The CIA was being mobilized.

The Israelis were in fact the first to start ringing the alarm bells. Hardly anybody had more to lose than they by the collapse of the

---

★ In her Cairo exile the Empress maintains that it was only later she realized the explanation of the Shah's moods at this time – he knew by then the gravity of his illness. But this knowledge left him uncertain what was the best course of action. One day he would decide that he must abdicate in favour of the Crown Prince; the next day he would change his mind, fearing that if he abdicated without disclosing his illness it would be interpreted as a sign of weakness, and the only result would be that the impending storm would fall on his son's head rather than his own. So he argued it back and forth in his own mind.

Shah's regime. He was an ally of long standing and shared interests, an invaluable partner in the exchange of intelligence and in trade, now running at about $400 million a year. The Shah's Iran was also a considerable purchaser of Israeli arms; even at a time when the Shah was busily coordinating oil policy with his OPEC partners, he was placing an order in Israel for small arms worth $600 million. Khomeini, on the other hand, had already established close relations with the Palestinians, some of whom were serving in his bodyguard, while others were helping to smuggle arms into Iran for use by the Mujahiddin Khalk, and even for the Fedayin Khalk. The Israelis knew too that the large Shi'a population in South Lebanon was as strongly opposed to their occupation there as were the Palestinians.

The Israeli mission in Tehran, headed by the former Mossad official Uri Lubrani, was called a 'Liaison Office', not an embassy, but it was more of a fortress than anything else. It was protected by barricades and steel doors, and there was an emergency escape route provided by an iron staircase which led to the roof and then across to an adjacent building which offered a descent into another street. The Israelis reported their apprehensions over what was going on, but when this was relayed to the Shah via General Afshar he sent the Israelis a message by Savak that they were to stop spreading alarmist rumours.

It is now known that four principal courses of action were, at this time, under consideration by those in and around government. The first was that the Shah should make a genuine effort to liberalize the regime. The second was to hit hard and to crush the incipient revolution by force. It was generally assumed, however, that it was too late for any move towards liberalization to be credible or successful, and by now army discipline was so suspect that coercion would be at best extremely hazardous. So a third course, which had many supporters, was that the Shah should take a long vacation, handing over control of the government to a regency council headed by the Empress Farah. If conditions improved, the Shah would be able in due course to return; if they did not, the Empress would continue to rule until the Crown Prince came of age.

This third solution was thought to be the one preferred by the Israelis, and by the Empress, who felt that the Shah's family (mother, sisters, brothers), with whom she had never been on good terms, were giving him bad and possibly fatal advice. It fitted in with her overriding concern, to preserve the throne for her son. This solution was also favoured by the influential head of the Pahlevi Foundation, Jaafar Sherif Emami; he calculated that he would probably be Prime Minister if such a regency were formed, which would enable him to play the role of *éminence grise* behind the throne.

A fourth solution, which appealed to some CIA elements, was for a military coup, rather on the lines of Ayub Khan's in neighbouring Pakistan. If the people wanted a republic, ran this argument, let them have it – the Shah would go into exile, a good Moslem general would be made president, and the ground would be cut from beneath the feet of the revolutionaries.

The CIA was formulating its own policy, which often differed from that of the State Department. The Pentagon was also involved, because the American Defence Chiefs looked on Iran as one of their principal garrison outposts, as well as being of course a lavish purchaser of American arms. So the American Military Mission assumed an importance equal to that of the Embassy or the CIA. In this connection it is interesting to note that the Congressional Committee set up to supervise intelligence activities should have released, after the Shah had gone into exile, a report from the Mission dated 28 September 1978, which expressed the opinion that the Shah would face no serious danger for at least ten years because nothing would challenge the basis of his authority, which was the army.

So the Americans were speaking with several voices. The Empress was uncertain what the Americans wanted, but she felt that they were not keen on her project for a regency. Some time around the beginning of August she was persuaded by Emami that the situation was so serious that it was her duty to try to awake the Shah to realities. They were not seeing much of each other in those days, the Shah keeping to his own wing of the Palace, but she went to visit him, primed with information about the demonstrations supplied by her family and friends. He brushed her pleas aside, assuring her that he had his own private sources of information and that her relatives were being deceived. But she insisted, and begged him to check. So, reluctantly, the Shah agreed, but looking around him he found there was nobody he could trust absolutely except his old valet. So this man was sent into the town to see what was going on. He made his reconnaissance and brought back his report: 'Your majesty, there are some people in the streets shouting, it is true, but they are obviously all communists who have been paid by somebody to demonstrate.' So the Shah went to Farah and told her that he now had his first-hand report, which showed that her apprehensions were greatly exaggerated. She burst into tears and left the room.

All the same, the Shah must have been to some extent shaken, because the next day he summoned his personal pilot and went alone with him on a helicopter journey over the capital. The streets were full of demonstrators. 'Are all those people demonstrating against me?' he asked his pilot, incredulously. The pilot refused to answer, but his silence was sufficient. The Shah returned to the Palace completely shattered. He began to think that there was nobody left he could trust.

This journey had a bizarre sequel the same night. The Shah went to his private suite of rooms, summoned the two officers from the Royal Guard who were always in attendance, and gave them strict instructions that nobody was to be allowed in without first being searched. One of the Guard officers later described what happened next to Bazargan, the first Prime Minister after the Revolution who was curious to find out everything he could about the last days of the Shah. According to this officer, the Shah repeated with significant emphasis: 'You understand, *nobody* is to be allowed in without being searched.' The officer, whose thoughts immediately turned to the one person most likely to appear, repeated 'Nobody?' 'Yes,' said the Shah. 'Nobody; not even the Empress.'

Guessing something of what the Shah must be feeling after his helicopter journey, the Empress decided at about 8 o'clock to go to see him, if possible to comfort him. She was wearing a cloak over her nightgown, but found to her great surprise that the doors leading to the Shah's suite were locked, with an officer standing guard in front of them. The officer, with tears in his eyes, explained that the Shah had given the strictest instructions that she was not to be allowed in without being searched. She indignantly refused to be searched, and went back to her own quarters. However, after a while she changed her mind and went back. 'Go ahead, search me,' she told the guard. She was weeping, and the guard, equally moved, could not bring himself to touch her. 'Go inside,' he told her, unlocking the door. She went in. What happened after that is not known.

During these early August days the Palace was the scene of almost continuous meetings to discuss the situation. General Afshar and Hoveyda, now appointed Minister of Court, always took part, as did Emami, the head of the Pahlevi Foundation. The Empress too was regular in her attendance, though the Shah was only occasionally present. Farah raised the question of a regency at some of these meetings, but in a tentative way, and she never mentioned it when the Shah was present; he had, as she well knew, no thought of leaving. She also mentioned it to the American Ambassador, William H. Sullivan, but he was not in favour of the idea.

On 13 August a bomb exploded in a Tehran restaurant which was much used by Americans. One person was killed and forty wounded, including ten Americans. A week later there was a horrible incident, which had a strong impact throughout the country. A blaze started in a crowded cinema in the oil town of Abadan, and 430 people were burned to death. There were immediate suspicions of arson; it was said that the doors had been locked to prevent anyone escaping and that the fire brigade had taken an inordinately long time to reach the scene. The city's police chief accused what he called 'Islamic Marxists' of responsibility, but a more popular view was that this was the work of Savak. The argument was that Savak wanted to terrorize the middle classes and chose this way of doing it. Hitherto the middle classes had been the bulwark of the Shah's regime; but now, with the economy of the country moving out of their hands and into the hands of the multi-nationals, with growing suppression and inflation, their loyalty was beginning to waver. Whatever the truth, during the days of mourning immediately following the fire Abadan saw fierce anti-government rioting, with attacks on public buildings and shouts of 'Death to the Shah!' Troops had to be moved into the city, and shots were fired over the heads of the demonstrators.

By now all the Palace debates had arrived at a conclusion. There was to be no regency and the Shah was to stay, but an attempt to liberalize the regime was to be made. Jamshid Amouzegar would be dropped and Jaafar Sherif Emami would become Prime Minister. This move had the backing of the Shah and the Empress.*

Emami was a politician of the old school, though not to be compared with Qavam or Mossadeq or Seyyid Zia. He was one of the last of the middle-weight politicians, clever, devious and ambitious, and though he had for a time been associated with Mossadeq's National Front, his long years in charge of the Pahlevi Foundation had made him as closely committed to the regime as anyone. He had already

---

* The Americans were not keen on this manoeuvre. I have seen the transcript of a testimony by Ambassador Sullivan in which he says: 'Thus the Shah named Sherif Emami as Prime Minister. Had he handed over to Bakhtiar at that time he might have deflected the revolution, but he didn't. The trouble was that Sherif Emami was a crook. The Shah had named him because he was supposed to have good relations with the Islamic clergy, but his relations were not as good as they were cracked up to be.'

served briefly as Prime Minister in 1960, and had been President of the Senate.

Even before he had begun to form his cabinet Emami started talking about his plans to liberalize. This was a mistake. Immediately three leading generals – Badri, Rahimi and Oveissi – came to the Palace and demanded to see the Shah. They insisted that to liberalize would be to court disaster; if one sector in the regime's defences was weakened this would allow the enemy to infiltrate and would lead to the collapse of the whole front. All this nonsense about liberalization must stop.

The Shah began to waver, but it was too late to go back, and on 27 August the changeover in the premiership was announced. However, the confused signals coming out of the Palace were demonstrated in the circumstances surrounding Chairman Hua's visit. The new Chinese leader had arranged some time before to stop over in Tehran on his way back from a visit to Yugoslavia. He arrived on 29 August, and a more inappropriate moment could hardly have been imagined. At the airport he vigorously assailed 'big power expansion, aggression and domination', but no sooner had he reached the Golistan Palace, where he was to stay, than he was waited on by the Minister of Court, who begged him not to make any more attacks on the Soviet Union.

Chairman Hua had supposed, with some reason, that he was about to set foot in a staunchly anti-Russian country, where remarks such as he had made at the airport would be welcome. What he had not been aware of was that the policy of rapprochement with China, and hence the invitation for him to visit Tehran, was the brain-child of the Shah's twin sister, Princess Ashraf. She was not only the most important woman in Iran but a figure of considerable weight internationally. She was head of Iran's permanent delegation to the United Nations, had been head of the UN Commission on Human Rights for two years, and had been tipped by many as a likely President of the General Assembly. She had fallen out with the Russian and Indian governments and so was keen to make up to China. But now the Shah and his ministers wanted to do nothing that might add any new complication. 'We are,' said Emami, 'like people walking barefoot through a field of broken glass.' So Hua had to tone down his speeches, and his scheduled press conference was cancelled. No communiqué was issued when he left for Peking on 1 September.

Another symptom of the prevailing confusion concerned the Foreign Minister, Abbas Ali Khalatbari. He was on his way to the airport to greet Chairman Hua when he heard on his car radio that he had been replaced in the new cabinet by Amir Khossrow Afshar. He told his driver to turn the car round and head for home.

Emami duly published his government's six-point programme, which was 'designed to create an atmosphere of reconciliation among all classes of the people.' Political prisoners were to be released, government salaries to be increased by forty per cent, 'legitimate' political parties allowed to operate and new elections to be held; human rights were to be respected and a sincere campaign to be waged against corruption. As a sop to religious opinion the Ministry for Women's Affairs, created by the Shah, was to be abolished, and the 'imperial calendar', linked to the Achaemenian monarchy, which had recently been introduced, was cancelled in favour of the Islamic Hijra calendar.

A week after Emami's installation, on 7 September, Tehran witnessed its biggest demonstration yet. An estimated 100,000 marched through the streets demanding the deposition of the Shah, the installation of an Islamic republic and the return from exile of Khomeini. Martial law was declared. The next day saw yet more huge demonstrations, in other big cities as well as Tehran, protesting against martial law. Troops opened fire. Government sources admitted a hundred dead, but opposition spokesmen claimed that the figure was much higher, even running into thousands.

Khomeni's *i'ilamiyahs* continued to pour into the country. He exhorted his followers not to challenge the army with force: 'Talk to the soldiers, have a dialogue with them. Bare your breasts, but do not fire. Do not throw so much as a brick against the soldiers.' He was also demanding that the whole Pahlevi family should be removed from Iran. This was a blow to the Empress, because it ended her hopes that some accommodation might be found which would enable her son to inherit with the Ayatollah's compliance.

On 10 September Emami presented his cabinet to the Majlis for approval, but his programme of liberalization had been overtaken by the continued rioting and by the imposition of martial law. Although the Majlis had never in the past showed much independence, it now began to reflect the mood of the country. Several of the deputies stayed away to avoid having to vote, but others shouted at Emami: 'We cannot accept you; your hands are stained with blood!' It was perhaps unfortunate that on this same day President Carter should have broken off from his labours at Camp David with President Sadat and Mr Begin to telephone to the Shah reaffirming the close and friendly relations between their two countries and the importance of Iran's continued alliance with the West. The President thought more liberalization would be a good idea.

Eventually, on 16 September, the new government was approved by 176 votes to sixteen, after Emami had promised that martial law would not be maintained for more than six months. Savak agents had to put pressure on deputies to vote, and even so a third of them were absent, and there were scenes of the utmost confusion, with running arguments about who had or had not voted, and which way.

Emami claimed he had evidence that the unrest was the result of a conspiracy hatched in a certain East European country. There had indeed been a meeting in Prague of the Tudeh Party's Politburo, but its purpose had not been that maintained by the Prime Minister. The old Tudeh leadership had been taken by surprise by the strength and effectiveness of the Islamic movement in Iran. It had gone on making its old-fashioned Marxist analysis of the situation, which bore less and less relation to the facts. So the Prague meeting was held to get rid of the old leaders and introduce new ones who would start a dialogue with the Islamic Revolution.

Once the army was called in to support the police, as it had been in Abadan after the cinema fire and in Tehran and other cities with the imposition of martial law, it found itself in the forefront of the struggle. This was something its commanders had always wanted to avoid, and the Chief of Staff, General Azhari, went to the Shah to complain. He and the other generals could claim with some justification that their warnings about the danger of a policy of liberalization had been proved right. Meanwhile the army continued to be the main target for Khomeini's i'ilamiyahs. 'You have opened fire,' said one of them, soon after the riots of 7 and 8 September. 'Very well – fire again. It is your own brothers and sisters who will receive your bullets, but they will be praying forgiveness for you.'


Something obviously had to be done about Khomeini, but what? I have already mentioned the Shah's attempts at this time to persuade the Iraqi authorities to muzzle Khomeini. Towards the end of September Khomeini decided to go to Kuwait, but the Kuwaiti government was alerted that something was going to happen because of an unusual amount of activity in the Shi'a community there. So the Minister of the Interior ordered the frontier to be closed and sent a message to Khomeini telling him they knew what he was up to.

Khomeini went back to Najaf and was then permitted to take a plane from Baghdad. He flew first to Damascus, and the Syrians would have been quite happy to let him stay, but he felt he would not be free there to continue his activities. Emami tried to lure him back to Iran by declaring a general amnesty, which was specifically stated to guarantee Khomeini freedom from arrest (this was in any case guaranteed to him, as an Ayatollah al-Uzma, under the constitution); but he was not to be trapped in this way. He was still hesitating where to go, thinking perhaps of Algeria, when he had a visit from Beni-Sadr, the head of the very active Iranian Student Committee in Paris. Beni-Sadr was a graduate of the Sorbonne, but was now giving all his time to politics. He had come to the same conclusion as Khomeini – that the motive power of the Revolution would have to be religion, because the mosque was the only place where the Shah's instruments of repression could not reach. So he made contact with Khomeini, and assured him that the Paris committee was well organized and would make all the necessary preparations for his reception. Khomeini accepted their offer and arrived in France on 6 October.

The French authorities would only grant Khomeini a residence permit for six months. When I was in Paris in December some members of his staff, including Yazdi and Ishraqi, discussed with me the problem of where he should go when his six months were up. I got in touch with a friend in Algiers to ask the Revolutionary Council to offer the Ayatollah a refuge, and no doubt this would have been arranged if the course of events had not rendered it unnecessary.

Khomeini's arrival in Neauphle-le-Château was one of the turning points in the Revolution. He was now exposed to the full attention of the world press and radio, which were understandably taking a great deal of interest in everything he said or did. He showed himself well aware of the advantages to be drawn from this exposure, timing his statements and interviews to catch the appropriate deadlines in America or anywhere else it seemed at that moment desirable to influence. In the course of the three months he spent in France Khomeini gave between four and five hundred interviews, which means an average of three or four a day. A large part of his time was spent in front of the television cameras. No American presidential candidate could have shown himself more conscious of the importance of the media.

One consequence of Khomeini's presence in Paris was to put the editors of Iranian newspapers in a quandary. It was difficult for Tehran to ignore an event which was making headlines everywhere else in the world, and on 10 October most papers carried agency reports of his arrival. *Etelaat* went further and printed a picture of the Ayatollah, but this was done without the knowledge or approval of the editor. Some of the printers had unearthed an old photograph of Khomeini and inserted it in the text on their own initiative. The next day troops moved into the office of *Etelaat* and declared that in future all news items would have to be cleared by a military censor before they could be printed. Journalists and printers promptly went on strike, but on 13 October a compromise was reached whereby the troops would be withdrawn provided that no criticism of the Shah or the army was printed.

Meanwhile liberalization was rapidly becoming indistinguishable from appeasement. As far back as 26 September the Shah had issued a directive instructing members of his family to put an end to their business activities and their control over charitable organizations and public institutions. On 22 October Emami announced the cancellation of Iran's $70-billion nuclear-energy programme. For a country which was one of the world's largest producers of oil and gas this programme had always appeared a grotesque waste of resources, but it was probably connected with the Shah's ambitions for Iran to possess nuclear weapons.

Later in the month the policy of throwing victims to the wolves was continued when thirty-four Savak officials were dismissed or retired. General Nassiri had been sacked as head of Savak in June and sent as ambassador to Pakistan; now he was recalled from that post. To underline the weakening of Savak's authority, over a thousand political prisoners, who had been released on 25 October as a gesture of clemency to mark the Shah's birthday, started court cases against the government, and were assured that they would be 'fully compensated' for their sufferings.

Either because he was badly informed, or because he felt that American interference could help to stem the flood, President Carter continued to make statements which only exacerbated the situation. On 10 October he told a news conference in Washington that he thought much of the opposition to the Shah was caused by his having 'moved aggressively to establish democratic principles' in Iran. On 31 October Carter was photographed on the White House lawn with Crown Prince Reza and announced that 'our friendship and our alliance with Iran is one of our important bases on which our entire foreign policy depends.' He praised the Shah's 'move towards democracy' and said it was being opposed by some people who didn't like democracy. This was a strange reading of events. Which better deserved the name of democracy – the Majlis produced by a fraudulent election, whose members were even now slinking away into hiding, or the mass participation of the people in direct political action?

On the same day as Carter met the Crown Prince, Emami felt compelled to denounce the strike of oil workers as an act of treason. It was admitted that oil production had dropped from 5.3 million barrels a day to about 1.5 million, and that refining operations had also been severely reduced. Troops were ordered into the oil installations to prevent sabotage.

As demonstrations continued at the beginning of November, neither the Carter administration nor the Shah could make up their minds what should be done. Ambassador Sullivan has testified that it was on the advice of Zbigniew Brzezinski that the Shah's son-in-law, Ardeshir Zahedi, Ambassador in Washington, was asked to go back to Tehran 'to hold the Shah's hand' and to stiffen his resolve. Zahedi was worried about leaving his Embassy at such a critical moment, but Carter told him, 'I will be Iran's ambassador in Washington in your absence.'

When Zahedi reached Tehran he went with the Shah in a helicopter over Tehran. It was a day of violent demonstrations during which the British Embassy was attacked and many cars and buses were left burning in the streets. Sullivan got an urgent message from the Shah for him to come to the Palace. His driver managed to make his way through the street fires, and he reached the Palace at about 6.30, but there was nobody at all on the gate. He wandered in and found the Empress, who took him to the Shah. The Shah told him there was now no alternative to military government; what would Washington think of that? Sullivan, who had seen this inevitable step coming, had consulted Washington and was able to tell the Shah that there would be no objection. General Gholam Reza Azhari, Chief of Staff of the Armed Forces, was at the Palace before Sullivan had left.★ The next day, 6 November, it was announced that Emami had been dismissed and that General Azhari had taken over.

General Azhari had been reluctant to take on this thankless task, but had been persuaded by Generals Rahimi and Rabi'i that it would be his duty. The first thing he did after accepting the charge was to tell Sullivan that he must help to achieve a peaceful solution of the crisis. He said he was prepared to become Prime Minister only to provide a

---

★ This is according to the recorded testimony of Ambassador Sullivan.

breathing space. 'A military government cannot last for long,' he said. 'A show of force can only be successful in a short run; then it must vanish. Please try to help us.'

The next few days of the new government were relatively quiet, but Azhari had been told by the Shah that the troops were not to fire on the crowds, only into the air, to avoid a degree of bloodshed which would finally discredit the throne. The crowds quickly realized this, and took full advantage of it.

Before news of the new government was made public, troops occupied all sensitive points in Tehran, including the main intersections, the radio station and newspaper offices. The Shah went on the air with what was supposed to be a gesture of conciliation: 'Your revolutionary message has reached me. I promise to make up for past mistakes, to fight corruption and injustices and to form a national government to carry out free elections.' He said military rule would only be temporary and that when it ended 'freedom and the constitution will be freely implemented.' It was not a very convincing performance, but the Shah obviously felt that the stick of military rule needed to be accompanied by some kind of carrot.

Khomeini's reaction to the military government was a statement in which he spoke ominously of the danger of 'a civil war between the army and the people.' Military rule, he said, was nothing new: 'We have always been living under military rule; the only difference is that now the military have come out in the open whereas before they were hiding in the Shah's pockets.'

By now everyone was looking around for alternative courses of action. Sullivan, on his own initiative, began making contact with opposition leaders, and General Muqadimi, now head of Savak and in the confidence of the Empress, advised the Shah that he should do likewise. So he got in touch with Karim Sanjabi, one of the old school of French-educated liberal constitutionalists, who had been a colleague of Mossadeq and was imprisoned for a time after the counter-coup. In the Kennedy-inspired period of liberalization, when Amini was Prime Minister, Sanjabi had re-formed the National Front, and though all political parties except the government Rastakhiz were illegal, it continued to operate as a group. The Shah saw Sanjabi and asked him to form a national government. Sanjabi consulted his colleagues in the National Front, but they all agreed that this would be impossible under martial law.

Sanjabi thought he ought to see Khomeini, and asked the Shah's permission to go to Paris (the Shah claimed that at their interview

Sanjabi kissed his hand, but Sanjabi denies this). Sanjabi spent two weeks in Paris, having talks with Khomeini, who made it plain that he was not prepared to make any concessions. Sanjabi came back to Tehran on 10 November and was about to hold a press conference to report on his discussions when he was arrested.

At about this time Sullivan got a telephone call from Azhari asking for an urgent meeting. When the Ambassador reached the Prime Minister's office he was surprised to be shown into an anteroom which was in darkness. When the lights were turned on he saw that Azhari was in bed, in pyjamas, and over the bed was an oxygen tent. The Prime Minister told Sullivan he did not think he would be able to carry on any longer because of the Shah's indecision. 'This country is not going to survive,' he said. 'We are not being allowed to make proper use of force.' On 12 November Sullivan sent a telegram to Washington giving his opinion that the Shah's days were numbered and some alternative would have to be found. But he never received an answer to this telegram, either from the White House or from the State Department.*

Meanwhile further concessions aimed at appeasing the demonstrators were made. On 7 November General Nassiri was arrested, and the next day it was the turn of Amir Abbas Hoveyda. Fifty-four former civil servants and businessmen were also arrested on charges of corruption and abuse of power. It was announced that there was to be an investigation into the business affairs of the Shah's brothers and sisters and into the Pahlevi Foundation. The tide was lapping very close to the throne, as Khomeini was quick to point out: 'The man who should be subject to investigation is the Shah himself, not his brothers and sisters or the Pahlevi Foundation. Bring him to court.'

Now came another of those turns in the wheels of fate which characterized the Iranian drama. Mehdi Bazargan was one of the few civilian politicians who enjoyed the confidence of Khomeini. He had belonged to the old National Front, but had later formed an Islamic Party. He had been arrested in 1961 and had defended himself courageously in court, attacking both the Shah and the Shah's father. Although, of course, his defence was not allowed to be published it became known and he became widely and deservedly respected.

---

* From the recorded testimony of Ambassador Sullivan.

Then, when President Carter came to power and started laying a great deal of emphasis on human rights, many politicians, Bazargan among them, thought this was an opportunity not to be missed, and so formed an Iranian Human Rights Committee, of which Bazargan was chosen to be chairman. But when martial law was proclaimed Bazargan was one of those arrested. One day in the middle of November, while he was still in Qasr prison, one of the Savak prisons, he was told that a messenger from the Shah was coming to see him.\* This was not the sort of news that people in Savak prisons like to hear, but when his cell door was opened he was astonished to find that his visitor was General Muqadimi, General Nassiri's successor as head of Savak – not a man with such an evil reputation as his predecessor but still not a visitor that a political prisoner receives with equanimity.

However, it soon became apparent that General Muqadimi had not come with sinister intent. 'I bring you a message from the Shah,' he said. 'His majesty is ready to reign and not to rule,' adding dramatically 'like the Queen of England! He is prepared to accept the role of a constitutional monarch because now that the great visions he had for his country have been brought to nothing, he is willing to let the Iranian people have their way. If a constitutional monarchy is what they want, then they can have it. Why do you not cooperate with him?'

Bazargan was a clever politican, and not to be stampeded. 'You tell me this while I am still in prison,' he said, 'where I have no means of contacting my friends. Am I supposed to discuss the Shah's proposal only with myself?' 'If you were to be released,' said Muqadimi, 'would you consider the proposal?' Bazargan said he would, so his release was ordered.

Two new leading Washington figures turned up in Tehran in mid-November – the Treasury Secretary, Michael Blumenthal, and the Senate majority leader, Robert Byrd of West Virginia. Blumenthal lunched with the Shah on 21 November, but when he got back to Washington his private verdict was 'You've got a zombie out there.' Senator Byrd's daughter had married an Iranian, so he was able to make enquiries which persuaded him that the briefing he had been given in Washington – that if the Shah stood firm the US would back him – was not relevant. Before he saw the Shah, he was warned by Sullivan that the question the Shah was certain to ask him was:

---

\* This information was given to me by Mehdi Bazargan, when I saw him in his Prime Minister's office and he went through some of his diaries with me.

did standing firm mean shooting people? That proved to be exactly what the Shah did ask him. The Senator's answer was noncommittal.

Meanwhile further measures of appeasement were being announced. The Shah repeated his pledge that there would be elections not later than June 1979 and that before then martial law would be ended. As an earnest of good intentions General Azhari increased the number of civilians in his cabinet from eleven to nineteen. Ten multimillionaires were arrested on charges of corruption.

The first official Russian comment on the crisis came on 19 November, when *Pravda* reported a warning by Brezhnev that any interference by the United States, 'especially military interference', in the internal affairs of Iran 'would be regarded by the Soviet Union as affecting the interests of its security.' Moscow's previous silence reflected the Russian leaders' continuing difficulty in working out a policy towards their southern neighbour which would be consistent both with communist ideology and with traditional requirements of Russian security in Asia.

They had, it seemed, achieved a breakthrough in the middle and late 1950s when, with the Egyptian arms deal, the revolution in Iraq and the collapse of the Baghdad Pact, they leapfrogged the 'northern tier' of states aligned with the West – Turkey, Iran, Pakistan. But with the Arabs' defeat in 1967, and later with Sadat's anti-Soviet stance, they began to look with renewed interest at the 'northern tier' countries. Turkey and Pakistan ceased to be bastions of pro-western stability; Afghanistan moved leftwards; new Soviet outposts to the south emerged in Aden and Ethiopia. And now there appeared to be promising symptoms in Iran.

But symptoms of what? To begin with, Moscow assumed that opposition to the Shah was along the classic lines of bourgeois revolutions – liberals demanding an end to autocracy and the restoration of the 1906 constitution. But by the beginning of 1978 it became clear that this simple interpretation would not do. I recall one high-ranking Soviet official saying to me: 'In the Middle East revolution always seems to come from the most unexpected quarters. The Egyptian revolution of 1952 came from the army, and as armies are there to protect the status quo you don't expect them to be the seed-beds of revolution. And then the Iranian revolution emerged from religion, and Marxists have to assume that religion is by its nature reactionary.'

Moscow was obliged to believe that sooner or later the religious trappings of the Iranian revolution would be dispensed with and a proper secular leadership would emerge. So it continued its traditional support for the Tudeh Party.

Then one day in late summer a most curious incident occurred. The Soviet Ambassador in Tehran, Vladimir Vinogradov, received a message that the Shah would like to see him. The Shah had tried to keep on good terms with the Soviets, supplying them with gas and oil and returning any defectors who sought asylum in Iran to their fate. His personal relations with Vinogradov had always been cordial; he had enjoyed the chance of an occasional informal discussion with him when he would let off steam about the Americans or chide Vinogradov about the so-called testament of Peter the Great, with its advice that Russia must expand southwards to the Gulf (a document which Vinogradov told him was a forgery concocted by the eighteenth-century transvestite French diplomat, the Chevalier d'Eon). But this time more serious matters were to be discussed.

Almost at once the Shah asked Vinogradov a direct question: 'What do you think of what is happening?' Somewhat taken aback, Vinogradov answered: 'Sir, I think your majesty knows better than I do.' 'But I want to hear your analysis,' said the Shah. 'Sir, I am sorry, but my analysis would have to be a Marxist analysis, and this might not please you.' 'I want to hear your Marxist analysis,' said the Shah. 'I don't mind hearing it.'

So Vinogradov, as tactfully as he could, began to talk about the class struggle in Iran, about the poor who were disappointed in their expectations of better things, the petite bourgeoisie, and the higher bourgeoisie who resented the foreign multi-nationals and being deprived of any share in government. He did not, however, say anything about corruption or the charges that the Shah was acting as an agent for the United States.

The Shah remained intent for a while, and then fired a question at Vinogradov which he was not prepared for: 'What would you do in my place?' Vinogradov felt obliged to answer: 'Sir, I was never a shah in my life. I am afraid I cannot be of any help to you.' But he did assure the Shah that the Soviet Union had no quarrel with him and would try to help Iran as much as it could. He pointed out that as far as contracts were concerned, the Soviets had been content with the leftovers of the West – things like iron and steel mills, power stations and railways, all of which needed a lot of hard work and yielded small profits. He quoted a Russian proverb to the effect that a strong neighbour is a security against trouble because he will be able to keep out intruders.

Vinogradov thought that the Americans were using the Shah against the Soviet Union, and that though the Shah sometimes tried to rebel against their tutelage, in the end he had to obey. He felt that in his heart the Shah thought the Americans despised him and that he tried to pick quarrels with them on minor issues as a way of releasing his frustrations and complexes.*

However, in spite of Brezhnev's fears, military intervention was not the line along which the Americans were thinking. They had come to realize that the situation could not be allowed to continue as it was. General Azhari was continually pressing them to do something. So it was that towards the end of November Bazargan, now a free man again and still Chairman of the Iranian Committee of Human Rights, was told that a delegation from the American Human Rights Committee was coming to Tehran and hoped to see him and some of his distinguished colleagues. The American delegation consisted of three men, and it was made immediately clear that what they wanted to talk about was politics, not human rights. Bazargan explained to them the attitude of himself and his colleagues. There were three essentials, he said. The Shah must disappear; there would have to be a regency council, and a government of known nationalists should be formed to prepare for elections.

After this first encounter the Americans asked if another meeting could be arranged, and this was done. The next day the three turned up, accompanied by someone from the American Embassy they addressed as 'John', but whom they did not introduce. A third meeting was arranged, and this was attended by a man from the Embassy called Lambrakis.† Bazargan meanwhile kept in touch with people who were close to Khomeini, including Ayatollah Muntazari, Hojat

---

* Information given to me by Ambassador Vinogradov in the course of a long discussion in the Russian Embassy in Tehran.

† According to the chapter on the CIA in Iran in John Kelly's *Counter Spy* George B. Lambrakis was one of the members of the Embassy staff in Tehran who 'have worked or collaborated with the CIA in a functional capacity.' Born in 1931, he had served in a number of countries, including Germany, Israel and Lebanon. From the list given by the same author, 'John' could possibly have been John Lamar Mills (Economic-Commercial Officer), or even Michael John Metrinko, stationed in Tabriz.

al-Islam Hashimi Rafshanjani, who was responsible for the Komitays now being formed in mosques everywhere, and Dr Nasir Menachi, later to become Minister of Information. After consultation with them a five-point programme was agreed upon, which Bazargan was to present to the Americans.

1. The Shah should leave the country, on the pretext of going for medical treatment or for a vacation.
2. A Regency Council should be set up composed of people 'nationally acceptable'.
3. A national government should be installed, liberal in composition and headed by someone generally acceptable.
4. The Majlis should be dissolved.
5. There should be fresh elections.

The Americans accepted all these conditions, but at the second meeting a disagreement arose. Bazargan proposed that the new Majlis should create a committee to consider revision of the 1906 constitution so that all references in it to the Shah should be removed and a republic inaugurated. The Americans rejected this, and the discussion became extremely heated.

A further meeting was held at the beginning of December, and this was attended by the American Ambassador, William Sullivan, himself. They went over the five points again, and Sullivan commented that he did not think Bazargan and his supporters would get a majority in a freely contested election. Bazargan said perhaps not, but he would accept the idea of forming a strong minority. On the disputed question of the constitution Sullivan argued that, while the idea of a committee to consider revision of the constitution was reasonable, he could not see why the issue of monarchy or republic had to be decided in advance. Several days later there was a final meeting, also attended by Sullivan. By then large numbers of Americans were leaving the country, and the situation in the oil industry was getting worse. The Americans agreed to everything Bazargan had proposed, but on two conditions – first, that there should be no attempt to interfere with the army, if the Americans gave a guarantee that the army would accept the new regime; and, second, that the current agitation would cease and law and order be restored. Another point raised at these talks, which was to cause a good deal of trouble later, was who was to be responsible for giving orders to the army commanders in the absence of the Shah; would it be the Regency

Council or the Prime Minister? It was interesting, incidentally, to see the Americans negotiating on behalf of the army and feeling themselves capable of giving guarantees in its name. There was some justification for the bitter comment the Shah was later to make that the Americans had been prepared to discard him 'like a dead mouse.'

Bazargan was pleased with what he had achieved in his talks with the Americans, but felt that he could go no further without consulting Khomeini. For one thing, if the agitation was to be stopped, Khomeini was the only man who could do it. So it was decided to send Ayatollah Muntaziri to Paris to report to Khomeini on the progress of the negotiations. He was also to ask Khomeini to suggest names for the Council of Regency (the Americans had suggested Ali Amini, which showed that they still did not understand the sort of people they were negotiating with). But Khomeini rejected everything. He said the negotiations were nothing but a trick, a compromise aimed at aborting the revolution.

Muharram, the Shi'a holy month, began on 2 December. The army ordered a curfew for 1 and 2 December. The word came from Khomeini: 'Defy the curfew!' Thousands obeyed his instructions and crowded into the streets. The troops opened fire and there were many deaths – twelve, said the government; sixty-seven, said the opposition. Azhari was shaken. After the first day's events he assured Sullivan that the people had got the message that the government meant business and would not come back for more punishment. But they did. On 2 December an estimated 400,000 came out, and there were mass demonstrations in Isfahan as well as Tehran. Azhari laid the blame on the Tudeh Party – 'atheists and saboteurs, not true Moslems.' Khomeini's message to the army was 'You kill us, but we forgive you; we forgive you, but you must awake to the fact that each day you are creating more *shahids* [martyrs].'

American policy was in complete disarray. Everybody blamed everybody else – Brzezinski blaming Vance, Vance blaming the military, the military blaming the CIA, and the CIA complaining that it was not being given a free hand. Carter complained to President Giscard d'Estaing of France about Khomeini's activities in Neauphle-le-Château. He also appointed George Ball, the former Under-Secretary of State, to make a long-range study of Gulf problems; it was his first report which was influential in getting American acceptance of the proposals put forward by Bazargan.

Ashura, the tenth day of Muharram, and the day on which Shi'is remember and mourn the martyrdom of Hussein at Kerbala, was expected by all to be a day of crisis. Khomeini had prophesied that 'torrents of blood' would flow, but the government had learned its lesson from the failure of the previous week's curfew and lifted the ban on demonstrations. Vast crowds, estimated by the opposition to number over two million, demonstrated peacefully in Tehran, but in Isfahan the mob attacked Savak offices and pulled down statues of the Shah. The police opened fire and there were numerous deaths, forty to fifty according to the government, with the opposition as usual putting the figure much higher.

Ardeshir Zahedi, now back in Tehran, was busily shuttling backwards and forwards between the Palace and the Americans. He remained in continual telephone contact with Brzezinski, assuring him that the situation was in hand – assurances which Brzezinski preferred to believe, although they were directly contrary to the advice coming from the Embassy and the CIA.* On his own initiative Zahedi decided to organize a counter-demonstration, and on 13 December a procession including ex-servicemen and well-to-do ladies in their furs moved through the streets of the capital on foot and in cars, compelling bystanders to display portraits of the Shah or in other ways to demonstrate their loyalty. It was not an impressive demonstration, and according to Zahedi's own account the Shah summoned him to his office that same evening and told him: 'We can't repeat 1953 today. We were poor then, and you could buy anyone in the street for two tomans. But today any wretched bazaar merchant has three or four million tomans.' The Shah had evidently not lost all his shrewdness.

Bazargan had become increasingly worried at the way events were shaping, at the escalating violence and the terrible toll of killed and wounded; so he decided to go to Paris to see Khomeini. As he later told me, 'I wanted to explain to him the whole picture as I saw it. I felt that so far we had succeeded, but we had to acknowledge that the whole army, from the generals down, was mobilized against the Revolution. We faced the prospect of civil war and of a massacre on an unprecedented scale. I explained my fears to Khomeini but his reply was: "You must not compromise. The ferment is now at its peak. This is the best guarantee for victory. If now you start talking about law and order the Revolution will lose everything. The people's enthusiasm will evaporate; they will go back to their homes and you will lose your

---

* From the recorded testimony of Ambassador Sullivan.

army of supporters." I said: "But, Seyyid, we could keep the people mobilized through the run-up to elections." He shook his head, but said nothing. I told him that, to clear my conscience, I wanted to ask him a direct question: was he absolutely convinced that he should go on? Could he guarantee our success against the army, the Americans, and Europe? He replied: "I have confidence in God." I said: "Well, we have always worked under your leadership, and we will continue to follow you, but I must confess that I am worried." Khomeini said: "I want to ask one thing of you. I want you to prepare for me a list of men whom the Revolution can trust and whom it can use when it is victorious." So I sat down with Yazdi, and we made a list of people suitable to act as councillors, ministers, governors, and so on. The names on that list in fact comprised the Revolutionary Council and the first post-revolution cabinet.

'Before I left Paris Khomeini appointed me his political representative in Tehran – there was as yet no Revolutionary Council, only the unofficial group round him at Neauphle-le-Château, men like Beni-Sadr, Ishraqi, Yazdi and others. His final instruction to me was that he wanted me to go to the south and organize a strike among the oil workers. I had been the Director of the Oil Company after nationalization in Mossadeq's time. He also asked me to prepare a report on what the Revolution's policy about oil should be. So I went back and organized a successful strike. It was this as much as anything else which brought the army and the Americans to their knees.'

On 29 December the Shah appointed yet another new Prime Minister, Shahpur Bakhtiar. He was a member of the National Front, but was in fact only third choice for someone to head a civilian government, two other National Front leaders, Karim Sanjabi and Gholam Hussein Sadiqi, having turned down the invitation. Bakhtiar had been involved in the negotiations conducted between Bazargan and the Americans, both directly and through his son-in-law, Dr Jafroodi, a former Senator and a Professor at the Tehran Technical College, at whose house one of the meetings with the Americans had taken place. Consequently, as soon as Bazargan came back from Paris with instructions from Khomeini that there was to be no compromise in the revolutionary path, it was a simple matter for Bakhtiar to take up the negotiations where Bazargan had left off. But, though Sullivan liked Bakhtiar personally, he was beginning to doubt his ability to cope with the rapidly changing situation. He described his appointment as 'a fig leaf'. Bakhtiar was confident he would be able to implement the programme agreed between Bazargan and the Americans, and he insisted also on the disputed condition, that he as Prime Minister would be empowered to give orders to the army commanders.

On 3 January a new emissary arrived from Washington. This was Air Force General Robert Huyser, Deputy Commander of US Forces in Europe. Although General Huyser had visited Iran a few times in the past, he knew little of the country or its leading personalities, nor did he speak Farsi. The purpose of his mission, which was strongly opposed by his immediate superior, General Alexander Haig, was to persuade the armed forces to transfer their loyalty from the Shah to Bakhtiar. It was proposed that he should occupy the same office as the Chief of Staff, General Abbas Gharabaghi, and ensure that the armed forces stayed loyal to the Bakhtiar government when the Shah had left. The Shah only learned that General Huyser was in the country some days after he had arrived. By then neither the Americans nor the Director of his own Personal Office, General Afshar Amini, were bothering to keep him informed of what was going on.

Huyser differed from Sullivan in his assessment of the situation. He believed that the armed forces would hold together, whereas Sullivan thought they would disintegrate at their first direct contact with the Ayatollah. But Sullivan believes that Huyser passed on the Ambassador's views as well as his own to the Pentagon.

When it became clear that Bakhtiar was planning the immediate implementation of so much of all that the demonstrators had for months been demanding and dying for – removal of the Shah, fresh elections, and so on – some of those in Paris began to be worried, as did Bazargan in Tehran. It seemed quite possible that a reform government would cut the ground from under the feet of the Revolution, particularly when Bakhtiar started to make other gestures, like suspending the delivery of oil supplies to Israel and South Africa, which showed a complete reversal of the Shah's policies. Another source of anxiety was a message sent by Carter via President Giscard (they had just met at the Guadaloupe Summit) to the effect that the Americans intended to give Bakhtiar their backing, and that as he had adopted the opposition's platform Carter expected that Khomeini would back him too. If he did not, Carter's message continued, the army would probably intervene, which would mean a military coup.

Khomeini's answer was that he was not going to back Bakhtiar. 'His appointment is illegal,' he said, 'since he was appointed by the Shah. Threats of military coups cannot frighten us, because there has already been one. Azhari's government was a military coup. Bakhtiar's government is no more than the façade for a military coup.

Bakhtiar is a puppet for the generals. If the army does intervene it will be under the control of the Americans, in which case we should consider ourselves at war with America.'

When the Shah heard that General Huyser had been in Tehran for some days without making any attempt to see him, he was naturally irritated. Eventually Huyser, accompanied by Sullivan, the Ambassador, did pay a call on the Shah, but, according to the memoirs the Shah wrote in exile, almost immediately Huyser, asked him 'When are you leaving, sir? Have you fixed a date?' In fact, on 6 January, the same day which saw the formal installation of the Bakhtiar government, the Shah issued a statement that he intended to leave for a vacation as soon as order was restored. He said he was tired, and needed a rest. A Regency Council would take over.

Bakhtiar was anxious for the Shah to go as soon as possible, since he felt that only when he was out of the way could he get the full cooperation of other politicians. The National Front had disowned Bakhtiar – had indeed expelled him from its ranks – but its leaders maintained contact with him by telephone. What the Shah was still ignorant of was the agreement that had been reached with the Americans on the eventual establishment of a republic. He was still insisting that even after he had left the country he should remain commander-in-chief of the armed forces, both in name and in fact. He claimed that he was the only coordinating link between all the separate commands. But the Americans realized that the Shah felt they had betrayed him, and now that they had committed themselves to the Bakhtiar government they had no intention of leaving the Shah in control of the armed forces. They were determined that, if there was to be a military coup, it should be undertaken by the whole army and not just by the Royal guards, and that it should be at a time decided on by them and not by the Shah. Plans for a coup were in fact far advanced, and papers found in the briefcase of General Afshar Amini after the Revolution showed that the planners were expecting to have to deal with up to 50,000 casualties. Huyser busied himself with arranging new appointments in the top command. Among others who were dismissed was General Oveissi, the Tehran martial law administrator and army commander. On 4 January it was announced that he was going to the United States 'for health reasons'.

On 9 January the Shah was reported to have ordered members of the royal family to transfer their private fortunes to the Pahlevi Foundation – a gesture which came late and meant little, since the Foundation had from the outset been one of the royal family's hunting-grounds.

Besides, they had other plans. Royalty, like other wealthy Iranians, had been busily transferring money abroad, and now they were borrowing money from banks in Tehran, which the banks were obliged to hand over even though they, and the borrowers, knew that the money would never be repaid. The Bank Omran, which was wholly owned by the Foundation and in 1977 had assets of over $1 billion, had for years acted as the private banker for royalty and selected important commoners. In these last days the Shah and members of his family withdrew $700 million from the Bank, and it was obliged to supply them with short-term loans amounting to $800 million. Not surprisingly, after the Revolution the Bank was declared bankrupt.

The Shah did not leave Tehran until 16 January, later than had been expected and than Bakhtiar had wished. The delay was partly due to the Shah's desire to take with him into exile some, at least, of the Crown Jewels. In particular he wanted the crowns used at his coronation for himself, the Empress and the Crown Prince. All these were now in the safes of the Central Bank (Bank Melli), but the employees of the Bank, like so many others, were on strike. The Shah ordered a detachment of the Royal Guards, known as 'the Immortals' (the same title assumed by the bodyguard of the Achaemenian kings), to force the Bank officials to open the safes. On six successive days this detachment went in its armoured cars to the Bank, defying the demonstrators, and six times it had to come back empty-handed. The royal treasure was kept in safes twenty metres underground, and the officials who knew the combinations had disappeared; so in the end all the elaborate safety precautions the Shah had installed defeated his own purposes, and he had to leave without the crowns. The jewels, reported to be insured for between $250 and $500 billion, stayed in the Bank.

Bakhtiar's Cabinet was approved by the Majlis on the day the Shah left. Three days before that he had announced a Regency Council, headed by an elder statesman, Jelaleddin Tehrani. Sanjabi and Bazargan were invited to be members but refused.

Once he had acquired theoretical control over the army Bakhtiar felt he was in a strong position. This new authority, he believed, gave him the power base he needed, not realizing that a politician cannot acquire a power base overnight as a gift or a loan. It was in fact Khomeini who was speaking from a position of secure strength. By now he had ample proof that the people would obey any instructions he gave them; he was their Imam and they were his *hawza*. It was he, not Bakhtiar, who had the power base and who possessed the true legitimacy which had, he always maintained, been usurped by the Shah. So, from Neauphle-le-Château, he denounced Bakhtiar, saying that obedience to him was obedience to Satan. He said he was setting up his own Revolutionary Council. Bakhtiar's ministers began to fall away, and even his own tribe, the Bakhtiaris, abandoned him and pledged their support to Khomeini.

The Shah had hoped to make his departure look as much as possible as if it was the start of a series of state visits. His ultimate destination was to be the United States, but he had in mind a number of intermediate stops. King Hussein of Jordan, who was to have been the Shah's first host, politely declined the honour, but the King of Morocco and President Sadat of Egypt accepted.

The Shah's party flew direct to Aswan, the winter resort on the Nile. The Egyptian authorities tried to make his arrival as impressive as possible, and some people were persuaded to come into the streets and cheer; but it was a fairly miserable occasion. The Shah himself was a sad and bewildered man, still unable to comprehend what had happened. He blamed his advisers; he blamed the Americans. He claimed that he had been surrounded by a hedge of hypocrites who had kept the truth from him. He was even ready at some moments to blame the Empress and accuse her of being a part of the conspiracy against him.

He now had two major concerns – to maintain communications with General Gharabaghi and the Royal Guards, which still consisted of two armoured divisions, and to discover whether Khomeini was planning to return to Tehran. He thought that whatever Khomeini did might be to his own advantage. If the Imam did go back to Tehran the army would deal with him; if he did not, he would lose face because it would look as if he was unsure of his reception.

While he was in Aswan the Shah still behaved as if he was a head of state. He had a three-man summit meeting with Sadat and ex-President Ford at which he brought out some of his grievances against the Americans. Carter, he said, had deceived him by continually saying in public that he was giving him full support while he was negotiating with the opposition behind his back. If there was any need to contact the opposition, he, the Shah, was in a better position to do this than the Americans. He added that it was strange that the King of Morocco, who had no obligation to do so, had offered to send troops to help him while the Americans, his supposed allies, had made no such offer. Ford sensibly asked what use extra troops would have been, since the Shah had had plenty at his command. As for the Shah's general complaints about American policy, there was, of course, nothing he could do except report them to Washington when he got back.

Khomeini's message to the Iranian people was that getting rid of the Shah was only a first step: 'It is not our final victory, but the preface to victory.' He called on the army to destroy its new sophisticated American weaponry, and on the people to continue their strikes and demonstrations against the Bakhtiar regime. As for Carter's suggestion that he should cooperate with Bakhtiar, he simply said that this was none of Carter's business.

Bakhtiar continued to show a misplaced confidence. He thought he had the army under his control, whereas in fact it was receiving its orders not from him but direct from the Americans. He felt he could defy Khomeini: 'I shall not give up my position to Ayatollah Khomeini,' he said, 'just as he would not give up his position to me.' This was not a particularly sensible remark. All the same, as he continued to implement the former opposition's programme – withdrawing from CENTO, asking for Iran to join the non-aligned countries, insisting that the Shah should never be allowed to return, and so on – there was increasing impatience among the exiles in France, and a feeling that the move to Tehran ought to be made without delay if the fruits of revolution were not to be stolen from them.

Yazdi told me that they got another message from the Americans, again sent via the French authorities, but this time Bakhtiar was involved too. The joint Carter–Bakhtiar message was 'Please don't go to Tehran as you are planning. If you do there is bound to be bloodshed.' Bakhtiar also sent a private message to Khomeini asking for three months' grace, in which time he promised to complete the programme they both wanted. But, he added, if Khomeini did come back there would certainly be a massacre by the army.

Bazargan was also sending messages to the Ayatollah. His suggestion was that Khomeini should announce the formation of a government in exile, declare a republic, and meanwhile let Bakhtiar do the dirty work of dealing with the army and preparing elections. Many of those round Khomeini were convinced by these arguments, being still haunted by their fear of what the army might do. But Khomeini said no; they should all go to Tehran. 'Give me two months,' was the new message from Bakhtiar. Khomeini said no. 'Give me three weeks.' Still no.

The Shah spent only five days in Aswan, and on 22 January flew to Marrakesh in Morocco. The assumption had been that he would only spend about another five days there before moving on to the States, but soon after he arrived he got a message from his son-in-law, Ardeshir Zahedi, the Ambassador in Washington, that the American authorities had changed their minds and he would no longer be welcome. So he had to stay in Morocco. But as well as being a disappointment for him, this was an embarrassment for his host. Students had demonstrated against the Shah on his arrival and continued to do so. With the Iranian Revolution exercising a fascination over Moslems everywhere, the Shah's presence was obviously going to be a liability for any government of an Islamic state. He told King Hassan that it was not convenient for him to leave because he was in continual touch with the Royal Guards, which had remained loyal, and he was expecting a summons to return to Tehran at any moment. If his return was effected from America it would look as if it had been engineered by the CIA. But after three weeks King Hassan felt obliged to send his ADC to the Shah to explain that, much as the King would like to give him asylum in Morocco, the situation had changed so much that, with regret, this had become impossible.

Morocco and the United States were closed to the Shah, but his influential American friends, Henry Kissinger and David Rockefeller, were able to arrange a sanctuary for him in Mexico. But here an unexpected complication arose. One of the actions of the new government in Tehran had been to cancel the light-blue imperial passports on which the Shah and his family had hitherto travelled. The Mexican authorities wanted to know what passports they would be travelling on. The Moroccans were unwilling to provide passports for the Shah and his family, because then the whole of his entourage would expect them too and all might use them to return to Morocco, which was something King Hassan most certainly did not wish. So there was an impasse.

One day the telephone rang in the Geneva office of Prince Sadruddin Aga Khan, the UN High Commissioner for Refugees. His secretary answered and told him that it was a long-distance call from somebody calling herself Queen Farah. This sounded improbable, but Prince Sadruddin picked up the telephone and recognized the voice. 'I'm sorry to trouble you,' said the Empress, 'but we have this difficulty over passports. The bureaucrats in Mexico say we must produce a piece of paper for them to stamp. Can you help us?' She told him that Princess Ashraf was in contact with Kurt Waldheim in New York over the problem, and she hoped that it would be possible for them all to be issued with UN or refugee passports. The wheel of fortune had indeed come full circle, with the Empress of Iran begging for her and the Shahinshah to be granted the status of refugees.

Meanwhile the situation inside Iran, following the Shah's departure, was becoming even more confused. Neither General Huyser nor the Iranian generals supporting the Bakhtiar government knew what to do. The only way that occurred to them for stopping the Ayatollah from carrying out his threat to return to Tehran was to order the closure of all airports. This was done on 25 January.

Khomeini's aides had been experiencing understandable difficulty in finding an aircraft to take him home, but eventually some wealthy Shi'a businessmen put up $3 million deposit which covered the hire of an Air France jumbo jet and the expensive insurance for it and its French all-male volunteer crew. As the airports had to be reopened on 30 January, since a continued closure would have brought the commercial life of the country to a standstill, the return of the Imam was fixed for 1 February.

There was serious rioting in Tehran and Tabriz, leading to more than a hundred deaths, during 26 and 28 January, and the day before Khomeini was due to arrive the commanders of the armed forces arranged for a massive show of strength in and over the capital by armoured units and the air force. But some army units at a base near Tehran mutinied, and the Royal Guards had to be sent in to restore control. The crowds in the streets greeted the soldiers with flowers. Without any doubt it was the willingness of almost the entire population of the principal cities to face martyrdom, indeed to welcome it – the 'Kerbala complex' – which ensured that the Revolution would triumph.

Khomeini boarded the Air France jet on the evening of 1 February and went straight to the upper section, where he performed his ritual ablutions (*wudu'*), said the prayers for those facing death, ate a little yoghurt, spread his *doshak* on the floor, and went to sleep. In the main section of the plane was his entourage (he had forbidden his wife or any of his supporters' wives to make the journey), as well as a large contingent of journalists, about a hundred people in all. There was a good deal of nervousness. 'Are they going to fire at us?' the crew wanted to know. Nobody could be sure.

Alone in his part of the aeroplane the Ayatollah slept till 5 o'clock, when he again performed the *wudu'*, repeated the dawn prayers and the prayers of those who expect to die, and ate a little more yoghurt. As the plane neared Tehran, Yazdi, who, like the other returning exiles, had been unable to sleep all night, went up to Khomeini and drew his attention to the view through the window over the city which he had not seen for nearly fourteen years.

It was an occasion of unbridled religious rejoicing, for which there has probably been no parallel in the modern world. If the Hidden Imam had in truth reappeared after eleven hundred years, the fervour could hardly have been greater. People were shouting, 'The soul of Hussein is coming back!', 'The doors of Paradise have been opened again!', 'Now is the hour of martyrdom!' and similar cries of ecstasy – though, as the Ayatollah Shariatmadari sardonically remarked, nobody had ever expected the Hidden Imam to return in a jumbo jet. When this comment was reported to Khomeini he was not amused.

Seeing the whole population of the capital in such a ferment, the government and army announced that they could not be responsible for the Imam's reception or for his security, perhaps calculating that, surrounded by a mob of millions, a frail old man of eighty stood little chance of survival, an outcome which would not have been wholly unwelcome to them – better he should be killed by his supporters' love than by the army's tanks. But the local Komitays took over and acted as guards around Khomeini, and the people showed a surprising discipline. However, the streets were so crowded that there was no hope of Khomeini's being able to make his way through them, so it was decided that he should continue his journey by helicopter. Although there had been a mutiny at the air force base, a helicopter and crew were produced, and Khomeini flew low over the heads of his wildly cheering supporters to the Husseiniyeh School, where he was to stay.

All authority apart from that emanating from Khomeini was melting away. Although Bakhtiar had not resigned yet, Khomeini ignored him and designated Bazargan as Prime Minister. General Gharabaghi reported to General Huyser that army units were joining demonstrators in the streets. Signals came from Brzezinski in Washington that it was time for a military coup; but it was too late – there was no army left to carry out a coup. So, after speaking to Washington, General Huyser decided that the only thing left for him to do was to disappear. This he did, leaving his Iranian colleagues to fend for themselves as best they could. But there was little they could do. As they reported to Gharabaghi, they were now generals without an army.

As a last resort Bakhtiar proclaimed a curfew. When he heard this, Khomeini took a piece of paper and wrote on it 'With the help of God, defy the curfew!' The paper was taken to the television station, and before it was occupied by some remnants of the army a picture of the piece of paper was shown on the television screens. The people poured out. It was the last day before the Islamic Revolution finally took over. General Gharabaghi telephoned to the Prime Minister Khomeini had appointed, Bazargan, and asked him to send a representative to whom he could hand over the army.* But army and government were now like phantoms.

Most of the junior officers had joined the other ranks and gone over to the side of the Revolution. Only senior officers, from the rank of colonel and upward, stayed loyal, and many of them were quickly killed or chose to commit suicide. General Badri, the commander-in-chief of land forces and before that commander of the Royal Guards, was shot by one of his officers. The commander of the navy, General Kamal Habibullah, disappeared, and is perhaps somewhere abroad. General Amir Hussein Rabii, the air force commander, was brought to trial and shot. The same fate befell General Amir Rahimi, the military governor of Tehran. Unlike some of the other senior officers (General Nassiri, for example, was prepared to reveal everything and implicate everybody to save his skin), Rahimi made a brave end, facing the firing squad with the cry of 'Long live the Shah!' General Ali Rashabi, commander of the Royal Guards, asked General Gharabaghi if he could borrow his command car, and drove off in it, only to meet a large crowd of demonstrators who surrounded the car and threatened its occupants. Rashabi shot himself with his service revolver. General Mohammed Ali Hatimi, director of civil aviation (a very important post in a country which had come to rely on air transport for most of its communications – the domestic airline had thirty-two jumbo jets) committed suicide.

The long duel between religion and empire, between Imam and Shah, was at an end.

---

* Information from an interview with Mehdi Bazargan.

# 15
## GUNS, BUT NO INFANTRY

THE LAST FLICKER of imperial rule in Iran had been when General Gharabaghi implored the new Prime Minister, Khomeini's nominee Mehdi Bazargan, to send somebody to take over the army from him. But in fact there was then no army to be taken over. Nor was it only the army which had evaporated; the whole apparatus of government had ceased to exist. Every element in the life of the country had come to a stop, waiting to know what the Imam wished done with it. Khomeini now exercised an authority far more absolute than that of any shah. The wealth and prestige of the country were at his disposal. Even those who had for long and independently opposed the Shah – the old politicians of the National Front and other groupings; the left, including the communists; the bazaar – now recognized their master. Internationally Khomeini was the new and incomparable hero for every revolutionary movement. Clearly a completely new chapter in Iran's history was opening. But what was the Imam going to write in it?

When I saw Khomeini in Paris at the end of 1978 I told him I had no doubt of his ability to demolish the old order, but I was not so confident about his ability to build a new one. 'If I may use military terms,' I said, 'you have shown that you command very effective artillery, but after your guns have done their work you need infantry to occupy the positions captured. Where are your infantry? In a revolution the infantry are the political cadres, the bureaucrats and technocrats who have to carry out the programmes which the re-volutionaries have been fighting for. Of course some of the old bureaucrats and technicians in Iran were corrupt and incompetent, but you will need the services of the good ones among them.'

Khomeini's answer was that Iran would not be deprived of the services of good Moslem technicians who had been trained in the West and who could come home and carry out programmes of moderniza-tion 'on the basis of Islamic principles.' When I pressed him to explain what the 'Islamic principles' governing the new government amounted to, he said 'liberty and justice'. I said I could see no conflict between us there.

But was his explanation sufficient? In the first days of the Revolution, many people, including politicians like Bazargan and Sanjabi, described Khomeini quite simply as 'a saint'. They saw him as a man of God who had thrust aside the forces of darkness, and who had thereby left the stage free for men of goodwill (like themselves) to take over the reins of government. These people believed that what the saint would do after his victory would be to spend a few days in Tehran and then go back to Qom, once again collect his *hawza* around him, and continue to instruct his disciples in religion as if all that had happened since 1963 could be forgotten. This was, indeed, Khomeini's own intention. Like so many military rulers who have seized power in the modern world and have proclaimed their intention to go back to barracks as soon as possible, Khomeini genuinely had no wish to rule. But, like so many of the soldiers, he found it was easier to wish for retirement to private life than to achieve it.

The fact is that the success of the Revolution had overthrown old focuses of authority without setting up new ones, apart from Khomeini himself. Any regime, if it is to survive, must have behind it some class or sectional interest, but in the early days of the Revolution in Tehran this did not exist. People like Bazargan (now seventy-five years old), Sanjabi and the others were leftovers from the Mossadeq generation. In spite of owing their present positions to the Ayatollah, they were isolated individuals, with no power base or organized following in the country.

If Khomeini understood this, it did not worry him. It was his firm belief that the first duty of the Revolution was to destroy everything connected with the Shah's regime; and in this he was proving remarkably successful.

The army had to be destroyed, not only because it was the creation of the Shah but because it represented the only real potential threat to the Revolution; both the exiled Shah and the Americans had their eye on it as the nucleus for a counter-revolution. Similarly the police had to be disbanded because they too had been instruments of the Shah's tyranny. The worst among them, from Savak, must suffer exemplary Islamic punishment (*qassas*) for their misdeeds.

When I spoke to him in Qom, Khomeini showed a utopian belief in a society's ability to live in harmony without compulsion. 'Certainly,' he told me, 'I could reimpose law and order on the country tomorrow, but this could only be done by means of the army and a new Savak-like police. Am I to resort to suppression, like the Shah? Our people have been in prison for thirty-five years; no government is going to put

them in prison again. They must be given a chance to express themselves as they wish, even if it means a certain degree of chaos.'

The army and the police were not the only casualties. All the old
bureaucracy had to be liquidated too. I remember Qotbzadeh saying
to me one day in his office in the Ministry of Foreign Affairs: 'The real
enemy I have to deal with is not outside – it is inside my ministry. The
civil servants have been doing their best to frustrate my efforts and to
carry on just as they did in the days of the Shah. I have to get rid of two
levels of officials and make use of the third layer.'

The intellectuals were not trusted, and in any case they had no
practical proposals for dealing with current problems. In these early
days, when Khomeini was accessible to all, he found himself daily
bombarded with grandiose plans drawn up by the intellectuals on
every conceivable subject, which had little or no relevance to the
country's needs. On the other hand, there were many technicians,
who had been educated abroad and who had remained abroad to avoid
working for a regime they detested, and officials from international
agencies such as the UN and the World Bank, who had, as Khomeini
conceded, much to offer. But most of these, having returned home
eager to see if the Revolution could make use of their services, sadly
came to the conclusion that the time for them was not yet.

The bourgeoisie, who had for the most part abandoned the Shah in
his last years, now found themselves in a world for which they could
feel no sympathy and which showed no sympathy for them. There
was chaos in the streets and in the markets; trade and credit had come
to a halt; there seemed nothing for them to do or to hope for.

So the vacuum was there, and though a Deputy Prime Minister
with responsibility for Revolutionary Affairs, Ibrahim Yazdi, had
been appointed, who was supposed to coordinate and reconcile all the
forces behind the Revolution, this proved no more than window-
dressing. There was only one authority in the country. As Yazdi
himself said to me, the Revolution consisted of one man, the Imam,
and the millions of his followers, with nothing in between.

The result was that when, after a few weeks, Khomeini did quit
Tehran and return to his home in Qom, he did not go as a private
citizen, or as a saint, or as a teacher about to reassemble his *hawza*
around him. The problems he was leaving behind him were too big
for any person or any group of people to cope with, so all Tehran went
to Qom with him. In fact if not in name, Khomeini remained the

government. In vain he protested that it was not his wish to be a ruler. But if he was not to be a ruler or a private citizen, what was he to be? The answer was of his own choosing. He would be an arbiter.

There was plenty of scope for arbitration. The new forces were divided. There was conflict between the mullahs and the intellectuals, and between the insiders and the outsiders. The intellectuals – men like Beni-Sadr, Yazdi, Shemran and Qotbzadeh – were not 'seculars', as they were sometimes wrongly labelled, for they too believed that the Revolution must have an Islamic character, but they had had a western education and naturally saw things differently from the mullahs. Then, as in so many revolutions, there was a rivalry between those who had remained all the time in Iran, facing the tortures of Savak and the bullets of the army, and those who had organized the revolution abroad and returned in triumph with the Imam. No one faction was strong enough to dominate the others. Some of the mullahs had strong local support, but none had a truly national following. Many of the intellectuals returning from abroad did not even own a house, let alone a power base. Beni-Sadr, for example, was still a lodger in his sister's house in Tehran when he was elected president, his only personal possessions there amounting to a few books he had brought back with him.

It seemed to Khomeini much better that the differences, often acute, between these various groupings should come out into the open while he was still alive and, thanks to his unique prestige, able to resolve them, rather than that they should fester and break out after his death – and he was feeling that his end could not be far off. So he set about creating a balance. As in the American Constitution there are checks and balances between the President, Congress, and the judiciary, so in revolutionary Iran there was to be a balance between the President and the Majlis, between the governmental machine and the mullahs.

Khomeini's nominee for the presidency was his loyal supporter, the head of his Paris Komitay and organizer of his Paris sojourn, Beni-Sadr. Not that he received Khomeini's endorsement in so many words; but few had much doubt about whom they were expected to vote for in the presidential election. On one occasion before the election, I had been invited to dine with Beni-Sadr at the house of his sister and brother-in-law. He was late in turning up, having been delayed by business at the Revolutionary Council, and I said I would go away and come back later. But as I was leaving the house I met Khomeini's grandson Hussein coming in. He greeted me: 'So you are going to have dinner with the first President of the Iranian Republic?' I told him he had just given me an important item of news, and though he tried to pretend that he had only been joking it was clear who Khomeini was going to vote for. Beni-Sadr duly got seventy-six per cent of the votes, and if Khomeini's wishes had been more explicit he would probably have got a hundred per cent.

If a representative of the laity was to enjoy the presidency, the mullahs were to have their reward in the Majlis. When a general election was held in March and May 1980, the Islamic Republican Party, led by Ayatollah Beheshti, was duly successful, gaining a majority of the 270 seats. At the same time, to give a more formal sanction to his own position, Khomeini decided that the 1906 constitution should be amplified by an amendment laying down that when a *faqih* (such as himself) was available, he should be the supreme authority in the state, but that in the absence of such a person this authority should rest in a committee, its members acting as trustees for the *faqih*.

In another move aimed at eliminating any threat to his authority, Khomeini disposed of the only other divine who enjoyed a large personal following, Ayatollah Shariatmadari. It was known that the Americans had been hoping to make use of Shariatmadari. Khomeini visited him, showed him documents which had been found in the imperial archives, and in half an hour it was all over. Shariatmadari disappeared from the scene.

But the delicate balancing act envisaged by the revolutionary arbiter did not work. What emerged was not a balance, but deadlock. Bazargan, Khomeini's first choice for the premiership, was its first victim. He resigned in November 1979, and when I saw him soon afterwards and asked what had prompted his resignation, his answer consisted simply of two Arabic words – words which, like so many others, have become part of the Persian vocabulary: *mudakhalat* (interference) and *muzahamat* (crowding). Bazargan always maintained that if he had been given five years he could have built up a strong party. The same sort of plea was heard from other old-guard politicians. But in a hurricane, who talks of five years' grace – or even of one?

Yazdi was another early casualty of the political deadlock, finding himself powerless as Minister for Revolutionary Affairs. He was undoubtedly handicapped because he had lived for a long time in America, but it is doubtful whether anyone else could have done better. He went to the Ministry of Foreign Affairs, but had no better luck there than its other occupants, Beni-Sadr, Sanjabi and Qotbzadeh.

As President, Beni-Sadr found that he was unable to appoint ministers of his choice, even though he was prepared to settle for control over only a few key posts, such as foreign affairs and economics. The mullah majority in the Majlis blocked all his nominations. In the end he had to accept as prime minister a man forced upon him by the mullahs, Mohammed Ali Rajai, whom he made no secret of thinking was totally unfitted for the job.

One bizarre consequence of this conflict between President and Prime Minister led to a good deal of misunderstanding abroad. After the war with Iraq had broken out, and when there was to be a debate about it in the Security Council, Beni-Sadr wanted to send as Iran's representative before the Council Ali Shams Ardakhani, then serving as Iran's ambassador in Kuwait, having been appointed to this post by Beni-Sadr when he was Foreign Minister. When he became President, Beni-Sadr had wanted to make Ardakhani Foreign Minister, but Rajai had refused to accept him. Now he refused to let him address the Council; it would, Rajai claimed, look as if the veto on Ardakhani as Foreign Minister was being sidestepped. To make quite certain that this did not happen, Rajai decided to go to New York himself. This he did, creating widespread speculation that the real purpose of his journey was to start up direct talks with the Americans about the hostages. But in fact he had no such intention; his New York trip was purely a reflection of Iran's internal power struggle.

Another element in the equation which has emerged to make a balance between the revolutionary forces even harder to maintain is the students. They are particularly interesting because it is probably from among them that future political groupings and political leaders will emerge. They are, as I can testify, very idealistic, proud of having captured the attention of the world, but astonishingly naive about many things. They really seemed to think, when I spoke to them, that the whole of the rest of the Islamic world was looking to them for leadership. Because of the intensity of their Islamic beliefs they have become allies of the majority of the Majlis, thus producing the paradox of mullahs and universities uniting against the so-called seculars, who might in any normal conditions be expected to provide the students with their natural leadership.

Another complication has been Khomeini's poor health. He is nearly eighty, and, after his return to Qom and more than one heart attack, the energy he showed in exile weakened. It became impossible for him to concentrate for more than twenty minutes at a time. Although all important questions continue to come to him for decision, his reactions are instinctive rather than thought out. He reads no reports. In the early days after his return to Qom he used to complain that every day he was being sent three reports – one from the Foreign Ministry about foreign security, one about internal affairs, and one on economic matters. He begged the officials in Tehran to stop sending them. 'I never read them,' he said.

In Qom there is no formal method of conducting business. The direct, personal relationship which Khomeini has maintained with the masses has rendered abortive all attempts at creating some sort of real political life in Iran. Every morning his supporters come to him from all over Iran, in buses, taxis, any way they can manage. He greets them from the roof of his house, and has a brief dialogue with their leader. It would be too much to expect that all this adulation has had no effect – Khomeini is but human, after all – and one result of it has been to persuade him that the more formal machinery of government is relatively unimportant. Institutions, he thinks, can take their time, for what are they compared with the fact that he and the masses are in constant contact and understand each other? He is the Imam, and the Imam has returned to his people.

Khomeini is extremely shrewd, but his single-mindedness at times leads him to adopt attitudes which can only make one gasp. 'The Revolution did not take place to provide people with food,' he told me. No doubt man cannot live by bread alone, but the problem of unemployment, already acute under the Shah, has grown worse since the Revolution, and those without work naturally want enough to eat, and the jobs which alone can provide that. Khomeini is not interested in economic theories. When challenged, he will, as I have said, point out that the officers who have seized power in so many Arab countries, and the princes who have inherited power, know as little about economics as he does; and as a *faqih* he fairly lays claim to more wisdom than they. But the others are susceptible to argument and to advice; how can anyone argue with absolutes, or offer advice to a *faqih* whose inspiration comes from somewhere outside?

Post-revolutionary Iran has been in desperate need of some form of economic planning. Although oil production has been cut back, there are still three million barrels of Iranian oil reaching world markets every day, which means a daily income of $120–150 million. There should be some agreed programme for making the best use of this revenue. President Beni-Sadr explained to me that there were many projects which had been started under the former regime and which it would have been sensible to complete – not all the enterprises sponsored by the Shah were inspired by *folie de grandeur*. For example, there was a $600 million project for new housing outside Tehran which would have provided much-needed homes for hundreds of families, and which could have been completed after the Revolution in three months of concentrated work. But nothing was done. Beni-Sadr would have liked to see the adoption of a short-term plan to cover worthwhile projects already started and capable of completion in about a year, and after that a long-term plan for orderly development.

But instead of this the people have continued to be summoned day after day for fresh and virtually uncontrolled demonstrations. How can a country be said to be governed where students are allowed to arrest a cabinet minister simply because they happen to have come across a document showing that once in the past he had met someone from the American Embassy?

It was to Khomeini, and not to Bazargan, that people went if they wanted something done. It was the Imam and his family, not the cabinet, who mattered in the eyes of the people. The fact that Khomeini was reputed to be easily swayed by the last person he spoke to made matters worse. Discussions would take place between Khomeini and a visitor or group of visitors, and subsequently bits of these discussions would be made public by the participants and presented as definite rulings by the Imam. The result was total confusion.

It has to be admitted that Khomeini showed enormous skill as a revolutionary strategist. He had the patience and determination required to effect the overthrow of a formidable regime. He showed a sensitivity to the moods and yearnings of his people which is almost unique in Persian history. This will always ensure him a prominent place in the story of our times. But his inability to consolidate the ground gained must severely detract from his claims to true greatness.

Those who know him appreciate that Khomeini is a kindly man, but he does not trouble to present the softer side of his nature to the world. When the Pope approached him on the subject of the American hostages his answer was a scathing attack in medieval language: 'Do not concern yourself with what is happening in Iran. Turn your eyes towards what is happening in America. Why did you remain silent when Jerusalem was occupied?' – and so on. It was not to be expected that Khomeini should learn the language of diplomacy, but he ought to have let his diplomats talk to other diplomats.

There can be no doubt that many of the excesses of the early days of the Revolution created a thoroughly bad impression in other countries, which neither Khomeini nor those closest to him did anything to counteract. There were arbitrary arrests, and an estimated 55,000 people were brought to trial, often in secret courts and without any opportunity to defend themselves. About 350 people were executed in the first three months, and executions have continued ever since, often on what appear to be the flimsiest charges and after trials which are a mockery of justice. Khomeini insists that these trials and sentences have been governed by *qassas* (punishment), not by *intiqam* (revenge), but the distinction is not always obvious.

Khomeini thinks and talks in terms of absolutes, and he is conditioned absolutely by his view of Shi'a history. He can never forget the tragic results of the battle of Siffin, and this has left in him a profound suspicion of anything to do with arbitration or compromise.

It is in foreign as much as domestic affairs that his inability to compromise has created complications which a wider knowledge of the world – or, should one say, a more worldly approach – could have avoided. Iran remains one of the biggest strategic prizes in the world, thanks to its geographical position and natural wealth. Whoever rules it – or fails to rule it – Iran will remain an area of conflict between the super-powers. But Khomeini quarrelled with Russia, and allowed the American hostage problem to be exploited by the mullahs, who for their own purposes wanted to keep the country in a perpetual ferment. The hostage problem was, in fact, ineptly handled on all sides.

Its mishandling was something of which I was to have direct experience. I hope I have been able to explain why I thought the occupation of the American Embassy was understandable, if not strictly justifiable, though I also thought that every political act should have an aim as well as a motive, and that the Revolution's mistake was its failure to make the world understand what it hoped to achieve by holding on to the hostages.

My own interest in the hostages was strictly journalistic, but because I had been inside the American Embassy, and talked to the students there as well as to other leaders of the Revolution, I found myself, at the beginning of 1980, while I was passing through London, approached by a well-known politician who was a friend of mine and who asked me if I was willing to go to Washington to meet the Secretary of State, Cyrus Vance, in connection with the question of how to get the hostages released. I explained that this was impossible, as I had only recently come back from Washington. My friend then asked if I was prepared to meet a representative of the American government in London. I said I was, provided he had nothing to do with the CIA. Was Harold Saunders suitable, asked my friend. I said he certainly was, as I knew him personally and respected him, having met him in Cairo when he was accompanying Henry Kissinger on his 1973 disengagement shuttle.

The next day the Under-Secretary of State arrived unofficially in London, and we had a private meeting at the flat belonging to my friend. Harold Saunders asked if I was ready to help President Carter, to which I replied that I was ready to help the Iranians, for I felt it was they who stood to gain most from a satisfactory solution of the hostage problem. It had become plain that the hostages were not only bedevilling Iran's relations with the outside world, but were also complicating the power struggle going on between rival factions inside Iran. It was by then generally – and correctly – assumed that one of the secular leaders would be rewarded with the presidency, while the mullahs would be allowed to maintain control in the Majlis. Qotbzadeh was hoping that a group of French lawyers, working on behalf of the Iranian government, of which he was Foreign Minister, would succeed in obtaining an order for the arrest of the Shah, who was then in Panama, and that this would enhance his chances of the presidency. But Qotbzadeh failed to realize that the only thing which counted was the backing of Khomeini, and this was to go to Beni-Sadr and not to him.

After Beni-Sadr had been duly elected at the end of January, the Americans thought he would be able to arrange for the release of the hostages – which only showed how little they understood the true position inside Iran. At the same time they tried to work through the United Nations, and the Security Council called on the services of the Secretary-General, Kurt Waldheim, who, with the prospect of a third term of office looming in 1982, was nothing loath. Meanwhile all sorts of volunteers were offering themselves as intermediaries, knowing that, thanks to the American media's obsessive interest in the hostages, this was the surest road to instant publicity.

The Americans were the more ready to clutch at any straw because they had no direct contact at all with the Iranians, and consequently reacted violently to every rumour coming out of the country. There was a moment, for example, before the UN mission arrived in Tehran, when the Americans were extremely agitated over reports that the students planned to kill all the hostages rather than hand them over to the mission, should this be ordered by their government. I was able to confirm from friends in Tehran and Qom there was absolutely no foundation for this rumour, but it was depressing to find a super-power not simply badly informed but totally unable to understand the thinking of a people with whom they had been in the closest contact for thirty years or more.

I had a number of other meetings with Harold Saunders and with various Iranian officials, but broke them off after the Tapaz raid had effectively sabotaged all attempts at mediation. But the Americans did not give up, and not long afterwards I was again contacted by the same friend who had arranged the original meeting with Harold Saunders. He had, he said, received a communication from Washington which seemed to him so strange that the only thing he could do was to hand it over to me. It turned out to be a directive, intended to be used by me in a new approach which it was hoped I would agree to make to the authorities in Tehran. It was indeed a strange document, and as an illustration of how far removed from reality American thinking had moved I cannot do better than quote it verbatim.

'The concept is to have Heikal go to Iran and present to Beni–Sadr a way to use rescue disaster to get the hostages released and the issue behind him. Heikal would persuade him of the unique opportunity this represents for him to ride the crest of Islamic nationalism, to solidify his own position. To the extent Khomeini shares the desire to be rid of the problem the concept could be presented to him.

'The themes Heikal can draw on are as follows:

'A. The success of Iran's revolution has been clearly and finally demon-strated with the humiliating defeat of the US government's rescue mission. God has shown the world that, no matter how powerful the enemy, righteousness accrues to the aggrieved party, and in this case the moral superiority of the Islamic Republic is there for all to see. Therefore:

'B. The American hostages have served the purpose Iran has wanted. They have served as a pretext to show the world dramatically the evils of the Shah's regime and the US government's support for it, and America's inability to mount the rescue operation is the second and final attestation to the justness of their being taken. (For example, the Iranian act brought about an American reaction which only underscored in its failure the message which Iran originally wanted to get across.) The hostages just are not needed any longer.

'C. The hostages will be released. Iran never intended them any harm anyway. The gesture dramatizes Islam's magnanimity and compassion. There was never any hatred for the American people, only the US government. (Let the hostages go now and make the Americans look even more foolish and inept. Perhaps fly them out via Tapaz along with newspaper correspondents and note down their disparaging comments, etc.) Iran and Islamic Republic emerge as both victorious and morally superior.

'D. The captors emerge victorious and are national heroes. They have not hurt anybody. They have honored the dictates of the Imam. They will be rewarded amply by the government, and recognized especially by the Imam. It may be the last time the captor force can be gotten off the compound without somebody in Iran losing face in the process.

'E. The release itself should be announced by Iran itself as being a dramatic act of clemency and mercy for the hostages, which was taken by Khomeini himself. The procedure for release affords Iran tremendous propaganda opportunity, cloaking the whole miserable five months in an aura of decency and mercy. Iran thus refurbishes the image of Islam, something all Moslems in the world would wish to happen. The US government, as opposed to the American people, is again scored for its enmity towards just causes, and in no way represents lessening of Iran's battle with US government or a compromise with it. End message.'

I was to get other messages from Washington after that, but my information from Tehran was that all lines of communication with the Americans had become hopelessly mixed up. The Iranians had no idea who was supposed to be talking to whom, or which of the many signals they were receiving represented the real American attitude. It was at this point that I and some others suggested that it would be more sensible to drop the idea of intermediaries. The Algerian role suggested itself as an alternative. Here was a country which already represented Iranian interests in America, which had a government that was both Islamic and revolutionary, and which was served in Washington by an extremely able ambassador, Abdel Karim Ghuraib. It proved to be he who was able to set in motion the process of negotiation which was brought to a successful conclusion in January 1981.

I think it has to be admitted that in the final analysis the Iranians lost more over the hostages than they gained. True, they had, through the hostages, humiliated their arch-enemy, America, but they were not, as they liked to boast, the first to humble a super-power. The real defeat for the Americans was the fall of the Shah. There was no need to add to that, and the continued detention of the hostages was used by America to isolate Iran and to make its rulers look both ruthless and incompetent.

I can understand Khomeini's point of view. When I said to him that taking the hostages was contrary to international law, his answer was to ask what benefit international law had ever brought to Iran. Had it prevented the Shah from laying his hands on the country's wealth? Had it stopped the Americans from violently overthrowing a constitutional Iranian government and killing its leaders? I had to admit that it had not. 'Very well,' said Khomeini. 'We do not consider that international law has ever been respected when it applies to Iran, and we do not see why we should respect it now ourselves.' However reasonable this argument might be, it was not one which was readily understood by the rest of the world, and as the dispute over the hostages dragged on it became less and less convincing.

# 16

# FIRE OVER THE GULF

IN ONE of his more exuberant moments Khomeini said that he 'would make the Gulf a ball of fire if anyone dares to touch us.' Whether this threat is carried out or not, it is certainly true that nowhere in the world did the sound of Khomeini's artillery have more ominous reverberations than in the Gulf. And this not just because one entire shore of the Gulf is Iranian territory, but even more because of the highly explosive mixture bequeathed to the area by the combination of geography and recent political developments.

The Gulf produces half of the oil that the rest of the world consumes. It has also come to be the importer of half the arms that industrial countries export. This uniquely sensitive two-way traffic of oil and armaments is largely in the hands of states so small that, though their revenues may be reckoned in billions, their populations can be reckoned in thousands. Nor are these small populations any longer homogeneous. Wealth has sucked into the Gulf many foreign immigrants, not least Iranian Shi'is, who have considerably diluted the original inhabitants.

In recent years the political structure of the Gulf had come to be organized on three distinct levels. At the lowest level were the small states strung along its southern and western shores – Kuwait, Bahrein, Qatar, the United Arab Emirates (UAE), and Muscat. The next level consisted of three medium-sized powers, all with outlet to its waters – Saudi Arabia, Iraq and Iran. But above these Gulf states proper brooded the ever-watchful eyes of the two super-powers, their fleets sailing the Indian Ocean, and their interests beyond the Straits of Hormuz so real that neither could allow the other to acquire the paramount position there which Britain had exercised in the century before the coming of oil.

In spite of the complexities and hazards of this three-tier structure, the smaller Gulf states had over the years adjusted themselves to it reasonably well. They had been content to leave the problems of super-power diplomacy to those more directly involved in it – Saudi Arabia, Iran, and the country to which they had always looked for leadership in the Arab world, Egypt. Their more immediate concern

was to stay on good terms with their larger neighbours, Saudi Arabia
and Iran, and as the Shah's ambitions to be recognized as sole policeman of the area became more obvious and emphatic it was his
goodwill especially they sought to cultivate. He, after all, was the
absolute ruler of thirty-seven million subjects, creator of a great
military and economic power, commander of the only sizeable navy in
Gulf waters, a man who daily hit the headlines with the splendour of
his court and the grandeur of his ambitions, the man who was wooed
by the West and who had helped to throw western economies into
confusion when he took a leading part in the campaign for vastly
increased oil prices, the man whose intelligence network knew everything and whose secret police were the object of universal dread –
their policeman, protector, and friend.

It became a custom for each Gulf ruler to pay an annual visit to the
court in Tehran. When what was to prove to be the last of such visits
took place, in August 1978, conditions had undergone a striking
change from what the rulers had become accustomed to: though he
could not know it, Sheikh Aisa bin-Sulman al-Khalifa of Bahrein
arrived just after the Shah had made the momentous helicopter flight
over the capital which gave him for the first time visual evidence that
the people were demonstrating against his rule. The Bahreinis first
realized that something was wrong when, after being met as usual by
the Shah at the airport, they went with him only as far as the Shahyad
Monument. Then, instead of continuing by car, they found two
helicopters waiting, one of which took the Shah to the Niavaran
Palace while the other took the visitors to the Golistan Palace. There
were whispers that this change in routine was made necessary by
demonstrations in the streets.

At the dinner given in their honour that evening the Bahreinis could
not help noticing the atmosphere of nervousness and tension. The
Empress was chain-smoking, and the Shah, who normally did not
touch cigarettes, was smoking too. During the meal the Shah al-
ternated between periods of complete silence, when he seemed to be
paying no attention to what was being said, and sudden outbursts of
recrimination: 'It is you small states that are the weak points in the
Gulf – you and the Saudis. You are responsible for the weakness of the
area. You are exposing it to the threat of communism. I've been told
that you are thinking of establishing diplomatic relations with the
Soviet Union. Why do you want to do this? Not that I mind – but if
you are going to establish relations with the Soviet Union you must
simultaneously start up relations with China – simultaneously, not a

minute later. The Chinese are the only people who know what is going on in the Soviet Union. I tell you, communism is spreading in the whole area of the Gulf. Some people say they can't detect any trace of it, but I tell you that if you scratch any tree in the area you will find it exudes the red fluid of communism.'*

The Empress spoke a great deal about her son, the Crown Prince, who had chosen flying as his career and was then undergoing his pilot's training at Houston, Texas. She said she worried all the time about the possibility of an accident. The only consolation was that when she woke in the morning she knew it was too early in America for him to have started flying, and when she went to bed at night his hours of training would have finished. During the day she had other matters to occupy her mind. But although the Shah had encouraged their son in his chosen career, the Empress felt that he ought to come back home and start the political training he must have before he inherited the throne. The Bahreinis came away extremely worried. They had not found anybody in the court or in the government who was prepared to talk to them seriously about anything.

The Bahreinis' anxieties were soon to be shared by the other Gulf rulers. Nor was the growing unrest in Iran the only reason for their disquiet. Another of the props on which they had come to rely, Egypt, was being knocked from under them. Their first misgivings had come at the beginning of 1977, with reports of food rioting in Cairo. All the Gulf rulers knew of the advice King Abdel Aziz had given to his sons before he died, that the health of the Arabs in general could be judged by the health of Egypt; if Egypt was sick, the whole Arab world was sick. What worried them now was not simply that Cairo had, for the first time for many years, seen serious riots, with considerable loss of life, but that the riots were officially said to be the work of communists. To the wealthy rulers of the Gulf the spectre haunting them was the spectre of communism.

But their concern over the Cairo riots was nothing to the astonishment with which they heard of President Sadat's proposal to visit Jerusalem. Some of them may have secretly admired his boldness, and have taken comfort from his Knesset speech. There he seemed to give nothing away, and to restate the point of view of almost all Arabs, including themselves, in a manner which they could readily endorse. But then came Camp David, where the results turned

---

* Information from an interview with Sheikh Mohammed al-Khalifa, Foreign Minister of Bahrein.

out to be very different from what they had been led to expect. The Americans made the blunder of trying to pressure other Arabs into backing the agreement, because Sadat had signed only on receiving a guarantee from Carter that he would persuade Saudi Arabia and Jordan to fall into line (and, if they did, obviously other Arab states, including the Gulf, would fall into line too). Carter gave the guarantee and immediately sent his Secretary of State, Cyrus Vance, off on a recruiting campaign – in fact, the first question President Sadat asked the American Ambassador, Herman Eilts, who came to see him off on his return journey to Cairo was, 'Has Vance left yet?'

He had, but his mission was a failure, as was a follow-up mission by Brzezinski, who did some rougher arm-twisting. Carter's misreading of the situation was due to a mixture of trying to be too clever and of naivety. While the Camp David negotiations were in progress King Khaled of Saudi Arabia was undergoing treatment in a Philadelphia hospital. Carter contacted him by telephone and asked him to give his blessing 'for peace'. An interpreter relayed the message and brought back the King's reply, which was that certainly he would give his blessing 'for peace'. This was seen by the King as a simple exchange of courtesies – how could he refuse to bless peace? – but was seized on by Carter as endorsement of a particular and highly controversial bargain then in the making.

For when the Saudis and their friends in the Gulf examined the Camp David agreements they could find nothing in it about Jerusalem; and for the Saudis, whose legitimacy depends on their role as guardians of the Holy Places of Islam, this was a fatal omission. Moreover, President Sadat's initiative coincided with growing evidence of what the Iranian Revolution meant in human terms. Rulers who had been for years accustomed to be the guests of the mighty in Iran – the princes, the generals, the millionaires – now found their former hosts turning up on their doorsteps, destitute and begging to be helped to catch a plane to Europe. In Dubai there was a regular traffic in small boats smuggling refugees from the southern coasts of Iran to safety on the Arabian side of the Gulf. Not only did the Gulf rulers hear on radio and television of the storm which was destroying an empire; like the courts of Europe after the French Revolution, they now heard from the lips of royalist émigrés terrible stories of what revolution means.

So by the beginning of 1979 the world to which the Gulf rulers were accustomed had changed out of all recognition. But there were further shocks to come. The Peacock Throne might have toppled; Egypt might have opted out of the Arab equation; but at least their third prop, the royal house of Saud, seemed to be standing firm. Then occurred one of the most extraordinary incidents in recent Middle Eastern history, and one which can be directly attributed to the influence of the Iranian Revolution. This was the attempt in December 1979 by a group of fanatics to take over the Great Mosque in Mecca.

A cardinal element in the belief of the Shi'is is, as has been seen, that the Imam will eventually return to fill the world with justice. But the idea of Mahdi, one guided by God, who will restore the faith and usher in a golden age, is a popular belief among Sunni Moslems also. The Mahdi whose followers conquered most of the Sudan in the 1880s is only one of many such leaders who have arisen throughout history. A well-known saying attributed to the Prophet Mohammed declared that at the beginning of every century (calculated by the Hijra calendar) a messenger will appear, bearing his (the Prophet's) name, and will be recognized by the people in the Great Mosque at Mecca between the *Hajar* (the Black Stone) and the *Maqam Ibrahim*. 1979 saw the beginning of the fourteenth century according to the Hijra calendar, just as the emergence of the Sudanese Mahdi marked the beginning of the thirteenth. As the new century approached there was a general atmosphere of expectancy among the pious. They recalled the Prophet's words and they were conscious of the resurgence of Islam, particularly in Iran; some, indeed, went so far as to identify Khomeini as the long-awaited Imam.

One of those strongly affected by this apocalyptic atmosphere was a Saudi Arabian called Juhaiman el-Oteibi, a man of commanding presence, a Wahhabi fundamentalist of the strictest and most puritanical sort. Although he had never been in Egypt, Oteibi had had a small book called *The Real Islam* printed by one of the small presses near el-Azhar. It attracted no attention. He had fallen out with the Saudi authorities and had been arrested, moved to Kuwait and deported. Then he came across a young man called Abdullah Qahtani. Here indeed was someone bearing the name of the Prophet, for Mohammed's father's name was Abdullah and Qahtan was the legendary ancestor of the Arabs. Oteibi persuaded Qahtani of the great destiny awaiting him, and took him round the tribes to present the Mahdi to them. There can be no doubt that he was activated by purely religious motives; had he wished to stage a coup he would have gone to Riyadh, not to Mecca. As it was, he collected about 400 people round him, armed tribesmen with a tradition of warfare and ready to die for the cause in which they now generally believed.

Oteibi, however, did not expect to die. He was convinced that when he showed Qahtani to the people in the Mosque they would recognize him for what he was and give him their acceptance (*bay'a*). He hoped that King Khaled would be in the Mosque at the time, and he planned to arrest him and perhaps take some other members of the royal house hostage. His preparations were made with military precision. Some months before the appointed day he began storing arms and supplies in the cellars beneath the Mosque. These *serdabs*, as they are called, provided an underground warren where he could work undetected. In the old days, when travelling was much more difficult than it is today, many pilgrims stayed behind in Mecca after the *haj* ceremonies were over, either because they were too ill to move or because they had no money for the return journey. In the cellars they could find refuge, but in these days of affluence and air travel the refuge was no longer needed.

When the day came, Oteibi and his followers entered the Mosque from their underground hideaway. He seized the microphone used by the preacher of the sermon and harangued the congregation: 'Your attention, O Moslems! Allahu Akbar! The Mahdi has appeared! He is here between the *Hajar* and the *Maqam*! Remember the words of the Prophet! Now is the time! This is the man! Bismillah ar-Rahman ar-Rahim!'

But his words fell on deaf ears. The people did not respond as Oteibi had thought they would. They watched in bewilderment, some leaving hurriedly, some staying out of curiosity, but there was no sign of a spontaneous move to give the people's *bay'a* to the Mahdi. Then the guards moved in, and the shooting started. Oteibi too was armed, and his followers knew what to do. They occupied the minarets, which gave them control over the entrances to the Mosque as well as its interior.

King Khaled had not been in the Mosque at the time, so escaped death or captivity, but he and his government were taken completely by surprise and had no idea how to act. This was, after all, the holiest place in the whole Islamic world. What would be the reaction if they used tanks to break open the doors of the Mosque, which the insurgents had closed? For days both the army and the National Guard showed themselves quite incapable of bringing the situation under control.

Evidence of the total confusion which reigned during this time is provided by the experience of King Hussein of Jordan. Like all Moslems, he was deeply shocked when he heard of what was happening in the Mosque, but unlike others he felt he was in a position to do something about it. For some years he had had, by agreement with the Saudis, one division of his army earmarked to intervene there in case of trouble. A special link had been established between the two kingdoms, and the commander of the Jordanian army, General Zaid ibn Shakir, immediately called up his opposite number in Riyadh, using the special code signal which had been agreed on for use in emergency. But he got no reply. For four days he went on trying to raise the Saudi commander-in-chief, but always without success. Finally he decided to try the ordinary telephone, in spite of the fact that conversations on it would of course not be confidential. This time he got through. He urged the Saudi general to open the special link so that they could talk in secret; had they not received his signals? Oh yes, he was told, we got your messages all right, but you must understand that we have been much too busy to answer them.

What the Saudi authorities were trying to do was to find a way of listening to the insurgents, who had retreated to the *serdabs*, and so learn what they were planning to do. They found an underground path which led them close to the insurgents, but as soon as troops tried to force their way in by it they found themselves exposed to fire from the defenders. So a team of foreign commandos specially trained for this sort of operation had to be flown in. By surrounding the whole area occupied by the insurgents, and with the use of sensitive listening devices and gas, they were eventually able to kill or capture all of them – but not until fifteen days after the first attack, and day by day the insurgents had been winning more sympathy inside and outside Saudi Arabia. As one Saudi officer said, 'If they had done this in any other place but the Holy Mosque in Mecca, I would have joined them.' He almost certainly spoke for many.

Iran, Egypt, Mecca – as they looked around them, the Gulf rulers must have seen little but shifting sands. Nor was this the end. Hard on the heels of the Mosque affair came news of the Soviet intervention in Afghanistan, with all the changes in the global balance of power which that implied – changes, too, which were taking place on their own doorstep.

The reaction of the Carter administration to events in Iran and Afghanistan involved, among other things, a strategic redeployment of American forces in the Gulf area. It was hoped that this would reassure the rulers that they were not being left friendless or unprotected, but it had the contrary effect of making them more alarmed.

The Carter administration had always shown itself ham-fisted in its approach to the Gulf's problems; the clumsy follow-up to the Camp David agreements has already been mentioned. Now the Gulf rulers were not being helped by the almost daily insistence that they were America's friends – the 'moderates' – and that it was as such that they deserved to be looked after. They feared that this designation could become the kiss of death. I have not met a single Gulf ruler who did not complain to me about having these damaging labels attached to him. Even Beni-Sadr told me: 'This terrible habit of describing me as a "moderate" could destroy me.'

Any American visitor to the Gulf, be he politician, soldier or diplomat, felt obliged on his return to tell the media that he had found in the Gulf a healthy spirit of cooperation, and that here was an area of the world where America could count on her friends. Two days before I arrived in one Gulf state recently the American Deputy Secretary of Defense had been visiting there. He had a preliminary talk with the ruler, and just before the second meeting was due to start the ruler was shown the transcript of a news bulletin from the Voice of America in which the Deputy Secretary was reported as saying that American forces were going to be granted certain facilities there. When I spoke to the ruler he was understandably indignant. 'To begin with,' he said, 'the information was not true. But, more important, even if it had been it should never have been published.' The rulers cannot help regretting the greater tact which was shown by the more experienced imperial power that the Americans have replaced – Britain.

In fact, the conclusion which most Gulf rulers tended to draw from America's plans for the rapid redeployment of its forces in the area was that Washington either thought their regimes were tottering, or had doubts about their 'loyalty' and was preparing to replace them by some more reliable nominees. The one thing they did not think likely was the danger the American moves were ostensibly meant to counter – a Russian move into the Gulf on Afghanistan lines – since they knew, and they knew the Russians knew, that this would mean a crossing of the tacitly acknowledged frontier dividing the two super-powers' spheres of influence, and so touch off World War Three.

The rulers consequently began to take their own steps to adjust to the changed conditions and to look to their own security. As a start, they obviously had to find ways of talking to the new regime in Tehran, but their first attempts to do this were far from encouraging. Two lines of approach were decided upon: the Foreign Minister of Kuwait, Sheikh Sabah el-Ahmed el-Sabah, should go on an official visit to Tehran, and the Foreign Minister of Bahrein, Sheikh Mohammed Mubarak al-Khalifah, should get in touch with Ibrahim Yazdi, the Iranian Deputy Prime Minister and Minister for Revolutionary Affairs, while they were both in New York for the United Nations.

Sheikh Sabah's visit was a disaster. He arrived in Tehran with considerable publicity, and, having correctly concluded that the real source of authority in the country was the Ayatollah, asked if he could see him. His request was granted. The usual escort of police motor-cyclists, troops, Foreign Ministry officials and so on went with him to the airport, where two helicopters were waiting to take the party to Qom. Sheikh Sabah was a bit puzzled to find that everybody was apparently to accompany him, but concluded that the authorities liked to give him proper treatment, and that as Qom probably lacked the manpower for a suitable cavalcade its ingredients had to be flown from Tehran. In Qom the whole party was transferred to buses and driven off to the Ayatollah's house. Sheikh Sabah wondered at what point the escort would melt away, but to his astonishment the whole lot of it piled into the house with him. It was clearly impossible for him to discuss anything of significance in front of this huge audience, and, as nobody suggested leaving the two of them alone, after an exchange of courtesies and compliments he asked permission to depart. His interview had lasted seven minutes. When he returned to Tehran and discussed what had happened with ministers, he was told: 'The Imam doesn't like to talk politics. He's there to give guidance.'

The Foreign Minister of Bahrein had rather better luck in New York. He saw Yazdi and had a frank talk with him. He complained that though the Gulf states were anxious to be on good terms with the new regime in Iran they continually found themselves attacked by it. They were accused of being imperialists and lackeys of the Shah, of oppressing their Shi'a minorities and allowing alcohol to be sold. 'But,' said Sheikh Mohammed Mubarak, 'we in Bahrein are a small country only trying to preserve our independence. When the Shah was there, naturally we were afraid of him. Who in Iran was not afraid of him? But we did not remain the Shah's men after he had left. You accuse us of cooperating with the Americans – certainly we try to cooperate with them, as with everybody else. As for our Shi'a subjects, this is an old argument which we used to have with the Shah. But as far as Bahrein is concerned let us not argue about statistics. You say the Shi'is are in a majority in Bahrein; we say they are in a minority. Let's leave it that they are fifty per cent. Then there is this question of alcohol. It is true that liquor is on sale in Bahrein, but not for our own people. You must realize that Bahrein is the first Arab country to move into the post-oil phase. Our own oil is exhausted, so we have to find other sources of revenue. We are turning Bahrein into a major centre for commerce and international communications. All the world is now passing through Bahrein, and we must be able to provide the sort of treatment travellers expect.'

Some at least of this message got across. But by the time the two Foreign Ministers reported back to their colleagues Yazdi had been dismissed, so that of the two meetings only that of Sheikh Sabah with Khomeini had any relevence, and that offered no cheer.

If talking to Tehran was difficult, finding a substitute protector for the policeman Shah, and an alternative to the policemen Americans, was even more of a problem. But quietly, without any fanfares, an Association of Gulf States came into being. In the spring of 1979 an inaugural meeting was held at the Saudi air base, Khamis Mishait, after which there were regular meetings of specialist ministers – for security, information, and so on – and an attempt to work out a common policy on such matters as foreign relations and oil. Later the Iraqis were invited to attend some of the meetings, not as full members, for there were some matters the Gulf governments preferred to discuss without them, but at least as potentially useful partners.

Sultan Qabus of Oman had some ideas of his own about what needed doing. In 1975, when relations between Iran and Iraq had improved, President Sadam Hussein visited Tehran, and he and the Shah discussed ways and means of ensuring freedom of navigation in the Gulf. The Shah wanted some form of joint defence planning, involving a combined naval force and bases, some of them in Oman. This was further than the Iraqis were prepared to go. But now, with the new regime installed in Tehran, the Sultan of Oman decided that the time had come to reactivate the Shah's plan. After all, over a thousand million dollars' worth of oil was passing each day through the Straits of Hormuz, which at one point are so narrow that the navigable channel is reduced to 600 metres, just sufficient space for two ships to pass. The world was showing understandable alarm at the implications of geography; Lloyd's had drastically increased insurance rates on shipping to the Gulf. What was feared was not so much a direct attack on the area by Russia but the possibility that the Straits might be mined, which would effectively block them to shipping, with disastrous consequences for all.

So Sultan Qabus, whose responsibility covered the southern shores of the Straits, decided that suitable precautions should be taken. What he had in mind was a force consisting of a flotilla of six or seven minesweepers and three squadrons of fighter and reconnaissance aircraft, on continuous patrol. However, he made the mistake of informing too many people of his plans. He told the Japanese, because they are wholly dependent on oil from the Gulf, but this annoyed his fellow rulers. If the plan was to be implemented, they said, they would prefer to do it on their own, and pay for it all, even if it was going to cost $100 million.

A significant feature of the new political scene in the Gulf is the involvement in it of Iraq. This reflects the profound change which has taken place in the alignment of forces in the Arab world over the past three or four years.

The natural fulcrum for the Arab world must always be Egypt, lying as it does across the bridge between North Africa and Asia, and possessing, thanks to the number and ability of its people, the necessary tradition of leadership. But when Egypt abdicates from its responsibilities as a leader, and chooses to go its own way alone, the rest of the Arab world inevitably regroups along sectional lines. And this is what has happened. The Maghreb has become absorbed in its internal squabbles – Morocco against Algeria, Tunisia against Libya. In the Fertile Crescent Syria has been directly involved in the Lebanese civil war and in a bitter quarrel with Iraq, while in the Arabian peninsula the Saudi Arabians have been trying to assert their leadership.

After the Revolution in Iran and President Sadat's journey to Jerusalem no Arab countries found a reassessment of their position more urgently necessary than Iraq and Saudi Arabia. A generation ago, in the days of Nuri Said and the Hashemites, all Iraq's ambitions were directed westwards, towards Syria, and towards realization of the dream of a single Fertile Crescent state which should unite the rival Umayyad and Abbasid capitals of Damascus and Baghdad. But now the centre of gravity had moved away from the Mediterranean to the Gulf, away from the Suez Canal to the Straits of Hormuz, and it was southwards and not westwards that the leaders of Iraq were directing their attention.

Iraq is, after all, one of the world's major oil-producing countries, and so potentially one of the richest. Originally its oil reached world markets through pipelines with their terminals on the eastern seaboard of the Mediterranean, but the wars with Israel and the troubles in Lebanon interrupted this flow, and now most of Iraq's oil is carried by tankers ploughing the waters of the Gulf.

Another consideration which brought Iraq and the Gulf states closer together was religion. A third of the population of Iraq is Shi'a, as are most Iranians, except for some of the minorities. Governments in Iran have always been firmly in Shi'a hands, and in Iraq since the foundation of the state after the First World War they have been in the hands of Sunni Moslems. In Syria, since General Hafez el-Asad came to power in 1971, the position has been reversed – a Sunni majority has been ruled by a government which is predominantly Shi'a. Although the Shi'is of Iran and Syria belong to different branches, being respectively Ja'afari and Nusseiri, to Sunnis this makes little difference. They are both Shi'is, and that is what matters.*

Casting their eyes northwards, the Gulf rulers saw that the government of President Sadam Hussein in Baghdad was hemmed in between the two Shi'a regimes of Iran and Syria, and that if by any chance it was replaced by a Shi'a government there would be a solid sea of Shi'ism from the confines of Pakistan to the Mediterranean. This was a prospect that alarmed them. So they began to pay increasing attention to their northern neighbour, Iraq, particularly since they found that the Saudis were preoccupied with the implications of the battle of the Mecca Mosque.

The leaders in Baghdad reciprocated this attention. Iraq has always felt that it had a leading role to play in the Arab world, and now realized that perhaps the Gulf rather than the Mediterranean was the area in which that role was destined to be played.

The Saudis were less certain of their role, held back by the

---

* Estimates of the number of Shi'is in the Gulf states vary, governments understandably tending to minimize their numbers and the Shi'is themselves to inflate them. For example:

|  | Total population | Government estimate of Shi'a percentage of population | Shi'a estimate of Shi'a percentage of population |
|---|---|---|---|
| Kuwait | 1,000,000 | 30 | 35 |
| Iraq | 12,000,000 | 36 | 70–75 |
| Bahrein | 250,000 | 50 | 60–70 |
| Saudi Arabia | 4,000,000 | 7 | 10–15 |

realization that, though their country is rich in resources, it is still in the process of organizing as a society and a state.★ Since the creation of the kingdom in 1932 its rulers have preferred to act as a strong number two to some other Arab state rather than strike out a line of their own. Thus, King Abdel Aziz ibn Saud was King Farouk's backer in the formation of the Arab League in 1944; King Saud supported Nasser in his opposition to the Baghdad Pact, and King Feisal stood staunchly behind President Sadat during and after the October war.

When the Saudis found themselves unable to go along with Sadat's Jerusalem initiative, they began by transferring their support to the new coalition developing between Syria and Iraq, and when this broke up they were prepared to continue their support on behalf of Iraq alone. But then Iraq became involved in a war. It was, in the end, Kuwait rather than Saudi Arabia which took the lead in rallying the states of the Arabian peninsula; its ruler sent a letter to all of them encouraging them not to be timid but to close their ranks. But at the Amman summit in November 1980 the Sheikh of Kuwait made a point of assuring President Sadam Hussein that this closing of the Arabian ranks was not directed against anybody.†

The war between Iraq and Iran took many people by surprise, but the seeds of it are plain to see in history. In recent years many ancient but dormant conflicts have broken out in open violence – Protestant and Catholic in Ulster; Maronite and Moslem in Lebanon; Chinese

---

★ See p. 76.

† The Kuwaitis have many qualities which justify them in taking an initiative. Their long tradition of trading has given them an understanding of money, and because the city was made up of several families which regarded themselves as equals there has been an openness in society which is not to be found in Saudi Arabia. Kuwait could boast a uniquely popular institution, the *diwaniyah*. This word, coming from the same root as 'divan', means a place for people to sit in. *Diwaniyahs* originated from the need fishermen and traders felt for somewhere where they could sit and talk when they came back from sea; and even when fishing and trade became subordinate to oil the *diwaniyahs* continued to flourish. Anybody could start one; all that was required was a room in a house where people could sit, and then the day for meetings to be made known. In their heyday, when there were up to four thousand *diwaniyahs*, any subject could come up for discussion – politics, literature, and specific local problems. Ministers as well as private individuals had their *diwaniyahs*, and speech was absolutely free; even attacks on the ruling family were permissible. Since the Constituent Assembly was suspended in 1976 these admirable institutions have perhaps lost some of their vigour, but the openness of society in Kuwait is also reflected in its press, which, though under increasing restraint, has today replaced the press of Egypt and Lebanon as the liveliest in the Arab world.

and Vietnamese. The hostility between Iraqis and Iranians could be seen as of that order.

As has been mentioned,★   the march of conquest of the Arab armies after the death of the Prophet Mohammed brought them into conflict with two ancient civilizations, Byzantium and Persia. The Umayyads in Syria absorbed the Byzantine Empire's population and its administration, the bulk of the people accepting both Islam and Arabism. Not so in Iran, where Islam − or rather a minority version of it − was accepted, but Arabism rejected. Through the centuries the border area between the Arabs in the land of the Twin Rivers and the Persians has been chronically disturbed, and never properly demarcated along its whole length.

The agreement signed in Algiers in 1975 between President Sadam Hussein and the Shah was supposed to settle all outstanding problems between the two countries. It did, in fact, resolve what had become Iraq's most urgent problem, the war in Kurdistan. President Sadam Hussein told me that when he went to Algiers he was authorized by his colleagues in the Revolutionary Council to make any concessions he might feel necessary to obtain the ending of the war, provided they did not involve the cession of any national territory or the safety of the Revolution. To illustrate how real the crisis was, he revealed that the Iraqi forces had by then only five heavy bombs left for their aircraft, and a thousand shells for their heavy artillery, and they had no prospect of getting additional supplies of ammunition from anywhere.

Fighting in Kurdistan duly came to an end. Concessions were made to Iran in the Shatt-el-Arab, but as part of an overall definition of the frontier, whereby Iraq was to receive about two hundred square

---

★ One problem in Saudi Arabia to which sufficient attention has not always been paid is the uncertainty over the rules governing inheritance to the throne. Until now it has been generally accepted that the throne should be occupied by the most eligible son of King Abdel Aziz. King Kahled has this sanction, and so has his half-brother, Prince Fahd, the Crown Prince. After Prince Fahd, the present line of succession would pass to other sons of King Abdel Aziz, starting with Prince Abdullah, the Commander of the Royal Guards, and then moving to Prince Abdel Muhsin and Prince Sultan, the powerful Minister of Defence. But all these brothers and half-brothers are of roughly the same age, and the problem will come when a ruler has to be found from the next generation. It is likely that the monarchy will then become hereditary in whichever branch of the family manages to establish its claim, and it is this looming controversy over the succession which accounts for the scarcely concealed rivalry between the various branches.

kilometres of territory. Joint commissions were set up to identify the area to be handed over.

When the Revolution took place in Iran the work of the commissions ceased abruptly. The Iraqis felt that they had kept their part of the Algiers bargain, but had not received the other part which was due to them. Nor did they find any encouragement in Khomeini's words or deeds. He did not, as they expected, return to their Arab owners the three islands at the western approaches to the Straits of Hormuz, Abu Musa and the Tunbs, which had been illegally seized by the Shah the day before Britain had withdrawn its protection from them in 1971. Mahmoud Dua'i, the Hojat al-Islam sent by Khomeini to Baghdad as the first ambassador of the revolutionary regime, was accused of encouraging the fanatical Da'wa Party.

More worrying to President Sadam Hussein and his colleagues were the implications of a telegram they received from Khomeini in answer to one they had sent congratulating him on the results of the plebiscite endorsing Iran's new Islamic constitution. After a vague acknowledge-ment Khomeini ended his telegram with the words 'Peace be on those who follow the right line' – the expression used by the Prophet Mohammed when writing to the non-Moslem communities in Arabia. It was impossible not to believe that the words had been deliberately chosen by Khomeini, and the only conclusion to be drawn was that he regarded the government in Baghdad as composed of infidels.

Inevitably the Iraqi government felt that the Shi'a community was being incited against it, and took strong measures to protect the state from disruption. Shi'is living in the sensitive areas adjoining Iran were sent across the frontier, and the same fate befell a number of leading Shi'is from other parts of the country. These received invitations to the Mansur Club in Baghdad, where they were told they were to meet President Hussein for discussions. On arrival, they were told that the venue for the meeting had been changed, so they were put into about twenty buses, driven to the frontier, and told to make their way to Tehran. Several of them were men of considerable property, but it all had to be left behind.

Tension on the border mounted. There were some armed clashes, after one of which Beni-Sadr was reported as saying 'If Iraqi provo-cation continues I cannot prevent my army from marching on Baghdad.' Just as in 1914 troops on both sides embarked for the front shouting 'Nach Paris!' 'À Berlin!', so along this forgotten frontier between two races and two creeds old hatreds revived.

The Iraqis feel confident that either Iran will suffer an internal collapse, or the present regime will be replaced by one from the army, which will recognize the reality of the military situation and be prepared to make peace. Of course, anything can happen, but because of its strategic importance it is unlikely that the super-powers would ever be prepared to stand idly by while Iran collapsed, or that any regime would be more willing to compromise than the government of mullahs has shown itself to be.

Khomeini believes in Islam as the universal verity which eclipses nationalism and is a unifying force. But a country like Iraq depends on nationalism for its survival – Iraqi nationalism and Arab nationalism. Take those away and it will split up among Sunnis, Shi'is, Kurds, and perhaps even smaller fragments. In the same way, in the other wing of the Fertile Crescent there are people at work only too eager to destroy the concept of Arab nationalism and divide up the area into a number of small sectarian states – Jewish, Maronite, Alawite, Druze, and so on. This is not a new idea, but it is the exact antithesis of all that the Arab nationalist movement has been struggling for in this century.

Indeed, one of the paradoxes of the Iraq-Iran war is that the spirit which has inspired the Iranian armed forces to resist is more nationalism than religion. True, the Iraqis have been as astonished as were the Shah's soldiers and police at the fanatical courage of some of the Iranians opposed to them. I have heard Iraqi generals telling President Sadam Hussein: 'They come at us like madmen!' But for the Iranians it has become a patriotic war, just as Stalin made the war against the Nazis a war for Mother Russia rather than for communism. Already Khomeini has seen the Islamic content of the Revolution he brought about diluted in his lifetime by the nationalism he professes to have so little time for.

# EPILOGUE

WHAT does the future hold? As long as Khomeini lives, things are not likely to change substantially. His prestige remains enormous, and he is able to keep the masses in a state of permanent alert which makes the consolidation of other power groupings in the country almost impossible.

The older-style politicians failed complete to get the five-year breathing space which they have admitted would be necessary if they were to build up a strong position for themselves. President Bani-Sadr failed to build up an effective power base to guarantee his position against the mullahs. The Mullahs can present a united front against the lay politicians, but they are divided by many personal and regional rivalries. In theory Khomeini has a destined successor in Ayatollah Hussein Muntazari. Earlier this would probably have been Ayatollah Mahmud Talaghani, who might have played a useful stabilizing role, but unfortunately he died a few months after the Revolution. Muntazari is a good and sincere man, but simple in the ways of the world. I was once talking to Yazdi in his presence, and when he heard us speaking in English Muntazari was horrified: 'Why are you using the language of infidels? Have you forgotten that the language of the Koran is Arabic? Have you forgotten that the language of the angels and of Paradise is Arabic?'

This leaves the communists and the army. Many people fear that it is the communists who will inevitably fill the vacuum resulting from Khomeini's disappearance. I think this is most unlikely, unless they are brought to power on the backs of an invading Soviet army; and that nightmare of the West can be ruled out because Iran, unlike Afghanistan, is very definitely not in an indeterminate area of super-power influence.

Moreover, communists in Iran suffer from several crippling disadvantages. In the first place, Khomeini or no Khomeini, the Shi'a Persians are a people who have religion in their bones, and for them the atheism of communism rules it out as an acceptable creed. Then the Tudeh Party's total commitment to Moscow has identified it with one of Iran's habitual enemies. In Tsarist days Russian expansionism was in continual conflict with Persian nationalism, and Stalin and his successors have demonstrated that Russia's predatory instincts are not dead. The Tudeh Party's backing for the Soviet puppet Azerbaijan and Gilan republics after the war has not been forgotten. Because of this the party has never played any significant part in affairs. In the great struggle over oil nationalization it was actually in opposition, and when the revolutionary movement got going in 1977 its leadership failed to understand its significance and were late in jumping on the bandwagon. The only time when communism attracted a sizeable number of recruits was in the aftermath of the counter-coup. At present communists are weakened by sectarian divisions. There are at least eleven different splinter groups of Marxists operating under various labels, but all very much on the periphery of political life.

What about the army? This remains the only organized force in the country, and its standing has been inevitably strengthened as a result of the war with Iraq. As General Walieddin Fellahi, Chief of Staff of the Iranian army, said to me: 'Thanks to the war the army has been purged of its sins. Today it is no longer the army of the Shah which fired on unarmed citizens, but the army which has successfully defended the integrity of the Motherland.'

Many people have been planning to make use of the army for their own purposes. Soon after the fall of the Shah the Americans began encouraging the minorities – Kurds, Baluchis, and others – hoping that the army would have to be rebuilt to cope with their insurrections, and that, when this had happened, it would turn on the mullahs in Tehran. But any validity this calculation may once have had has been destroyed by the war. Nor are the exiled politicians and generals who claim to have contacts with elements in the army likely to find much comfort. If there is a cell of resistance in the army it will operate on its own and not on direction from outside. Conspirators are not normally willing to hand over the prize they have won to someone else.

The Iranian Revolution, like the French and Russian Revolutions, has found itself quickly having to face an external as well as an internal threat, and it may well be that war will help to consolidate this revolution as it did the earlier two. Much will depend on the social and class affiliations of the new breed of officers and NCOs who have gained promotion as the result of the Revolution and the war. It may also be that history will repeat itself in other ways, and that there is even now somewhere in the ranks of the revolutionaries a Bonaparte waiting to seize his chance.

# INDEX

# ABOUT THE AUTHOR

Mohamed Heikal was born in 1923. He went to school in Egypt and studied economics, journalism, and law at university. After traveling widely as a reporter, he became editor of *Akher Saa* in 1949 and of *Al Ahram,* the leading newspaper of the Arab world, in 1957. He was offered ministerial posts by Nasser but declined them until, in 1970, he was appointed minister of information. He also served as minister of foreign affairs. He resigned from *Al Ahram* in 1974 over a difference of opinion on policy with President Sadat, and has now turned to a full-time writing career.